CELTIC DAILY PRAYER

CELTIC DAILY PRAYER

A Northumbrian Office

◆

Compiled by
Andy Raine and John T. Skinner of
the Northumbria Community

MarshallPickering
An Imprint of HarperCollins*Publishers*

Marshall Pickering is an Imprint of
HarperCollins*Religious*
Part of HarperCollins*Publishers*
77-85 Fulham Palace Road, London W6 8JB

First published in Great Britain
in 1994 by Marshall Pickering

10 9 8 7 6 5 4 3 2

Andy Raine and John T. Skinner assert the moral right
to be identified as the authors of this work

A catalogue record for this book is
available from the British Library

ISBN 0 55 02845-9

Typeset by Harper Phototypesetters Limited
Northampton, England
Printed and bound in Great Britain by
HarperCollinsManufacturing Glasgow

Contents

Introducing the Office

'A Northumbrian Office' is a compilation of prayers (old and new), meditations and readings from the Bible. These have not just been selected at random, but were chosen as a focus for Christian friends who had a commitment to pray together for God's purposes in Northumberland.

In publishing the office at this time we are making what we have already come to value available to a wider group of praying people. The readings are not intended to replace your own prayer – after all, we are told to 'pray without ceasing' – but to provide a helpful discipline and the sense of companionship with many others who will be praying in a similar way.

The office is intended as a small gift to the whole Church. We hope it will enrich the prayer and spiritual life of all who use it.

Praying the Morning Prayer

We begin in the name and presence of the One God, three in one, Father, Son and Holy Spirit.

'One Thing' declares our intention to become focused on God with all our heart, all our emotions and will, all our mind and all our strength.

'To whom shall we go?' confesses our dependency on God and His word to us.

Scripture references – Each day will have passages from Psalms, Old Testament and New. Often they are only a verse or two long to allow the reader to digest them more carefully. It is good to pause for a few moments after each reading and ask inwardly, What is my response to that? Does it make sense to me? or, What have I learnt? After doing this it is good to read the accompanying commentary for that day. (Some people find the morning is too rushed to spend long pondering the Scriptures, and leave them instead until the evening prayer. The important thing is to find a rhythm that works for you.)

Meditations – the same meditations are used according to what day of the month it is. (So, on the 4th day of each month the Prayer of Abandonment is used, for example.) With frequent use of the office each of these will gradually become familiar friends, also.

Prayers – This is now the opportunity to pray whatever is on your mind or heart, offering to God concerns of the day, your personal needs, prayers for other people. This would be the appropriate time to pray for the needs mentioned in the daily entry of the Northumbria Community's prayer guide, which is issued three or four times a year.

Many of our folk have developed the practice of keeping a 'prayer-pot' with small slips of paper in it on which are written the names of friends, family members , or anyone we may want to pray for from time to time. Three strips are then drawn from the pot, prayed for in turn and then a) disposed of, b) returned to the pot, or c) carried around that day – whichever seems appropriate.

Christ as a Light – This is one of many settings of the prayer known as St Patrick's Breastplate. It speaks of the Name and Presence of Jesus as powerful protective clothing. The

Celtic understanding is that it is just as important to clothe ourselves with the awareness of the Presence, as it is to put on outward clothing to face the day!

Peter's Song – is a beautiful blessing for each day, creating in us an expectancy that we will be made aware of 'wonders' of all kinds, and return safely to give thanks.

We commit our day to God in His Name, in the name of Father, Son and Holy Spirit.

Midday Prayer

The midday office is especially designed for use in the middle of a busy working day. For this reason it is short, and can be prayed in the time it takes to boil a kettle – especially if already committed to memory.

Sometimes I deliberately pray midday prayer on my feet, moving around the kitchen to remind me that I work as I pray and pray as I work. Other people may spend quite a few minutes over these prayers, with long pauses in between, grateful to come to a complete pause, an oasis of silence in the middle of the day's demands.

(I had some hesitancy in retaining the 'thee' and 'thou' forms, but Psalm 90 and 'Teresa's Bookmark' already were worked in that way, and were ideal in their context for midday prayer, so it seemed convenient that they would be consistent with the usual form of the Our Father. I apologize to anybody who finds this has made the liturgy inaccessible – to me it is just one more way of highlighting the contemporary relevance of the treasure of prayer from long ago.)   A.R.

Evening Prayer

Prayer does not begin by ignoring our difficulties and darkness, but by gathering them to us and offering them to God from the outset. We look to Him with expectancy: with simple trust, or in desperate hope, we declare, 'Lord, today I believe.'

It is useful to read these prayers slowly, pausing between the verses to offer the circumstances of our life, or of our day, to God.

The Scripture references are those of the day, which may be used instead (or as well) in the morning. Some people enjoy reading the passages twice in one day with opportunity to reflect on them from time to time in between. For others it is an opportunity to re-use a favourite page of notes with its readings or to revise a previous month's which were particularly helpful. (If an additional or alternative set of readings is to be used only occasionally the series entitled 'Consider my Meditation' is to be recommended since these will specifically correspond to the meditation for the day of the month.)

Read your appropriate Psalm, Old and New Testament passages and respond to these, then read the commentary on the same page.

Next, turn to the **meditation** for this day of the month. Each month you use them the more familiar these will become.

For **'Prayers'** you may wish to pray for whatever events or people are listed in your diary, any names you take from a 'prayer-pot' full of concerns for others. It is also a good time to recall those you have met through the day, and any needs they have. These may be prayed for now, or written down and added to the 'prayer-pot' for another day.

Some people at this time will wish to pause, if they are praying alone, to write in a journal, recording whatever seems to have been of significance during the day.

Evening prayer ends with the Psalm **'In the Shadow'**, and then Columba's blessing, which reminds us to be at peace with each other, determining that, for our part at least, there will be no ill-feeling between ourself and another person.

Communion

This is intended as a resource. Some will read the prayers in times of quiet or reflection. Others who are accustomed to leading communion services may find their order adapts easily for use with small, intimate groups on retreat or at a house-mass. In other places this order would be used for special occasions such as the feast-day on which one of the Celtic saints is remembered in particular. Some celebrants will borrow only parts of the 'Celtic' communion service and incorporate them into their normal order for communion.

If copies of this Northumbrian Office Communion are given to a congregation to use, some care may be needed to plan where any music should be introduced, and when it is preferable for people to stand, kneel or sit. No such directions are given in the text as it stands. This is not an attempt in any way to reconstruct early Celtic liturgy, or to be an example of what it might have become had it not become suppressed. Much of their Eucharistic liturgy had developed on precisely the same lines as that of the Roman or Eastern branches of the Church. Where it varied it was likely to do so from one occasion to another, from one place to another, from one celebrant to another. Prayers would be very familiar ones employed as appropriate, or extemporary, in any case. All we have sought to do is give an example of how prayers and readings from Celitc and contemporary sources may be blended together in a way that captures a little of the simplicity, depth and vitality of Celtic Christianity.

Family 'Shabbat'

There are separate notes accompanying the 'Shabbat' itself, giving precise instructions for its use.

Here I wish only to make some relevant observations.

Part of our intention in preparing a Shabbat was to enter into the experience and emphasis of the early Celtic Churches who typically observed Sunday as Sabbath, honouring Sunday as the day of the Resurrection and beginning it with Eucharist, but then working for whatever was left of the day. An anthology of passages from Exodus, Leviticus, Numbers and Deuteronomy called the *Liber ex Lege Moisi* was one of the most frequently copied of texts. So, other than the Jewish peoples throughout history, the Celtic Church was probably the most profoundly affected by these Scriptures of any people. They were a 'people of the book', and these texts were amongst the most popular.

Another reason for adopting the regular, or occasional, use of Shabbat was, for us, its focus on the honouring of women.

The woman presides, and leads the prayers of blessing. She is uniquely the person whose prerogative it is to light the candles. She prays for herself, intercedes for her children wherever they may be and commits them to God's care.

The blessing of the bread and wine only marks the commencement of the meal. It is not the focus of the Shabbat prayer. Here only is a concession made to the man – he may pronounce this blessing.

I remember many years ago being struck by a paragraph in a book written by someone from a community in Ann Arbor. It said that traditionally in our society we have had different and distinct ways of honouring men and women. Most of the necessary boundaries of preserve have been superseded. Women and men are able to do, or are encouraged to do, many things which in times past would have been impractical. The differences and constraints are going, but it would be sad if in the process we lost the possibility of honouring men and women differently. Expectations about dress or behaviour vary from generation to generation and country to country. Whatever we choose as a distinctive dress, behaviour or privilege is likely to be *arbitrary* now. With modern technology there are few 'heavy' jobs only men could tackle, nor are we so convinced that men are ill-suited for homemaking or nurturing roles. More and more people choose to have smaller families so women are not as inevitably constrained by child-rearing for year after year.

The marks of honour, the different roles, we choose to give may be different from what they were before, but it is important that some exist, or that if necessary we invent them!

The true celebration of our personhood demands it.

The first Easter Workshop at which we introduced Shabbat for our community we did in the context of a main dinner. The cooks had chosen lamb and herbs to give it something of the flavour of a Passover meal, and when the food was ready everyone would need to be in place to eat whilst it was still hot. Everyone was called in in good time, and the children came in as a group, sitting all together with their friends. This had not been our intention originally; we had kind of assumed each family could try to sit together and include those with no family present. Instead, we just gave each woman or girl their own candle, or two if they were married, and to those who were mothers extra candles to represent their children. Each man or boy had a tiny bread-roll to break and share. One by one, many of the women came to ask could they take an extra candle to light for a child they had miscarried, or aborted, a child who had died or they had given up for adoption. Each thought they were the only one to have asked. In some cases the youngsters sitting separately deferred any need for explanations. What a tremendous healing it was! We hope it will be a blessing to some of you as well.

MORNING PRAYER

Morning Prayer

Opening Sentences

One thing I have asked of the Lord,
This is what I seek:
That I may dwell in the house of the Lord
All the days of my life;
To behold the beauty of the Lord
And to seek Him in His temple.

Call: Who is it that you seek?

Response: **We seek the Lord our God.**

Call: Do you seek Him with all your heart?

Response: **Amen. Lord, have mercy.**

Call: Do you seek Him with all your soul?

Response: **Amen. Lord, have mercy.**

Call: Do you seek Him with all your mind?

Response: **Amen. Lord, have mercy.**

Call: Do you seek Him with all your
            strength?

Response: **Amen. Christ, have mercy.**

Declaration of faith

To whom shall we go?
You have the words of eternal life,
And we have believed and have come to know
That You are the Holy One of God.

Praise to You, Lord Jesus Christ,
King of endless glory.

Scripture readings

Psalm
O.T. Reading
N.T. Reading

Meditation of the day

Prayer

Canticle

Christ as a light
Illumine and guide me
Christ as a shield
O'ershadow me
Christ under me
Christ over me
Christ beside me
On my left and my right
This day be within and
Without me
Lowly and meek yet
All-powerful
Be in the heart
Of each to whom I speak
In the mouth of each
Who speaks unto me
This day be within and
Without me
Lowly and meek yet
All-powerful
Christ as a light
Christ as a shield
Christ beside me
On my left and my right.

Blessing

May the peace of the Lord Christ go with you,
    wherever He may send you,
May He guide you through the wilderness,
    protect you through the storm.
May He bring you home rejoicing
    at the wonders He has shown you,
May He bring you home rejoicing
    once again into our doors.

MIDDAY PRAYER

Midday Prayer

Opening Sentences

Let the beauty of the Lord our God be upon us.
Establish Thou the work of our hands.
Establish Thou the work of our hands.

The Lord's Prayer

Our Father, who art in heaven,
Hallowed be Thy name;
Thy kingdom come,
Thy will be done
On earth as it is in heaven.
Give us this day our daily bread,
And forgive us our trespasses
As we forgive those who trespass against us.
And lead us not into temptation,
But deliver us from evil.
Amen.

Declaration of faith

We believe and trust
In God the Father Almighty.
We believe and trust
In Jesus Christ His Son.
We believe and trust
In the Holy Spirit.
We believe and trust
In the Three in One.

Canticle

Teach us, dear Lord, to number our days
That we may apply our hearts unto wisdom.
Oh, satisfy us early with Thy mercy
That we may rejoice and be glad all of our days.
And let the beauty of the Lord our God
     be upon us
And establish Thou the work of our hands.
And let the beauty of the Lord our God
     be upon us
And establish Thou the work of our hands,
     dear Lord.

Blessing

Let nothing disturb thee,
Nothing affright thee;
All things are passing,
God never changeth!
Patient endurance attaineth
To all things;
Who God possesseth
In nothing is wanting;
Alone God sufficeth.

EVENING PRAYER

Evening Prayer

Opening Sentences

My soul waits for the Lord
More than those who watch
For the morning.
More than those who
Watch for the morning.

Call: Out of the depths I have cried to You.

Response: **O, Lord hear my voice.**

Call: With my whole heart I want to praise You.

Response: **O, Lord, hear my voice.**

Call: If You, Lord, should mark iniquities.

Response: **Who could stand? Who could stand?**

I will wait for the Lord
My soul waits,
And in His word
Do I hope

Profession of faith

Lord, You have always given
Bread for the coming day,
And though I am poor,
   Today I believe.

Lord, You have always given
Strength for the coming day,
And though I am weak,
   Today I believe.

Lord, You have always given
Peace for the coming day,
And though of anxious heart,
    Today I believe.

Lord, You have always kept
Me safe in trials,
And now, tried as I am,
    Today I believe.

Lord, You have always marked
The road for the coming day,
And though it may be hidden,
    Today I believe.

Lord, You have always lightened
This darkness of mine,
And though the night is here,
    Today I believe.

Lord, You have always spoken
When time was ripe,
And though You be silent now,
    Today I believe.

Scripture readings

Psalm
O.T. Reading
N.T. Reading

Meditation of the day

Prayer

Canticle

> In the shadow of Your wings
> I will sing Your praises, O Lord.

The Lord is my light, my salvation;
Whom shall I fear?
The Lord is the refuge of my life;
Of whom shall I be afraid?

> In the shadow of Your wings
> I will sing Your praises, O Lord.

One thing I ask of the Lord,
One thing I seek;
To dwell in the presence of my God,
To gaze on Your holy place.

> In the shadow of Your wings
> I will sing Your praises, O Lord.

I believe I shall see the goodness
Of the Lord in the land of the living.
O wait for the Lord!
Have courage and wait,
Wait for the Lord.

> In the shadow of Your wings
> I will sing Your praises, O Lord.

Blessing

See that ye be at peace among yourselves,
     my children,
And love one another.
Follow the example of good men of old
And God will comfort you and help you,
Both in this world
And in the world which is to come.

MEDITATIONS

Day 1

It is a difficult
 lesson to learn today,
to leave one's friends
 and family and deliberately
practise the art of solitude
 for an hour or a day
  or a week.
 For me, the break
  is most difficult . . .

And yet, once it is done,
 I find there is a quality
to being alone that is
 incredibly precious.

 Life rushes back into the void,
  richer,
   more vivid,
    fuller than before!

   Anne Morrow Lindbergh

Day 2

There is a contemplative
  in all of us,
almost strangled
  but still alive,
who craves quiet
  enjoyment of the Now,
and longs to touch
  the seamless
garment of silence
  which
makes whole.

Alan P. Tory

Carmelite vow

Let each stay in or near
  his own cell
meditating, day and night
  on the law of the Lord,
    and vigilant in prayer,
  unless otherwise employed
    by the Holy Spirit.

Day 3

The Cry to God as 'Father'
  in the New Testament
is not a calm acknowledgement
  of a universal truth about
God's abstract fatherhood.

It is the Child's cry
   out of a nightmare.

It is the cry of outrage,
   fear, shrinking away,
when faced with the horror
      of 'the world'
   – yet not simply or exclusively
      protest, but trust as well,

'Abba Father'
   all things are possible
      to Thee . . .
                    Rowan Williams

Day 4

Prayer of abandonment to God

Father, I abandon myself
   into your hands.
Do with me what you will,
Whatever you do, I will thank you,
I am ready for all, I accept all.
Let only your will be done in me,
   as in all your creatures,
And I'll ask nothing else, my Lord.

Into your hands I commend my spirit;
I give it to you
   with all the love of my heart,
For I love you, Lord,
   and so need to give myself,
To surrender myself into your hands
   with a trust beyond all measure,
   because you are my Father.
                    Charles de Foucauld

Day 5

The Methodist Covenant prayer

I am no longer my own, but Thine,
Put me to what Thou wilt,
   rank me with whom Thou wilt;
put me to doing, put me to suffering;
let me be employed for Thee
   or laid aside for Thee;
let me be full, let me be empty;
let me have all things,
   let me have nothing;
I freely and heartily yield all things
   to Thy pleasure and disposal.

And now, O glorious and blessed God,
   Father, Son and Holy Spirit,
Thou art mine, and I am Thine.
   So be it.
And the covenant
   which I have made on earth,
   let it be ratified in heaven.
                 Amen.

Day 6

From 'If I only love Jesus'

I praise the wounds
   and the blood of the Lamb
  that heals the weakness
   of my body,
I praise the wounds
   and the blood of the Lamb

that heals the weakness
    of my soul,
I praise the wounds
    and the blood of the Lamb
    that heals the weakness
    of my spirit!

Praise be to the blood of the Lamb
    in His forgiving power,
Praise be to the blood of the Lamb
    in His cleansing power,
Praise be to the blood of the Lamb
    in His saving power,
Praise be to the blood of the Lamb
    in His releasing power,
Praise be to the blood of the Lamb
    in His victorious power,
Praise be to the blood of the Lamb
    in His renewing power,
Praise be to the blood of the Lamb
    in His protecting power.

For him who believes
    in the power of the blood of Jesus,
    nothing is impossible.

I praise the blood of the Lamb
    that covers all my sins
        so that they can no
        longer be seen,
I praise the blood of the Lamb
    that cleanses me
        from all my sins
        and makes me
        white as snow,
I praise the blood of the Lamb
    that has power to free me
        from all my bondages

and chains of sin.
I praise the blood of the Lamb
  that is stronger
    than my own sin-infested blood
    and remoulds me
    into the image of God,
I praise the blood of the Lamb
  that is victorious
    over all powers that seek to
    oppress me,
    over every power of the enemy.
I praise the blood of the Lamb
  that protects me from all
    the devious attacks of the enemy.
I praise the blood of the Lamb
  that prepares for me
    the bridal garment.

I praise the blood of the Lamb
  that makes all things new.
    Hallelujah! Amen.
                    M. Basilea Schlink

Day 7

For him who believes
  in the power
  of the blood of Jesus,
nothing is impossible!

'The Lord shall surely
  perfect that thing,
  that thing
  which concerneth thee.'

To him who believes
in the power
of the blood
of the Crucified Lamb,
nothing shall be called impossible!

Blessed be the Lamb
that was slain before
the foundation of the world.

Day 8

I find Thee enthroned in my heart,
my Lord Jesus.
It is enough.
I know that Thou art throned
in heaven.
My heart and heaven are one.

Alistair MacLean

Day 9

Isaiah 58:6–12

Is not this the kind of fasting
I have chosen:
to loose the chains of injustice
and untie the cords of the yoke,
to set the oppressed free
and break every yoke?

Is it not to share your food
with the hungry
and to provide the poor wanderer

with shelter –
when you see the naked to clothe him,
   and not to turn away
      from your own
      flesh and blood.

Then your light will break forth
      like the dawn,
   and your healing
      will quickly appear;
then your righteousness
      will go before you,
   and the glory of the Lord
      will be your rear guard.

Then you will call,
      and the Lord will answer;
   you will cry for help,
      and he will say:
      Here I am.

If you do away
      with the yoke of oppression,
   with the pointing finger
      and malicious talk,
and if you spend yourselves
      on behalf of the hungry
   and satisfy the needs
      of the oppressed,
then your light
      will rise in the darkness,
   and your night
      will become like the noon-day.

The Lord will guide you always;
   he will satisfy your needs
      in a sun-scorched land
   and will strengthen your frame.

You will be like a well-watered garden,
   like a spring whose waters never fail.

Your people will rebuild
      the ancient ruins
   and will raise up
      the age-old foundations;
you will be called
      Repairer of Broken Walls,
   Restorer of Streets with Dwellings.

Day 10

What mean these stones?

Land of my fathers,
how I long to return,
to touch thy earth,
and find again thy sacred paths,
well-walked with the Gospel of Peace,
veiled now in the shadow of mediocrity.

   'What mean these stones'
   which beset thy coastline,
   who in twisted agony cry out
   in praise and supplication of Him
   and the renewal of the faith
   that bled to secure them there?

Yet we would walk again
      thy sacred paths,
repair thy ancient ruins,
restore thy broken altars,
raise up the foundations
of many generations.

Hear this, you lands of the south
who hold men in captivity
by your empty words
and well-worn myths,
who neglect to see justice
for the poor, the widow,
    the fatherless.

Look to the North –
for lo your Redeemer comes,
clothed in the poverty of the few
who dare to speak His name,
    without vanity,
in a whisper,
    ' lest the earth should tremble
Holy, Holy, Holy is the Lord.

Poor of Yahweh, arise,
take up the ancient mantle
which has awaited your day;
clothe yourself within its humility,
for you have been set
as a stumbling block for many.

Day 11

Jeremiah's field

Weep, weep not for me,
    but weep for yourselves
    for the day has ended.
Weep not for me,
    for the night must come
    before the morning.
This is the time, the time
    for seeking the Lord,

This is the time, the time
  for weeping before Him.
Now is the time, the time
  for returning.

  Set up the waymarks!
    turn your hearts
    towards the highway.
  Turn again,
    turn again,
  O virgin Israel.
  Return to the Lord.

Day 12

Isaiah 30

In returning to Me,
  and waiting for Me,
  shall you be saved.
In quietness and confidence
  is your strength.
But we would trust ourselves
and stand in our own strength
and we shall be ashamed
  upon that day.

But the Lord still waits for you
  to show to you His love
  as He has said.
And He, He will conquer you,
  so that He may bless you
  with Himself.
Blessed are they
who wait upon the Lord
for they shall weep no more,
  neither be afraid.

O my people in Jerusalem,
   weep no more,
for the Lord
   shall be gracious unto you,
   and show to you His love,
   as He has said.
And though He give to you the bread
and water of adversity,
with your own eyes
   you shall see your King,
   and you shall say,
   you shall say:
Blessed is He! Blessed is He!
Blessed is He who comes
   in the Name of the Lord!
Blessed is He! Blessed is He!
Blessed is He who comes
   in the Name of the Lord!

Tear down your images
and the idols that you have made,
for the Lord has prepared a fire
   to cover the earth.

And the glory of the Lord
   shall descend upon His hill
   upon that day.
And the law of the Lord
   shall go out from Zion
   in His name.
And all the nations of the earth
shall bow before the One
   they have pierced.
And the poor of the earth
   shall rejoice:
   Messiah has come!

Jesus! Emmanuel!
Blessed is He who comes
    in the name of the Lord.
Lion of Judah,
Blessed is He who comes
    in the name of the Lord.

Tear down your images
and the idols that you have made,
for the Lord has prepared a fire
    to cover the earth.

Day 13

From **Judges 1:14–15**

And so it was that Achsah kept urging Othniel
her husband to ask from her father a field. She
lighted from off her ass, and Caleb said to her,
'What is it that you want?' And she said to him,
'Give me a blessing, for you have given me this
dark, desert land; now give me also springs of
water.' And her father gave her the upper and
the nether springs.

Day 14

From **Judges 1:14–15, Numbers 24:1–10,** *and* **Psalm 26:3–4**

Every curse becomes a blessing
to the people of God's choosing.
He who spoke it shall perform it,
He shall bring on us the blessing,

though the enemy may fight.
My Jesus has done all things
    right.

In the dry and desert places
Jesus is our souls' oasis.
He will give us of His plenty,
fill the vessels once so empty,
    pour His waters on the ground,
    living waters gushing round.

See the land so black and barren
God will make a watered garden,
fruitfulness where once
    was parchedness,
light to break into the darkness,
    Upper springs
        and nether springs
    in the field
        that Father's given.

Satan tries, but cannot block it,
powers of Hell could never stop it.
Darkness flees as light is given.
God establishes His heaven
    in our hearts, and in this place
    shows the radiance of His face.

Day 15

Matthew 12:43-45

When the unclean spirit
    has gone out of a man,
he walketh through dry places,
    seeking rest and findeth none.

Then he saith,
I will return into my house
   from whence I came out;
and when he is come,
   he findeth it empty,
   swept,
      and garnished.

Then he goeth,
   and taketh with himself
   seven other spirits
   more wicked than himself,
      and they enter in
      and dwell there:
and the last state of that man
   is worse than the first.

Even so shall it be
   unto this wicked generation.

'Legend says that when Satan raised his giant
battle-axe against Heaven's gates, God's shaft of
lightning struck it from his hand. The flaming
axe fell into the North Sea, and was changed
into the thousand-acre island of Lindisfarne.

Through the centuries this bit of lore concerning
God's victory inspired those who lived on, or
visited the island, to keep Satan's power
underfoot . . .'

   Lord, show us the things that are binding the
   work You have called forth on Holy Island.
   Help us to loose *YOUR* work,
      and let it go
         in resurrection power.

Day 16

St Aidan's prayer for the Holy Island of Lindisfarne

Lord, this bare Island,
  make it a place of peace:
Here be the peace
  of men who do Thy will:
Here be the peace
  of brother serving man:
Here be the peace
  of holy monks obeying:
Here be the peace
  of praise by dark and day:
Be this Island Thy Holy Island:
I, Lord, Thy servant, Aidan,
  make this prayer:
Be it Thy care.
Amen.

Day 17

  Here am I, Lord,
I've come to do Your will.
  Here am I, Lord,
in Your presence I'm still.

Day 18

Primeval fire fused a cradle of rock:

Borne by the rocking tides,
Smooth sand folded its hollows.

Frail seeds flew
  on the winds' shoulders;
Blessed by soft rain
  and warmth of sun
Grass and herb
  bound the shifting dunes.

Lastly, men came, led by Christ
To build a home for restless souls,
A beacon to shed forth His light.

  Lord of rock and tide,
  Of sun and air,
  Light of men:
  May your blessing rest
  On this your house.

Day 19

a haven

Lord, take this song
  and fill it with Your presence.
Let it bring a word of hope
  to weary care-full hearts.
Take this song
  and fill it, Lord.
Fill it with Yourself.

Lord, take my life
  and fill it with Your praises.
Let me speak a word of peace
  that Jesus brings in me.
Take this life
  and fill it, Lord.
Fill it with Yourself.

Lord, take this place
 and fill it
 with Your blessing.
Let it be a haven
 where the
 poor in spirit
 sing.
Take this place
 and fill it, Lord.
Fill it with Your praise.

Day 20

Even though the day be laden
and my task dreary and my
strength small, a song keeps
singing in my heart.
For I know that I am Thine.
I am part of Thee. Thou
art kin to me, and all my times
are in Thy hand.

Alistair MacLean

From **Psalm 31:14–15, 21**

I trust in Thee, O Lord,
 I say, Thou art my God.
My times are in Thy hand,
 my times are in Thy hand.

Blessed be the Lord
 for He hath wondrously shown
His steadfast love to me,
 His steadfast love to me.

Day 21

Seven times a day, as I work upon this hungry
farm, I say to Thee,

'Lord, why am I here? What is there here to
stir my gifts to growth? What great thing can I
do for others – I who am captive to this dreary
toil?'

And seven times a day Thou answerest,

'I cannot do without thee. Once did my Son
live thy life, and by His faithfulness did show my
mind, my kindness, and my truth to men. But
now He is come to my side, and thou must take
His place.'

Hebridean Altars

Day 22

Enrich, Lord, heart,
   hands, mouth in me
With faith, with hope
   and charity,
That I may run, rise,
   rest in Thee.

G. Herbert

Day 23

As the rain hides the stars, as
   the autumn mist hides the hills,
happenings of my lot hide the

shining of Thy face from me.
Yet, if I may hold Thy hand in the
   darkness, it is enough.
Since I know that, though I
   may stumble in my going,
Thou dost not fall.

Alistair MacLean

The Lord is thy keeper,
   the Lord is thy shade;
The sun shall not smite thee by day,
   nor the moon by night;
The Lord shall preserve thee,
   thy soul from all evil;
The Lord shall preserve thee,
   thy going and thy coming,
From this time forward, and
   even for ever more.

As it was, as it is, and as it
   shall be
Ever more, God of grace,
   God in Trinity!
With the ebb, with the flow,
   ever it is so,
God of grace, O Trinity,
   with the ebb and flow.

Traditional Gaelic from
Alexander Macneill, Fishsalter, Barra

Day 24

Saviour and friend, how wonderful art Thou!
My companion upon the changeful way.
The comforter of its weariness.

My guide to the eternal town.
The welcome at its gate.
                    Alistair MacLean

As the moorland pool images the sun, so in our
hours of self-giving thou shinest on us, and we
mirror thee to men. But of the other land, our
heaven to be, we have no picture at all. Only we
know that thou art there. And Jesus the door
and the welcome of each faithful one.
                    Alistair MacLean

Day 25

Of all in earth and heaven
the dearest name to me
is the matchless Name of Jesus
the Christ of Calvary!
   The Christ of Calvary!
   The dearest name to me
   is the matchless Name of Jesus
   the Christ of Calvary.
I cannot help but love Him
or tell His love to me
for He became my ransom,
the Christ of Calvary.
   The Christ of Calvary!
   The dearest name to me
   is the matchless Name of Jesus
   the Christ of Calvary.
I could not live without Him,
His love is life to me.
My blood-bought life I give Him,
the Christ of Calvary.
   The Christ of Calvary!

The dearest name to me
is the matchless Name of Jesus
the Christ of Calvary.

Tune: Annie Laurie

Day 26

My Master's face

No pictured likeness of my Lord
    I have;
He carved no record
    of His ministry
  on wood or stone,
He left no sculptured tomb
    nor parchment dim
but trusted for all memory of Him
  men's heart alone.

Who sees the face but sees in part;
Who reads the spirit which it hides,
    sees all;
  he needs no more.

Thy life in my life, Lord,
    give Thou to me;
and then, in truth,
    I may forever see
  my Master's face!

William Hurd Hillyer

Day 27

Arise, my love, my fair one,
and come away with me.
Arise, my love, my fair one,
and come away with me.

For lo, the winter is passed
and the rain is gone away.
Come away with me,
   Come away with me.

The flowers appear on the earth,
the time for singing has come,
and the voice of the turtle-dove
is heard in our land.

Come away with me.

The fig-tree puts forth its fruit,
the vines are in blossom,
they put forth their fragrance,
O come away with me.

Arise, my love, my fair one,
come away with me.
Arise, my love, my fair one,
come away with me.

O come away with me,
Come away
   with me.

Extract taken from the song *Arise, my love* by John & Ross Harding. Copyright © 1975 Kingsway's Thankyou Music, PO Box 75, Eastbourne, E. Sussex, BN23 6NT, UK. Used by permission.

Psalm 84

How lovely is Thy dwelling-place,
  O Lord of hosts, to me.
My soul is longing and fainting
  the courts of the Lord to see.
My heart and flesh, they are singing
  for joy to the living God.
How lovely is Thy dwelling-place,
  O Lord of hosts, to me.

Even the sparrow finds a home
  where he can settle down.
And the swallow, she can build a nest
  where she may lay her young.
Within the courts of the Lord of hosts,
  my King, my Lord, and my God.
And happy are those who are dwelling where
  the song of praise is sung.

And I'd rather be a door-keeper
  and only stay a day,
than live the life of a sinner
  and have to stay away.
For the Lord is shining as the sun,
  and the Lord, he's like a shield;
And no good thing does he withhold
  from those who walk his way.

How lovely is Thy dwelling-place,
  O Lord of hosts, to me.
My soul is longing and fainting
  the courts of the Lord to see.
My heart and flesh, they are singing
  for joy to the living God.
How lovely is Thy dwelling-place,
  O Lord of hosts, to me.

Lady Poverty in the eyes of Juniper, friend of Francis, fool of God

If I am truly poor, then I am dependent on others for everything, and I feel useless and worthless, and I realize deep within that everything is a gift from the Father. Then in this attitude of complete dependence, I become useful again, for then I am empty of selfishness and I am free to be God's instrument instead of my own. In poverty I begin to value everything rightly again. I see how little really matters, and I see that only that which glorifies God is of value.

I write these words in pain, Lady Poverty, for I have wept bitter tears because I was poor and had to beg from others, and I felt like a burden to people and to God . . . And I have grown weary of Christ's words not to worry about tomorrow. But in His grace I have surrendered to God's sovereignty and providence, and it has made me free.

. . . Lady Poverty, I love you. You, my Lady, take all the sting from being poor. In your embrace I am rich indeed, for I have someone to love. I have you. Perhaps, my Lady, that is why I keep submitting, surrendering my desire to control my life, my need to provide for the future. You have stolen my heart and made me happy, and your love makes up for all the pain that loving you involves.

. . . and we know it is all worthwhile because
when we look into your eyes, we see Christ
Himself.

Murray Bodo

Day 30

Saranam (Refuge)

Receive our thanks
    for night and day,
For food and shelter,
    rest and play.
Be here our guest,
    and with us stay,
  Saranam, saranam, saranam.

For this small earth
    of sea and land,
For this small space
    on which we stand,
For those we touch
    with heart and hand,
  Saranam, saranam, saranam.

In the midst of foes
    I cry to thee
From the ends of earth,
    wherever I may be,
My strength in helplessness,
    oh, answer me,
  Saranam, saranam, saranam.

Make my heart to grow
    as great as thine,
So through my hurt
    your love may shine,

My love be yours,
   your love be mine,
Saranam, saranam, saranam.

For those who've gone,
   for those who stay,
For those to come,
   following the Way,
Be guest and guide
   both night and day.
   Saranam, saranam, saranam.

Day 31

From **L'Abri**

But in addition to these conversations and discussions, something else was happening. People were finding it hard to 'shake off' what they were living through.

They were *there* while we were praying for things that they later found had been given . . .

They were being given (*not by us*, but by God's answers to prayers), a demonstration that God exists . . .

It was a combination which could never be 'planned' or 'put on' as an exhibit . . . it had to be real.

. . . a completely new work . . . would never have been possible if we had not been uprooted completely in every way, and if in that uprooting we had not decided to pray for God's solution and leading every step of the path as it wound through unknown territory.

We also prayed that if it grew, God would send us the workers of His choice, rather than our trying to advertise or get people to help us . . . So *not* to advertise, but simply to pray that God will send those of His choice, and keep others away, is a *different* way of doing things.

We don't say everyone ought to work this way, we simply say we feel we were led by God to do this as a demonstration that He is able to bring the people to a place – even a tiny out-of-the-way place . . . – and only to bring the ones He wants to have there for His purposes.

Edith Schaeffer

AN ORDER FOR
HOLY COMMUNION

An Order for
Holy Communion

Opening Sentences

Whoever is on the Lord's side let them join with
me, that we may come to the visions of God.

The preparation

All: **Enkindle, we beseech thee, O Lord, the
light of our understanding, and pour
forth love into our hearts, that we may
be able to love thee worthily.
Amen.**

All: **Create a clean heart within me, O God,
so that it may become thine abode and
the resting place of the Holy Spirit. I
know, O Lord, I know indeed that thou
art beautiful and so it is presumptuous
of me to invite majesty so great into the
dwelling of so defiled a heart; but I
invite thee in order that thou mayest
cleanse it, and afterwards, I beg thee, if
it please thee, depart not from me, and
even unto old age and grey hairs leave
me not.**
Amen.

Prayers of penitence

Leader: There is one God and one mediator
between heaven and earth, the man Christ
Jesus, who gave himself as a ransom for all
people.

All: **We are guilty and polluted, O God, in spirit, in heart, and in flesh, in thought, in word, in act, we are hard in thy sight in sin. Put thou forth to us the power of thy love, be thou leaping over the mountains of our transgressions, and wash us in the true blood of conciliation.**

Leader: Pour down upon us from heaven the rich blessing of Your forgiveness. Grant to us, Thou Saviour of Glory, the fear of God, the love of God and His affection, and the will of God to do on earth at all times as angels and saints do in heaven.

In the name of Father, Son and Holy Spirit. Amen.

Canticle

I praise the wounds
   and the blood of the Lamb
  that heals the weakness
   of my body,
I praise the wounds
   and the blood of the Lamb
  that heals the weakness
   of my soul,
I praise the wounds
   and the blood of the Lamb
  that heals the weakness
   of my spirit!

Praise be to the blood of the Lamb
in His forgiving power,
Praise be to the blood of the Lamb
in His releasing power,
Praise be to the blood of the Lamb
in His victorious power,
Praise be to the blood of the Lamb
in His renewing power,
Praise be to the blood of the Lamb
in His protecting power.

I praise the blood of the Lamb
that makes all things new.
Hallelujah! Amen.

The Ministry of the Word

The Old Testament Reading

The New Testament Reading

The Gospel

All: **I pray you good Jesus that as you have
given me the grace to drink in with joy
the word that gives knowledge of you,
so in your goodness you will grant me
to come at length to yourself, the source
of all wisdom, to stand before your face
for ever.**

The Ministry of the Word

Declaration of faith

All: **There is no other God, there never was
and there never will be, than God the
Father, unbegotten and without
beginning, the Lord of the Universe, as
we have been taught, and his son Jesus
Christ whom we declare to have always
been with the Father and to have been
begotten spiritually by the Father in a
way that baffles description before the
beginning of the world, before all
beginning; and by him are made all
things visible and invisible. He was
made man, defeated death, and was
received into heaven by the Father, who
has given him power over all names in
heaven, on earth, and under the earth;
and every tongue will acknowledge to
him that Jesus Christ is the Lord God.
We believe in him and we look for his
coming soon as judge of the living and
the dead who will treat every one
according to their deeds. He has poured
out the Holy Spirit upon us in
abundance, the gift and guarantee of
eternal life who makes those who
believe and obey sons of God and joint
heirs with Christ.**

**We acknowledge and adore him as one
God in the Trinity of the holy name.**

Intercession and Thanksgiving

Let us call upon the Name of the
Lord in prayer and thanksgiving,
trusting in the Holy Spirit
to lead and guide us.

All: **Our Father, who art in heaven,**
Hallowed be Thy name;
Thy kingdom come,
Thy will be done
On earth as it is in heaven.
Give us this day our daily bread,
And forgive us our trespasses
As we forgive those who trespass
against us:
And lead us not into temptation,
But deliver us from evil.
Amen.

The Ministry of the Sacrament

The Peace

President: Christ, King of Tenderness
Christ, King of Tenderness
Bind us with a bond
that cannot be broken
Bind us with a bond of love
that cannot be broken.

My brothers and sisters,
the peace of our Lord Jesus Christ
be with you.

All: **And also with you.**

The Preparation of the Gifts

President: May Christ the bread of heaven
bless this bread.
May Christ who is the true vine
bless this wine.
May Christ that feasted his disciples
bless this supper.

All: **Blessed be God for ever.**

The Eucharist Prayer

President: The Lord be with you.

All: **And with thy spirit**

President: Lift up your hearts.

All: **We lift them unto the Lord.**

President: Let us give thanks to the Lord.

All: **It is meet and right to do so.**

President: Thanks be to thee, holy Father of
glory,
Father kind, ever-loving, ever-powerful
because of all the abundance, favour and
deliverance
that thou bestowest upon us in our need
through thine ever-living and true son
our saviour, Jesus Christ.
He is the lamb slain
before the foundation of the world,
the perfect sacrifice for all our sins;
Therefore, with angels and archangels
and with all the company of heaven,
we proclaim thy great and glorious name,
for ever praising thee and saying,

All: **Holy, holy, holy Lord,**
God of power and might,
heaven and earth are full of thy glory,
Hosanna in the highest.

Blessed is He who comes in the name of
the Lord,
Hosanna in the highest.

President: Accept our praises, heavenly Father,
through thy son our saviour, Jesus Christ;
and as we follow his example and obey his
command,
grant that by the power of thy Holy Spirit
these gifts of bread and wine
may be to us his body and blood;
who in the same night that he was betrayed
took bread and gave thee thanks;
he broke it and gave it to his disciples
saying,

'Take, eat; this is my body
which is given to you; do
this in remembrance of me.'

In the same way, after supper
he took the cup, and gave thee thanks;
he gave it to them saying,

'Drink this, all of you;
this is my blood of the new
covenant, which is shed for
you and for many for the
forgiveness of sins. Do this,
as often as you drink it, in
remembrance of me.'

All: **Christ has died:**
Christ is risen:
Christ will come again.

President: Almighty God, our heavenly Father,
    in your tender mercy,
    send us the Spirit of the Lamb,
    send us the loving Spirit of the Lamb.

All: **Jesus, Lamb of God:**
        have mercy on us.
    Jesus, bearer of our sins:
        have mercy on us.
    Jesus, redeemer of the world:
        give us your peace.

President: If thou are thirsty, drink the Fount of
    Life.
    If thou art hungry, eat the Bread of Life.
    Blessed are they who hunger for this Bread
    and thirst for this Fount.

After Communion

All: **Almighty Father, Son and Holy Spirit,**
    Eternal, ever-blessed, gracious God,
    To me, the least of saints, to me, allow
    That I may keep a door in Paradise;
    That I may keep even the smallest door,
    The furthest door, the darkest, coldest
        door,
    The door that is least used, the stiffest
        door,
    If so it be but in thine house, O God!
    If so it be that I can see thy Glory
    Even afar and hear thy Voice, O God!
    And know that I am with thee,
        thee, O God.

President: I bless you, in the Name of the
        Father, the Son,
and the Sacred Spirit,
the One and the Three.
May God give you to drink of his cup;
may the sun be bright upon you,
may the night call down peace
and when you come to his household
may the door be open wide for you to go in
to your joy.

President: Go in peace to love and serve the
        Lord

All: **In the Name of Christ,**
Amen.

FAMILY SHABBAT

Family Shabbat

This is a 'family prayers' based on the prayers for Shabbat. It could be used each Friday evening at the beginning of a shared meal, or whenever the family wish to break bread together with their friends and guests.

The order has three sections:

1 The lighting of candles – led only by women/girls
2 The breaking of bread – led only by men/boys
3 Thanksgiving before sharing a meal – prayed by anybody.

If no meal is planned use 1 or 2. If no candles, no women, or it is not appropriate, use 2 and 3. If no men, no bread or wine, or it is not desirable to break bread, use 1 and 3. Or each section could be used individually.

Candles

A single candle may be used for simplicity, but these prayers are only to be used by a woman (or girl). This is her privilege exclusively. If you have enough candles and holders the following is the normal practice. Each woman or girl lights a candle of her own (remembering also to pray for, or give thanks for, her own mother). A married woman also lights another candle for her husband, and one for each of her children, and these she sets in front of her. A single or divorced woman, or a widow, will light only one candle, plus ones for any children she may have who are still living.

The blessing is done outwards palm-down,

and the prayer of blessing said by whichever women or girls have candles lit. It may be said together. (The bracketed section is said only by a woman praying for her children.) The intimate prayer is said with eyes covered, perhaps one at a time, by the womenfolk.

Then, 'Thou art our trust, O King of kings' as hands are taken from eyes may be said by all the women together, looking at the candles.

Usually the rest of these prayers would be said by the woman in whose home you are gathered, but any female person will do, and a small girl could repeat them if desired. Do all this as quickly or as slowly as you feel is appropriate to the occasion or to your needs as a household. It need only take a few moments.

Bread and wine

These prayers should only be used by the menfolk, and a man or boy should have the bread or wine before him, breaking the bread and passing it to the next person. He may eat first or last as desired.

The same procedure is followed with passing and drinking the wine.

A shared table

Food may have been prepared for the guests, or they may even have brought food as well to contribute to the shared meal, but in any case you should endeavour to sit at one table, and leave one spare place-setting, or one seat free. This is to welcome the Christ who comes in the guise of the stranger or 'unexpected' visitor. This reminds us that we long for the coming of

Christ, His returning, and yet honour His presence with us; also, it teaches us to treat with honour whoever may come and be given the place prepared as His.

The woman:

Blessed are You, Lord, High King above all kings,
    our Father for ever and ever.
Thine, O Lord, is the greatness, the power, the
    glory, for ever and ever. Amen.

(Lighting candles) Let Thy face, O Lord, shine
    forth upon us, and be Thou merciful unto us.

(Moving hands forward with circular motion
    outwards from candles, three times): The
    peace of God . . . and of Christ . . . and of
    the Holy Spirit . . . be upon us (*and upon our*
    children, us and our children) for ever more.

(Covering eyes with hands): I do not think that I
    shall fear Thee when I see Thee face to face.

(Removing hands from eyes, and looking at
    candles): Thou art our trust, O King of kings.

I pray that no envy and malice, no hatred or
    fear, may smother the flame.
I pray that indifference and apathy, contempt
    and pride, may not extinguish its light.
Be with us by day, be with us by night,
    and as darkness covers the earth
    keep our lights shining brightly.
We are on a journey, for our hearts have run
    before us to Your Kingdom;
once far off, we have now been brought near.

See how good and joyful a thing it is
    to dwell together in unity!

The man:

(Taking bread): Blessed are You, Lord,
   High King above all kings, for through Your
   goodness we have this bread.
You have given us Your peace, and set a hunger
   in our hearts. Restore our strength.
Give new energy to tired limbs,
   new thought to weary minds.

(Share bread)

(Taking wine): Blessed are You, Lord,
   High King above all kings, for through Your
   goodness we have this wine.
We thank You for Your loving kindness
   which has filled our days
   and brought us to this time and place.
May the wine restore our souls,
   giving new vision to dry spirits,
   new warmth to cold hearts.

(Share wine)

(Before eating): Bless, O Lord, this food we are
   about to eat,
and we pray you, O God,
that it may be good for our body and soul,
and if there is any poor creature
hungry or thirsty walking the road,
may God send them in to us
so that we can share the food with them,
just as Christ shares His gifts with all of us.

JANUARY READINGS

JANUARY READINGS

Consider my meditation

Day 1 Psalm 46:6–11
        Ezekiel 10:6–18
        Mark 1:35–37
Day 2 Psalm 1:1–3
        1 Samuel 1:12–17
        Luke 8:40–46
Day 3 Psalm 27:7–10
        Isaiah 49:13–16
        Romans 8:15
Day 4 Psalm 119:105–109
        Jeremiah 31:6–9
        Luke 23:39–46
Day 5 Psalm 89:19–29
        1 Samuel 16:17–22
        Philippians 4:12–13
Day 6 Psalm 116:12–14
        Genesis 49:10–11
        Luke 7:42–48
Day 7 Psalm 18:25–29
        Isaiah 35:3–8
        Philippians 3:12–4:1
Day 8 Psalm 78:70–72
        Exodus 2:11–15
        Matthew 18:32–35
Day 9 Psalm 147:1–3
        Proverbs 23:12–17
        Matthew 18:12–22
Day 10 Psalm 106:7–12
        Joshua 4:1–24
        Mark 9:17–24
Day 11 Psalm 31:9–13

Jeremiah 32:6–15
Luke 22:54–65
Day 12 Psalm 127:1–2
Isaiah 30:15–18
James 5:11
Day 13 Psalm 126:4–6
Isaiah 43:18–21
Jude 20–23
Day 14 Psalm 109:25–29
Numbers 23:5–12
1 Corinthians 1:20–30
Day 15 Psalm 142:5–7
Numbers 24:2–9
Matthew 21:18–22
Day 16 Psalm 107:35–37
Malachi 3:2–4, 7–12
Luke 10:17–21
Day 17 Psalm 17:5–7
Isaiah 40:3–5
Mark 1:15–18
Day 18 Psalm 84:3–7
Malachi 3:16–18
Romans 8:14–17
Day 19 Psalm 107:28–31
2 Kings 4:8–10
Mark 6:30–31
Day 20 Psalm 87:5–7
2 Kings 4:1–6
Ephesians 5:15–21
Day 21 Psalm 55:16–17
Daniel 6:10–14
1 Thessalonians 5:16–18
Day 22 Psalm 3:3–5
2 Samuel 22:20–21
1 Corinthians 13:12–13
Day 23 Psalm 121:1–4
Isaiah 42:1–4

John 12:20–21
Day 24 Psalm 18:30–36
Habbakuk 3:17–19
Luke 19:37–41
Day 25 Psalm 119:111–12
Ezekiel 3:1–3
Luke 9:24–38
Day 26 Psalm 115:2–8
Numbers 6:24–26
John 6:66–68
Day 27 Psalm 45:10–11
Song of Songs 2:8–14
Revelation 19:6–8
Day 28 Psalm 36:5–9
Nehemiah 13:19–22
Luke 12:32–34
Day 29 Psalm 141:1–2
1 Kings 17:6–16
Matthew 10:38–42
Day 30 Psalm 46:1–11
1 Kings 18:4
John 6:31–34
Day 31 Psalm 118:22–26
Isaiah 28:16
John 2:22–3:3

Day 1

Psalm 46:6-11   Ezekiel 10:6-18   Mark 1:35-37

The world gives itself
up to incessant activity
merely because
it knows of nothing
better.
The inspired man
works among
its whirring wheels
also, but he knows
whither the wheels
are going.
For he has found
the centre
where all is
stillness . . .

Paul Brunton

This month the Scripture passages have been chosen to complement the meditations we use each month on that particular date. Instead of study notes there are songs or quotations to stimulate us to action or to quiet.

Consider my meditation

Day 2

Psalm 1:1-3   1 Samuel 1:12-17   Luke 8:40-46

(These verses may be sung to any of the tunes used for 'When I survey the wondrous cross', and are brought us by Wild Goose of Iona!)

Inspired by Love and Anger

When trouble strikes and fear takes root
And dreams are dry and sense unsound
When hope becomes a barren waste,
Then doubts like mountains soar around.

Our wandering minds believe the worst
And ask, as faith and fervour fade,
'Has God now turned his back on us,
Forsaking those he loved and made?'

God says, 'See how a woman cares,
Can she forget the child she bore?
Even if she did, I shan't forget
Though feeling lost, I love you more.'

Day 3

Psalm 27:7–10   Isaiah 49:13–16   Romans 8:15

God says, 'See how a woman cares,
Can she forget the child she bore?
Even if she did, I shan't forget
Though feeling lost, I love you more.

'My dearest daughter, fondest son,
My weary folk in every land,
Your souls are cradled in my heart
Your names are written on my hand.'

Then praise the Lord through faith and fear,
In holy and in hopeless place,
For height and depth and heaven and hell
Can't keep us far from his embrace.

Day 4

Psalm 119:105–109   Jeremiah 31:6–9
                        Luke 23:39–46

A healthy child is
somehow very much
like God. A hurting
child, his son.
from Calvin Miller's 'The Singer'

In 'The Singer' Earthmaker and his Troubadour
sit down on the outer rim of space and look
at our planet. Earthmaker holds it to his ear . . .

'They're crying, Troubadour,' he said. 'They
cry so hopelessly.' He gave the tiny planet to
his Son who also held it by his ear. 'Year after
weary year they all keep crying. They seem
born to weep then die.'

Then with his nail he scraped the
atmosphere and both of them beheld the
planet bleed. Earthmaker set earth spinning on
its way and said, 'Give me your vast infinity,
my Son; I'll wrap it in a bit of clay.'

And so the Son became one of us.

Day 5

Psalm 89:19–29   1 Samuel 16:17–22
                   Philippians 4:12–13

A covenant sealed with blood commits both
parties to each other for ever. All they have
belongs to the other, and they will lay down
their life on the other's behalf.

Christ has many services to be done;
some are easy, others are difficult;
some bring honour, others bring reproach;
Some are suitable to our natural
inclinations and temporal interests,
others are contrary to both.
In some we may please Christ and please
  ourselves,
in others we cannot please Christ except by
  denying ourselves.
Yet the power to do all these things is assuredly
  given us in Christ, who strengthens us.

Therefore let us make
  the Covenant of God our own.
Let us engage our heart to the Lord,
and resolve in His strength never to go back!

the Covenant Service

Day 6

Psalm 116:12–14 Genesis 49:10–11 Luke 7:42–48

The Love of Jesus took Him to Calvary where
He forgave, and offered hope even as He
suffered.

We need to receive His mercy, but also to
show it to others. Jesus is Shiloh, the Awaited
One to whom all will gather. His wounds are
for our cleansing, His Blood the cup of our
salvation.

Hear the challenge of this Chuck Girard
song:

Don't shoot the wounded,
they need us more than ever.
Sometimes we just condemn them,
and don't take time to hear their story.
Don't shoot the wounded,
some day you might be one.

Day 7

Psalm 18:25–29   *Isaiah 35:3–8*
Philippians 3:12–4:1

Why do we call impossible what God calls
   possible?
Why do we call unforgivable what God has
   forgiven?
Why do we compromise with what God calls
   sin?
How we need to know God's heart, and reach
   out in His love and wisdom to others.

It's easy to love the people who are standing
   hard and fast,
Pressing on to meet that higher calling.
But the ones who might be struggling, we tend
   to judge too harshly
And refuse to try and catch them when they're
   falling.
We put people into boxes and we draw our hard
   conclusions
And when they do the things we know they
   should not do
We sometimes write them off as hopeless and
   we throw them to the dogs.
Our compassion and forgiveness sometimes seem
   in short supply . . .

Day 8

Psalm 78:70–72   *Exodus 2:11–15*
                    Matthew 18:32–35

We can love them and forgive them
  when their sin does not exceed our own
For we too have been down bumpy roads before.
But when they commit offences outside the
  boundaries we have set,
We judge them in a word and we turn them out,
  and we close the door.
Myself, I've been forgiven for so many awful
  things,
I've been cleansed and washed and bathed so
  many times
That when I see a brother who has fallen from
  the way
I just can't find the licence to convict him of his
  crimes.

C.G.

Day 9

Psalm 147:1–3   *Proverbs 23:12–17*
                    Matthew 18:12–22

Don't shoot the wounded!

That doesn't mean we turn our heads when we
  see a brother sin
And pretend that what he's doing is all right.
We must help him see his error, we must lead
  him to repent,
Cry with those who cry, but bring their deeds
  into the light.

For it's the sick that need the doctor, and it's the
    lame that need the crutch;
It's the prodigal who needs the loving hand.
For a man who's in despair there should be
    kindness from his friends
Lest he should forsake the fear of almighty God
and turn away from God and man.

C.G.

Day 10

Psalm 106:7–12   Joshua 4:1–24   Mark 9:17–24

Stumbling Blocks and Stepping Stones
(a song from Wild Goose of Iona)

Unsure, when what was bright turns dark
And life, it seems, has lost its way,
We question what we once believed
And fear that doubt has come to stay.
We sense the worm that gnaws within
Has withered willpower, weakened bones,
And wonder whether all that's left
Is stumbling blocks or stepping stones.

Day 11

Psalm 31:9–13 Jeremiah 32:6–15 Luke 22:54–65

In the midst of negative circumstances we have
to try hard to remember God's promises, remain
true to Him, make sure there is something left to
come back to and hold on to.

In Jeremiah's case he bought a field when it
seemed a foolish step.

Where minds and bodies reel with pain
Which nervous smiles can never mask,
And hope is forced to face despair
And all the things it dared not ask;
Aware of weakness, guilt or shame,
The will gives out, the spirit groans,
And clutching at each straw we find
More stumbling blocks
   than stepping stones.

Day 12

Psalm 127:1–2   Isaiah 30:15–18   James 5:11

To have confidence in God is a hard lesson to
learn. When all goes well our gratitude quickly
evaporates and becomes carelessness. When
life is troubled our reflex is to try and right
things ourselves, employing only human
reckoning of resources available. Our greatest
strength is not to struggle, but to trust there
will be a way forward.

Where family life has lost its bliss
And silences endorse mistrust,
Or anger boils and tempers flare
As love comes under threat from lust;
Where people cannot take the strain
Of worklessness and endless loans
What pattern will the future weave –
Just stumbling blocks?
   no stepping stones?

Day 13

Psalm 126:4-6   *Isaiah 43:18-21*   *Jude 20-23*

As Caleb's daughter was an asker, so we need
to take courage and seek for springs not only
for our own survival, but that others may
know the life of God. The life ahead of us is
new, and it is even the ancient springs which
will bring waters that are always fresh and
new.

We must ask boldly of our Father:

Where hearts that once held love are bare
And faith, in shreds, compounds the mess;
Where hymns and prayers no longer speak
And former friends no longer bless;
And when the church where some belonged
No more their loyalty enthrones,
The plea is made, 'If You are there,
Turn stumbling blocks
   to stepping stones.'

Day 14

Psalm 109:25-29   *Numbers 23:5-12*
            1 Corinthians 1:20-30

God loves paradoxes and contradictions. When
we are weak, we are strong. Every curse
becomes a blessing, and stumbling blocks can
be turned to stepping stones; the valley of
Achor where all was destroyed can be a
doorway of hope.

Ah God, you with the Maker's eye,
Can tell if all that's feared is real,
And see if life is more than what
We suffer, dread, despise and feel.
If some by faith no longer stand
Nor hear the truth your voice intones,
Stretch out your hand to help your folk
From stumbling blocks to stepping stones.

Day 15

Psalm 142:5-7   *Numbers 24:2-9*
                Matthew 21:18-22

The following song from the third chapter of
the book of Malachi was given in 1978 as a
prayer for the Islanders. Lindisfarne, long
dubbed the 'Holy Island', still needs a witness
to each succeeding generation, and God will
have a presence there in His people.

The Island's inhabitants walk often
unknowingly in the field of an on-going
spiritual conflict.

When the work is done,
When comes the day of the Refiner's fire,
When they are purged like gold and silver
To offer Me an offering in righteousness
Then shall the offering of My people in My holy
    place
Be pleasant unto Me, the Lord your God,
As in the days of old,
    and as in former years:
A place of peace,
    a dwelling-place for man and God.

Day 16

Psalm 107:35–37   *Malachi 3:2–4, 7–12*
Luke 10:17–21

Why should the former glory of these holy
places be greater than what can happen in
these latter days? Look at Haggai chapter 2,
and you find it need not be so. There again
God reminds us the first tenth of our income,
at least, must be dedicated to Him – or we are
robbing Him.

   Can we afford to do this?
   Can we afford not to?

When the time is come,
When they return to Me in everything they do
And I am first,
   then will heaven's windows open wide
And pour a blessing bigger than you can contain.
Then shall the offering
   of My people in My holy place
Be pleasant unto Me, the Lord your God,
As in the days of old,
   and as in former years:
A place of peace,
   a dwelling-place for man and God.

Day 17

Psalm 17:5-7   Isaiah 40:3-5   Mark 1:15-18

It is by God's grace that our feet don't lose
contact with the path we set out to follow. We
say, 'Here I am, Lord' when He calls. He calls
continually to the willing and the unwilling. It
is not so much our ability He has need of, but
our availability.

I see a Man walking by the seashore,
whistling gently to the waves of those
who will come to restore the ruined
places, who're crying,
'PREPARE YE THE WAY!

PREPARE YE THE WAY, PREPARE YE THE
WAY,
PREPARE YE THE WAY OF THE LORD!
Prepare ye the way, Prepare ye the way.
Prepare ye the way of the Lord!'

Jesus stands on the shore and whistles
for his people to respond, wave upon
wave. He calls them to bind the
broken-hearted, and build up waste places.

Bryan Pollard, 30.4.78

Day 18

Psalm 84:3-7 Malachi 3:16-18 Romans 8:14-17

Each of us has the potential to become a son
of God, an heir to all that is His, for each of
us, male or female, in every place, has been
made in His image, with chance to choose
Him.

Only after we have yielded to Him can we
   reflect the face of Christ.
What kind of stones will Holy Island offer
   on His return?

When I the Lord shall come
To gather jewels for My diadem
Shall I find stones, resistant, hard and rough?
Or gems prepared and radiant with My glory?
And shall the offering of My people in My holy
   place
Be pleasant unto Me, the Lord your God?
As in the days of old,
   and as in former years:
A place of peace,
   a dwelling-place for man and God?

So hearken unto Me
   and follow Me with all your heart.

Day 19

Psalm 107:28–31   2 Kings 4:8–10   Mark 6:30–31

Time for everything but prayer

Why is there so little anxiety to get time to
pray? Why is there so little forethought in the
laying out of time and employments so as to
secure a large portion of each day for prayer?

Why is there so much speaking, yet so little
prayer? Why is there so much running to and
fro, yet so little prayer? Why so much bustle
and business, yet so little prayer? Why so
many meetings with our fellow-men, yet so
few meetings with God?

Why so little being alone, so little thirsting

of the soul for the calm, sweet hours of
unbroken solitude, when God and his child
hold fellowship together as if they could never
part?

It is the want of these solitary hours that not
only injures our own growth in grace but
makes us such unprofitable members of the
church of Christ, and that renders our lives
useless.

Horatius Bonar

Day 20

Psalm 87:5–7   2 Kings 4:1–6   Ephesians 5:15–21

In one single quiet hour of prayer the soul will
often make more progress than in days of
company with others. It is in the desert that
the eye gets the clearest, simplest view of
eternal certainties; it is in His presence alone,
it is then that the soul gathers in wondrous
refreshment and power and energy.

And so it is also in this way that we become
truly useful to others. It is when coming out
fresh from communion with God that we go
forth to do His work successfully.

In nearness to God we get our vessels so
filled with blessing, that, when we come forth,
we can not contain it to ourselves but must, as
by a blessed necessity, pour it out
whithersoever we go.

Horatius Bonar

Day 21

Psalm 55:16–17   *Daniel 6:10–14*
1 Thessalonians 5:16–18
(From the Covenant Service)

O God our Father, who hast set forth the way
of life for us in Thy beloved Son: We confess
with shame our slowness to learn of Him, our
reluctance to follow Him. Thou hast spoken
and called, and we have not given heed; Thy
beauty has shone forth and we have been
blind; Thou hast stretched out Thy hands to us
through our fellows and we have passed by.
We have taken great benefits with little thanks;
we have been unworthy of Thy changeless
love.

Have mercy upon us and forgive us, O Lord.

Day 22

Psalm 3:3–5   *2 Samuel 22:20–21*
1 Corinthians 13:12–13

It was only Nicodemus who was told to be
born again, the adultress who was told
'Neither do I condemn you, go, and sin no
more', but we all identify with them and learn
from the conversation Jesus had with them.

This song was a prophecy for one man, but
we can all learn from it:

Reservoir

You place my feet upon a larger place, Lord,
You give my hands a greater task for You.
You set my eyes upon the far horizon
and in my heart I know Your word is true.

You place a reservoir within my heart, Lord,
    that all my tears
        would come from a different place:
that all my ways would minister Your grace
    to those who long
    to see Your face.

Day 23

Psalm 121:1–4   Isaiah 42:1–4   John 12:20–21

Even as the tide comes in and goes out again,
so we are drawn to retreat into silence and
aloneness with God, then released to be
involved in the going and activity again.
    Most of the world would like to see
something of Jesus, but how we fail to show
Him through our life! How seldom when we
speak is it what He has given us to be said!

So in my life may I know Your approval;
So may I move out with Your commendation,
that my words may be filled with Your grace and
    truth
From the reservoir within my heart.

You place a reservoir within my heart, Lord,
    that all my tears
        would come from a different place:
that all my ways would minister Your grace
    to those who long
    to see Your face.

Day 24

Psalm 18:30-36   *Habbakuk 3:17-19*
Luke 19:37-41

I'm not defeated. I'm an overcomer. I want to
live to give glory to You, God. All creation
resounds with Your praise and longs to be finally
reconciled. I am part of Your purposes.

You cause my heart to soar like an eagle,
You teach my feet to conquer like a deer.
All I survey shall echo with Your praise,
and Lord,
  I know that *I* must know You here.

You place a reservoir within my heart, Lord,
  that all my tears
    would come from a different place:
that all my ways would minister Your grace
  to those who long
    to see Your face.

Teach us, Lord, to cry with Your tears, as well as
our own.

Day 25

Psalm 119:111-112   *Ezekiel 3:1-3*
Luke 9:24-38

God's life in our life is always a miracle.
Something which is known to have been from
the beginning, this we have heard, and seen
with our own eyes, something we have touched
and have carefully watched, the Word who is
life, this we share with those whose lives touch
our own.

Suddenly the miracle seems possible – to
them, and once again to us also.

I knew a blind man
whom a surgeon
helped to see.
The doctor never had a
lover such as he.
It is in such a way
that singers love
composers.
                    Calvin Miller

Day 26

Psalm 115:2–8 Numbers 6:24–26 John 6:66–68

If we have truly looked at God then we are
different – there is a difference for always. An
old man and his wife had been married for
many years. Content in each other's company
they rarely needed to speak.
   Another man, speaking of his way of
praying, has said, 'I looks at Him, and He
looks at me, and we're happy together.'

My eyes, my eyes have seen the King.
my eyes, my eyes have seen the King.
The vision of His beauty
   has pierced me deep within;
to whom else can I go?

                    J.T.S.

Day 27

His Bride is a corporate Bride made up of all
those who love Him and put Him before
everything else. He loves us and longs to spend
time alone with us. He loves to hear us speak
to Him, and we love Him because He loves us
first, and drew us to Him.

My heart, my heart desires Him,
my heart, my heart desires Him.
He's touched something inside of me
that's now reaching out for Him,
and I know that I must go.

Day 28

The following passage is from *The Last Battle*,
the seventh and final of the Narnia stories by
C. S. Lewis:

Farewell to Shadowlands

'Farther up and farther in!' roared the
Unicorn, and no one held back. They charged
straight at the foot of the hill and then found
themselves running up it almost as water from
a broken wave runs up a rock out at the point
of some bay. Though the slope was nearly as
steep as the roof of a house and the grass was

smooth as a bowling green, no one slipped.
Only when they had reached the very top did
they slow up; that was because they found
themselves facing great golden gates. And for a
moment none of them was bold enough to try
if the gates would open. They all felt just as
they had felt about the fruit – 'Dare we? Is it
right? Can it be meant for *us*?'

But while they were standing thus a great
horn, wonderfully loud and sweet, blew from
somewhere inside that walled garden and the
gates swung open.

Day 29

Psalm 141:1–2   *1 Kings 17:6–16*
                Matthew 10:38–42

Francis of Assisi said that he was in love with
a lady whose name was Poverty. In the
meditation Brother Juniper talks about his own
more stormy relationship with Lady Poverty.

He has learnt to trust God and catches
glimpses, in this trust, of a deeper reality, of
heaven itself.

Farther up and Farther in

Perhaps you will get some idea of it if you
think like this. You may have been in a room
in which there was a window that looked out
on a lovely bay of the sea or a green valley
that wound away among mountains. And in
the wall of that room opposite to the window
there may have been a looking-glass. And the
sea in the mirror, or the valley in the mirror,

were in one sense just the same as the real
one: yet at the same time they were somehow
different – deeper, more wonderful, more like
places in a story: in a story you have never
heard but very much want to know.

C. S. Lewis

Day 30

Psalm 46:1–11   1 Kings 18:4   John 6:31–34

We cry out to God to be our refuge and
strength, our hiding place. We find others who
have also taken refuge in Him, and are
beginning to build from what is broken.
    Gerry Tuohy's song has captured the flavour
of what God has built in Ireland, and has
spoken also to us concerning Northumberland.

God called forth a people
And we responded to His call,
'Rebuild this ancient ruin,
Restore my city walls.'

He has led us day by day.
As we listened to His voice,
And we were fed on finest wheat,
And manna from the skies.

When we started, we were strangers,
We hardly knew each other's names.
Now we are brothers and sisters,
And we will never be the same.

Day 31

Psalm 118:22-26   Isaiah 28:16   John 2:22-3:2

God called forth a people
And we responded to His call,
'Rebuild this ancient ruin,
Restore my city walls.'

As we built, brick by brick
We discovered the cornerstone
And as we let Him mould and fashion us,
He built us up in love.

Now we have seen,
And we have heard,
That the Lord our God is great
For a wilderness has been transformed
Into His holy place.

FEBRUARY READINGS

Devoted to Him

Brother Lawrence
Day 1   Psalm 80:17
        Judges 6:14-24
        Revelation 3:20

Michel Quoist
Day 2   Psalm 139:7-8
        Ruth 1:16
        1 John 4:16, 18

Marjorie Milne
Day 3   Psalm 149:1-4
        Songs of Songs 1:4
        Matthew 11:16-17

Ian Petit
Day 4   Psalm 119:105
        Isaiah 11:1-2
        John 5:30

Catherine Baird
Day 5   Psalm 119:107
        Isaiah 53:11
        Mark 1:16-17

Madelaine L'Engle
Day 6   Psalm 119:96
        Judges 6:11-16
        John 1:43-50

Henry Drummond
Day 7   Psalm 119:112
        Joshua 24:15
        Matthew 10:29

Monk of Farne
Day 8   Psalm 91:1
         Jeremiah 33:3
         Romans 8:38-39

Ann Kiemel
Day 9   Psalm 91:2
         Daniel 4:29-37
         John 8:36

Oscar Romero
Day 10 Psalm 91:9-10
         Nehemia 9:1-3
         John 8:2–11

Ronald Rolheiser
Day 11 Psalm 35:19-24
         Genesis 4:10-16
         Revelation 4:1

Fr James Kavanagh
Day 12 Psalm 35:27-28
         Song of Songs 5:4
         Luke 13:29

Florence Converse
Day 13 Psalm 35:14
         Ezekiel 22:29-30
         Romans 12:21

Pat Lynch
Day 14 Psalm 8:4-5
         1 Samuel 3:4-7
         Luke 11:1-4

Glenn Clark
Day 15 Psalm 8:6
         Genesis 8:22
         Philippians 4:8

Thomas H. Green
Day 16 Psalm 8:3-4,9
         1 Kings 19:11-12
         Matthew 6:28-30

Horatius Bonar
Day 17 Psalm 63:1,8
         Song of Songs 7:11
         Luke 9:10

Arthur Burt
Day 18 Psalm 63:1-2
         Ezekiel 47:3-5
         Acts 4:15-21

Jeanne Guyon
Day 19 Psalm 63:3-7
         1 Samuel 10:10-11
         Acts 17:28

Thomas Merton
Day 20 Psalm 62:11-12
         Isaiah 58:5-6
         Matthew 6:5

Clement of Rome
Day 21 Psalm 62:4,8
         Isaiah 53:7
         1 Thessalonians 3:1-8

Carlo Cerrotto
Day 22 Psalm 48:3
         2 Samuel 12:5-7
         James 3:10-14

Malcolm Smith
Day 23 Psalm 61:5
         2 Kings 2:6
         2 Corinthians 13:5

Roland Walls
Day 24 Psalm 61:4
       Isaiah 60:1
       Matthew 16:28,7:8

C. S. Lewis
Day 25 Psalm 61:1-3, 6-8
       Song of Songs 3:1-4
       1 Corinthians 2:9-10

Ralph Wouldbam
Day 25 Psalm 125:2
       Song of Songs 8:6
       John 16:15

Henri J. M. Nouwen
Day 27 Psalm 122:8
       Daniel 6:19-23
       Phiilippians 1:3-5

Larry & Pearl Brick
Day 28 Psalm 127:2
       Isaiah 58:10-11
       Luke 2:8,18

Catherine de Hueck Doberty
Day 29 Psalm 138:8
       Song of Songs 4:12
       Mark 6:30-32

Day 1

Psalm 80:17   Judges 6:14-24   Revelation 3:20

This month the readings are from the writings of different Christians, both contemporary and from the past, all of them ***Devoted to Him.***

Pray remember what I have recommended to you, which is, to think often of God, by day, by night, in your business, and even in your diversions. He is always near you and with you; leave Him not alone. You would think it rude to leave a friend alone who came to visit you: why then must God be neglected? Do not then forget Him, but think of Him often, adore Him continually, live and die with Him; this is the glorious employment of a Christian; if we do not know it we must learn it.

Brother Lawrence
The Practice of the Presence of God

Day 2

Psalm 139:7-8   Ruth 1:16   1 John 4:16, 18

Lord, you seized me and I could not resist you.
I ran for a long time, but you followed me.
I took by-paths, but you knew them.
You overtook me. I struggled. You won.
Here I am, Lord, out of breath, no fight left in me,
    and I've said 'yes' almost unwillingly.
When I stood there trembling
  like one defeated before his captor,
  your look of love fell on me.

The die is cast, Lord, I can no longer forget you.
In a moment you seized me,
    in a moment you conquered me.
My doubts were swept away, my fears dispelled.
Nothing matters to me,
    neither my comfort, nor even my life.
I desire only you, I want nothing but you.

Michel Quoist
Prayers of Life

Day 3

Psalm 149:1-4   *Song of Songs 1:4*
Matthew 11:16-17

Christ 'in giving Himself to us has become our fellow-pilgrim on life's journey.' But He said 'I piped to you and you would not dance.' In the face of this Christ I felt myself 'so heavy footed and drowsy.' I asked him, therefore, to wake me, 'rouse me, let me dance hour by hour to your piping in all I do all day long,' concluding 'I have trusted in Him and I am helped, therefore my heart danceth for joy and in my song I will praise Him. So make us Thine that we may be a chalice of joy.'

Marjorie Milne
from 'Glastonbury Journey' – Brian Frost

Day 4

Psalm 119:105　　　*Isaiah 11:1-2*　　　*John 5:30*

I am forever speculating about how much
Jesus knew. As God, of course, he would know
everything. Did that knowledge affect his
human knowledge? I tend to side with those
who say that his human knowledge was
incomplete. I find comfort in thinking of him
also in the dark, following blindly the Father's
will. He was asked to fail, to be conquered, to
be hounded out of the city and to die as a
criminal. Could he see through all that to the
victory to follow? It is difficult to tell. I find it
good to wrestle with such questions, and in
prayer to ask the Lord to enlighten me. What
happened to the Master will surely happen to
the disciple; we, too, will suffer hardship, and
perhaps for no apparent reason.

Ian Petit
The God who speaks

Day 5

Psalm 119:107　　　*Isaiah 53:11*　　　*Mark 1:16-17*

When Jesus looked o'er Galilee,
So blue and calm and fair,
Upon her bosom, could He see
A Cross reflected there?

When sunrise dyed the lovely deeps,
And sparkled in His hair,
O did the light rays seem to say:
A crown of thorns He'll wear?

When in the hush of eventide,
Cool waters touched His feet
Was it a hymn of Calvary's road
He heard the waves repeat?

But when the winds triumphantly
Swept from the open plain,
The Master surely heard the song:
The Lord shall live again!

Catherine Baird

Day 6

Psalm 119:96   Judges 6:11-16   John 1:43-50

We are all asked to do more than we can do.
Every hero and heroine of the Bible does more
than he would have thought it possible to do,
from Gideon to Esther to Mary. Jacob, one of
my favourite characters, certainly wasn't
qualified. He was a liar and a cheat; and yet
he was given the extraordinary vision of angels
and archangels ascending and descending a
ladder which reached from earth to heaven.

In the first chapter of John's Gospel,
Nathanael is given a glimpse of what Jacob
saw, or a promise of it, and he wasn't qualified
either. He was narrow-minded and
unimaginative, and when Philip told him that
Jesus of Nazareth was the one they sought, his
rather cynical response was, 'Can anything
good come out of Nazareth?' And yet it was to
Nathanael that Jesus promised the vision of
angels and archangels ascending and
descending upon the son of man.

Madelaine L'Engle
Walking on Water

Day 7

Psalm 119:112   Joshua 24:15   Matthew 10:29

Every hour a kingdom

Every hour a *kingdom* is coming in your heart, in your home, in the world near you, be it a kingdom of darkness or a kingdom of light.

The Bible does not say

The Bible does not say that everybody who is not a Christian is a notorious sinner; but it says that the man who lives outside that is wasting his life. He may not be doing wrong, but his life is lost.

No small sin

There is no such thing in the world as a great sin, but there is no such thing as a small sin. The smallest sin is a fall, and a fall is a fall from God, and to fall from God is to fall the greatest height in the universe.

Henry Drummond
A Mirror Set at the Right Angle

Day 8

Psalm 91:1   Jeremiah 33:3   Romans 8:38-39

So, precisely because I am a sinner, I have fled to thee; since there is nowhere I can flee from thee to save thee, Thou dost stretch out thine arms to receive me and bend down thy head to kiss me; thou dost bleed that I may have drink, and open thy side in thy desire to draw me within.

What then shall separate me from the love of Christ, and prevent me from casting myself into his embrace, when he stretches out his hands to me all day long? Shame at the sinfulness and impurity which defile me? No, indeed; a shame that would separate me from my Lord would be fatal. I will rather run to him as he beckons me to come, and by touching him I shall be cleansed from all impurity of body and soul. Should I fail to do so I would hear the words of Wisdom reproaching me: 'I stretched out my hand and thou didst not look; thou hast despised all my advice, and I shall laugh at thy destruction.' No, Lord, not so! I will gladly run to thee albeit a sinner, albeit unclean, for with thee there is merciful forgiveness; thou wilt wash me in thy blood, and I shall be made whiter than snow. I will enter into thee and not stay without, for outside thee there is no salvation.

Monk of Farne

Day 9

Psalm 91:2   *Daniel 4:29-37*   *John 8:36*

YES, i deal with guilt every day
    what counts is my heart's desire,
    only that my heart's motives be pure,
    and that i strive for that . . . day after day.

the devil must know guilt is my most vulnerable
    place. Some days he is most successful in
    destroying my creative energy and vitality
    – just in that very way.

YES to the fact that Jesus understands it all.
   He has never willed me to carry guilt.
YES to realizing that carrying guilt is a greater
   sin than the failures that caused it . . .
   that it negates all Christ paid to set us free.

YES to surrendering this area of my life to God,
   and not picking it up . . .
   over and over again.

Ann Kiemel
Yes

Day 10

Psalm 91:9-10   Nehemiah 9:1-3   John 8:2-11

How easy it is to denounce structural injustice,
institutionalized violence, social sin? And it is
true, this sin is everywhere, but where are the
roots of this social sin? In the heart of every
human being. Present-day society is a sort of
anonymous world in which no one is willing
to admit guilt and everyone is responsible.

   Because of this, salvation begins with the
human person, with human dignity, with
saving every person from sin. Individually
there are among us here no two sinners alike.
Each one has committed his or her own
shameful deeds, and yet we want to cast our
guilt on the other and hide our own sin. I
must take off my mask; I, too, am one of
them, and I need to beg God's pardon because
I have offended God and society. This is the
call of Christ.

   How beautiful the expression of that woman
upon finding herself pardoned and
understood: 'No one, Sir. No one has

condemned me.' Then neither do I, I who
could give that truly condemning word,
neither do I condemn; but be careful, brothers
and sisters, since God has forgiven us so many
times, let us take advantage of that friendship
with the Lord which we have recovered and
let us live it with gratitude.
Oscar Romero of El Salvador

Day 11

Psalm 35:19-24   Genesis 4:10-16   Revelation 4:1

If the Catholicism that I was raised in had a
fault, and it did, it was precisely that it did
not allow for mistakes. It demanded that you
get it right the first time. There was supposed
to be no need for a second chance. If you
made a mistake, you lived with it and, like the
rich young man, were doomed to be sad, at
least for the rest of your life. A serious mistake
was a permanent stigmatization, a mark that
you wore like Cain. *I have seen that mark on
all kinds of people:* divorcees, ex-priests, ex-
religious, people who have had abortions,
married people who have had affairs, people
who have had children outside of marriage,
parents who have made serious mistakes with
their children, and countless others who have
made serious mistakes. There is too little
around to help them. We need a theology of
brokenness. We need a theology which teaches
us that even though we cannot unscramble an
egg God's grace lets us live happily and with
renewed innocence far beyond any egg we

may have scrambled. *We need a theology that teaches us that God does not just give us one chance, but that every time we close a door he opens another one for us.*

Ronald Rolheiser
Forgotten among the Lilies

Day 12

Psalm 35:27-28   Song of Songs 5:4   Luke 13:29

I still believe in the power of the priesthood, where sinful men are helped by sinful men. I believe in an authority that stoops to wash a poor man's feet. I believe in a banquet where sinners learn to love, eating in company with their God. I believe in parents who teach their children the beauty that is life. I believe in the words that God has left for men, words that can fashion hope from darkness and turn bitter loneliness into love. And I believe in man, fashioned in mystery by God. I believe in the beauty of his mind, the force of his emotions, the fire and loyalty of his love. I know his weakness, his cowardice, his treachery, his hate. But I believe in him and his thirst for acceptance and love.

Most of all I believe in God and the power of His victory in Christ. I believe in a Resurrection that rescued man from death. I believe in an Easter that opened man to hope. I believe in a joy that no threat of man can take away. I believe in a peace that I know in fleeting moments and seek with boldness born of God. I believe in a life that lingers after this, a life that God has fashioned for His friends.

I believe in understanding, in forgiveness, in mercy, in faith. I believe in man's love for woman, and hers for him, and in the fervour of this exchange I hear the voice of God. I believe in friendship and its power to turn selfishness to love. I believe in eternity and the hope that it affords.

Fr James Kavanagh
A Modern Priest Looks at His Outdated Church

Day 13

Psalm 35:14   Ezekiel 22:29-30   Romans 12:21

How can you hope to make the imperfect things perfect, unless you keep before your eyes the vision of God, who is perfection? The prayer that is only against evil destroys itself. If you look at nothing but sorrow and sin, your heart may be at first full of love and pity, but presently anger – righteous perhaps, but still anger – will enter and begin to crowd out love; and then despair will come and deaden pity, and at last will even smother righteous anger. And then there will be silence; for the heart that is filled with despair cannot pray.

It is not enough to know that the world is full of evil, we must know also that God is good.

Christ is a part of all the poverty and misery because He was born into it and didn't try to get away from it. If you put Him in the background, with the sin and sorrow all in front, how he shines and makes courage and hope! Yes! And if you put Him in the front,

with the darkness all around Him, how He
shines again! Either way, He is the light in the
picture.

Florence Converse
The House of Prayer

Day 14

Psalm 8:4-5   *Luke 11:1-4*   *1 Samuel 3:4-7*

Notice that not once did Jesus make his
disciples pray. He just kept praying until at last
they could contain their hunger no longer and
asked him to teach them how to pray. The
question came from the twelve, indicating that
they were now ready to listen and to hear.
Jesus must have jumped at this opportunity of
holding before them his model of prayer. It is
interesting to note that he gave them a
formula, neat and tidy. It was almost as if he
was getting them into practice so that later on
their own prayer life could develop. It is also
interesting to note that in this first prayer
taught by Jesus there is no sentimentality,
piousness or rhetoric. It is simple, direct and
filled with nobility and sureness. It contains
simple praise and intercession.

Pat Lynch
Awakening the giant

Day 15

Psalm 8:6   *Genesis 8:22*   *Philippians 4:8*

After a farmer plants wheat he does not lie awake nights worrying lest radishes come up. He knows that it is the nature, or we might say the *virtue*, of wheat to grow wheat. It is the virtue of acorns to grow oak trees. And it is the virtue of prayers that are based upon that which is true, honest, just, pure, lovely and of good report, to come into fulfilment. Such a fulfilment is in accord with the inevitable unfoldment of all moral law. We do not have to argue or get excited or perspire over trying to make four plus four equal eight. It is the virtue of such a combination to become eight. It is the law of mathematics, irresistible and inevitable as the tides.

In the same irresistible, tidal way, trust to the inborn virtue residing in these laws of the true, the honest, the just, and the pure in your list of desires, and give them completely to God. Relinquish them into His hands, and go off and leave them. Do not worry about them, do not even pray for them for the next few weeks. Give them as completely as the farmer gives his wheat to the soil, after the soil has been properly ploughed and harrowed. Later on, when the weeds begin to come up, we may have to get into these prayers with a cultivator and re-mellow the soil of our faith a bit, but now, go off and leave them entirely.

Glenn Clark
I will lift up mine eyes

Day 16

Psalm 8:3-4, 9   1 Kings 19:11-12
Matthew 6:28-30

I find it good just to let my gaze wander,
without any concern for time and without any
attempt to force concentration. Gradually one
part of the woods catches my attention, and
then one tree, and eventually one branch on
the tree. My scattered thoughts come to focus
on a single experience, and then dive deeper
and deeper into that one reality (the universe
in a blade of grass). Oftentimes the result is
that my attention is absorbed by some small
flower or leaf at my feet which I had not even
noticed before – and I am at peace!

Thomas H. Green
Opening to God

Day 17

Psalm 63:1,8   Song of Songs 7:11   Luke 9:10

Why is there so little anxiety to get time to
pray? Why is there so little forethought in the
laying out of time and employment so as to
secure a large portion of each day for prayer?
Why is there so much speaking, yet so little
prayer? Why is there so much running to and
fro, yet so little prayer? Why so much bustle
and business, yet so little prayer? Why so
many meetings with our fellow-men, yet so
few meetings with God?

Why so little being alone, so little thirsting
of the soul for the calm, sweet hours of
unbroken solitude, when God and His child

hold fellowship together as it they could never part? It is the want of these solitary hours that not only injures our own growth in grace but makes us such unprofitable members of the church of Christ, and that renders our lives useless. It is not in society – even Christian society – that the soul grows most rapidly and vigorously. In *one single* quiet hour of prayer it will often make more progress than in days of company with others. It is in the desert that dew falls freshest and the air is purest. So with the soul. It is when none but God is nigh; when His presence alone, like the desert air in which there is mingled no noxious breath of man, surrounds and pervades the soul; it is then that the eye gets the clearest, simplest view of eternal certainties; it is then that the soul gathers in wondrous refreshment and power and energy.

And so it is also in this way that we become truly useful to others. It is when coming out fresh from communication with God that we go forth to do His work successfully.

Horatius Bonar
Words to Winners of Souls

Day 18

Psalm 63:1-2   Ezekiel 47:3-5   Acts 4:15-21

THE MAN
who has a great God
is little in his own eyes
BUT
the man who comes
to know God as He is,

becomes nothing
in his own eyes!

THE CHRISTIAN LIFE is not hard to live
– it's utterly impossible to live!
Only One can live it!
    LET HIM! IN YOU.

If you were arrested for being a Christian,
    is there enough evidence to convict you?
ARE YOU COMMITTED AS A CHRISTIAN?
Have you gone beyond the point of no return?

Arthur Burt
Pebbles to slay Golliath

Day 19

Psalm 63:3-7   1 Samuel 10:10-11   Acts 17:28

Some persons, when they hear of the prayer
of the quiet, falsely imagine the soul remains
stupid, dead, and inactive. But unquestionably
it acteth therein, more nobly and more
extensively than it had ever done before, for
God Himself is the Mover and the soul now
acteth by the agency of His Spirit . . . Instead,
then, of promoting idleness, we promote the
highest activity, by inculcating a total
dependence on the Spirit of God as our
moving principle, for in Him we live and
move and have our being . . . Our activity
should therefore consist in endeavouring to
acquire and maintain such a state as may be
most susceptible of divine impressions, most
flexible to all the operations of the Eternal
Word. Whilst a tablet is unsteady, the painter

is unable to delineate a true copy: so every act
of our own selfish and proper spirit is
productive of false and erroneous lineaments,
it interrupts the work and defeats the design
of the Artist.

Mme Jeanne Guyon

Day 20

Psalm 62:11-12   *Isaiah 58:5-6*   *Matthew 6:5*

Sometimes contemplatives think that the
whole end and essence of their life is to be
found in recollection and interior peace and
the sense of the presence of God. They
become attached to these things. But
recollection is just as much a creature as an
automobile. The sense of interior peace is no
less created than a bottle of wine. The
experimental 'awareness' of the presence of
God is just as truly a created thing as a glass
of beer. The only difference is that
recollection and interior peace and the sense
of the presence of God are spiritual pleasures
and the others are material. Attachment to
spiritual things is therefore just as much an
attachment as inordinate love of anything else.
The imperfection may be more hidden and
more subtle: but from a certain point of view
that only makes it all the more harmful
because it is not so easy to recognize.

Thomas Merton
Seeds of Contemplation

Day 21

Psalm 62:4,8   *Isaiah 53:7*
                    1 Thessalonians 3:1-8

Clement of Rome

Suppose there is friction and bad feeling in
your church – what should you do, especially
if you are involved in the arguments and
divisions yourself? Further, let's suppose that
you are in the right, that the trouble is not
your fault, and that you are a mature and
compassionate person. In that case, I suggest
that you should say to the elders and members
of the church: 'If I am in any way the cause of
this trouble, even if unwittingly, or if my
presence will in any way serve to perpetuate
it, I will move to another congregation . . . I
will go away anywhere you wish, and do
anything the congregation says – anything, if it
will contribute to peace among Christ's flock
and its pastors.'

Anyone who adopts this attitude will
deserve a high reputation amongst Christians,
and God's approval.

Veronica Zundel
The Lion of Christian Classics

Day 22

Psalm 48:3   *2 Samuel 12:5-7*   *James 3:10-14*

Where would we have been without this
Church? Who would have handed down to us,
across twenty centuries, the teaching of our
dear Lord Jesus? Who would have encouraged

us in the truth, reassured us in the path we
had undertaken?

The Church already was founded before we
appeared on the scene, and had we not come
on the scene would have gone on being saints
and sinners, capable of high ideals and base
enormities, the dwelling place of peace and a
jungle of violence.

But one thing is sure: if we should fail,
overwhelmed by our sins and our faithlessness,
the Church will not have failed. The 'little
remnant' will have arrived none the less. God
Himself is the guarantor.

Carlo Carretto
I, Francis

Day 23

Psalm 61:5   2 Kings 2:6   2 Corinthians 13:5

Christ, and only Christ, was the All in All.
Paul was saying that Christ living in a believer
was an observable fact, and that new believers
could learn by observing more mature
believers. Paul spoke of a Lord who could be
practically followed – and lived – with the
help of the lives of those gone before.

That which had been a spring of life within
me now leaped boldly, laughing in my spirit,
sending my doubts scurrying in disarray and
confusion. I laughed at my fleeting doubts. 'Are
you so shocked that what Paul preached actually
worked? Are you horrified that Paul expected
Christ to be seen in Him? Much of what you
call humility is a form of religious pride!'

Malcolm Smith
Follow Me

Day 24

Psalm 61:4   Isaiah 60:1   Matthew 16:28-17:8

In this momentary lifting of the veil, a
foretaste of the Resurrection glory, the true
meaning is given – the glory of such
humiliation. Here faith is given a glorious
icon. Each detail is a stroke of the brush, a
precious gem.

The true external value of the God who in
Christ hides himself in identifying himself with
us in all our fragility, insignificance even to
death, is the God who by so doing transforms
our nature with his own glory and majesty. By
the way of solidarity and temptation he leads
us into glory. He 'transfers us from the
kingdom of darkness into the kingdom of his
Son.'

Roland Walls
The Royal Mysteries

Day 25

Psalm 61:1-3, 6-8   Song of Songs 3:1-4
1 Corinthians 2:9–10

In speaking of this desire . . . I feel a certain
shyness. I am almost committing an indecency.
I am trying to rip open the inconsolable secret
in each one of you – the secret which hurts so
much that you take revenge on it by calling it
names like nostalgia and romanticism and
adolescence, the secret also which pierces
with such sweetness that, when, in every
intimate conversation, the mention of it
becomes imminent, we grow awkward and

affect to laugh at ourselves, the secret we
cannot hide and cannot tell.

C. S. Lewis

Day 26

Psalm 125:2   Song of Songs 8:6   John 16:15

The love of Christ is not a different love from
the eternal fire in the heart of God or that
which flows between the three persons of the
Trinity. We are loved passionately by God. The
self-sacrificing love between the three persons
is the joy at the centre of God. What is the
response from us to such love? To silently
wonder. We enter into the ebb and flow of this
divine love. The Holy Spirit enables us to
know something of the reality of this love in
the depths of our heart.

Ralph Wouldham

Day 27

Psalm 122:8   Daniel 6:19-23   Philippians 1:3-5

In solitude we can come to the realization that
we are not driven together but brought
together. In solitude we come to know our
fellow human beings not as partners who can
satisfy our deepest needs, but as brothers and
sisters with whom we are called to give
visibility to God's all-embracing love. In
solitude we discover that community is not a
common ideology, but a response to a
common call. In solitude we indeed realize
that community is not made but given.

Henri J. M. Nouwen
Clowning in Rome

Day 28

Do you ever start thinking,
'Lord, do I really have to love these people ?
Oh, I can't take it any more?'
Do you ever want to peg out?
   does it ever let up?
   is the war ever over, Lord?
   when is it going to get easy?

Jesus said His yoke is easy,
   and His burden is light.
He never said there won't be a yoke or
     burden,
   but that's alright.

The yoke is going to hold you,
   and a burden's made to bear.
Lord, when the load gets heavy on me,
I know You'll be there; I know You'll be there.

I tried to speak the truth in love today
   to someone walking the wrong way;
   it fell on stoney ground.
It seems the more I try to follow you,
   the more the enemy rages:
   he's not going to win.

I know You'll be there, I know You'll be there.
                    Larry & Pearl Brick
           from the 'See-Through Servant' album

Day 29

Psalm 138:8   Song of Songs 4:12   Mark 6:30-32

My island teaches me new truths, or deepens
the truths I already know. Like life, the island
is never the same. Who of us has not known
those 'naked days' when we feel the world is
against us, that its prying eyes strip us naked
and leave us crucified: days when we feel we
could give anything for a little privacy; days of
sorrow and pain when we want to hide and
have no place to hide?

But if one reads the Scriptures and comes
across its lovely poetic words about a 'garden
enclosed', a 'fountain sealed', and wonders
about it all, then my island will reveal the
secret of those holy words, and it will lead
gently to contemplation, which is the key to
that garden. Someday, unseen and unheard,
the Bridegroom will come into such a garden.
Then one will understand what it is to be all
his.

Catherine de Hueck Doberty
I Live on an Island

MARCH READINGS

Ask for the Old Paths

Day 1 Psalm 61:2–3
       Proverbs 18:10
       Ephesians 1:18–21
Day 2 Psalm 34:7–8
       Isaiah 6:1–3
       Matthew 25:15–23
Day 3 Psalm 3:3–4
       Job 38:4–13
       John 1:3–5
Day 4 Psalm 139:11–12
       1 Kings 18:21
       Romans 13:11–14
Day 5 Psalm 91:4–8
       Daniel 1:20
       Luke 10:18–20
Day 6 Psalm 139:5–8
       Deuteronomy 33:27
       Luke 23:33–34
Day 7 Psalm 96:11–13
       Jeremiah 33:3
       1 John 1:1–5
Day 8 Psalm 23:3–4
       Joel 2:25
       John 4:28–30
Day 9 Psalm 139:15–17
       Isaiah 66:3–4
       Hebrews 11:24–25
Day 10 Psalm 148:3–8
       Joel 3:14–16
       Acts 26:16–18
Day 11 Psalm 94:16–20

Day 1

Psalm 61:2–3   Proverbs 18:20   Ephesians 1:18-21

The readings for this month are fairly short, designed for meditating upon a mouthful at a time.

Jeremiah 6:16 tells us to *Ask for the old paths* and the commentary on these pages will largely be the stories and prayers of the Celtic saints.

We begin by slowly examining the much-used Celtic discipline of putting on St Patrick's Breastplate, calling on God to protect His servant.

I bind unto myself today
  the strong name of the Trinity
by invocation of the same,
the Three in One and One in Three.
I bind this day to me for ever,
by power of faith, Christ's Incarnation,
His baptism in the Jordan River;
His death on cross for my salvation;
His bursting from the spicèd tomb;
His riding up the heavenly way;
His coming at the day of doom;
I bind unto myself today.

Translation in verse
Mrs C. F. Alexander

Day 2

Psalm 34:7–8   Isaiah 6:1–3   Matthew 25:15–23

In 2 Kings 6:15–17 Elisha's servant has his spiritual eyes opened and can see what the man of God knew all along, the presence of angels defending them. 2 Samuel 5:23–24 tells us of David's army not moving until given the signal of the sound of angelic hosts marching overhead. Patrick knows himself to be in the company of all those who love and serve his God, all ranks of angels, earlier saints and elders, old testament men of faith, martyrs and monastics. All that matters is God's approval.

I bind unto myself the power
of the great love of the Cherubim;
the sweet 'Well done' in judgement hour;
the service of the Seraphim,
Confessors' faith, Apostles' word,
the Patriarchs' prayers, the Prophets' scrolls,
all good deeds done unto the Lord,
and purity of virgin souls.

Day 3

Psalm 3:3–4   Job 38:4–13   John 1:3–5

All of nature is invested with the loving care of an infinitely creative God. Each act of creation reflects some aspect of His love and strength. God is BIG, but still cares about every detail of what He has created, and so He cares for us. We can look to Him for direction. Jesus was able to say that He spoke what He was given to speak (John 8:26) and if we too can be sensitized to what is from Him (John 10:4-5) we will find the fear of the Lord is indeed the beginning of wisdom (Proverbs 15:31-33).

I bind unto myself today
the virtues of the starlit heaven,
the glorious sun's life-giving ray,
the whiteness of the moon at even,
the flashing of the lightning free,
the whirling wind's tempestuous shocks,
the stable earth, the deep salt sea,
around the old eternal rocks.
I bind unto myself today
the power of God to hold and lead,
His eye to watch, His might to stay,
His ear to hearken to my need,
The wisdom of my God to teach,
His hand to guide, His shield to ward;
The word of God to give me speech,
His heavenly host to be my guard.

Day 4

Psalm 139:11-12 1 Kings 18:21 Romans 13:11-14

Patrick's life really was in danger at the time he first prayed the Breastplate, but all the solitaries and people of prayer know that the biggest battles can be the ones inside – 'fightings and fear, without, within.'

Come swiftly, O Lord, to the dark moments when we are lost. Make us aware of Thy presence. Strengthen us to resist the urges and pulls to deeper darkness. Stir us to move away

from the dark moments of sinfulness toward
the light of Thy forgiveness. Come quickly, O
Lord, as we call – or forget to call – and keep
Thou close to us and keep us close to Thee
this day and night and as far as the days and
nights stretch before us, through Christ. Amen.

James W Kennedy
'Holy Island – A Lenten Pilgrimage'

Against the demon snares of sin,
the vice that gives temptation force,
the natural lusts that war within,
the hostile men that mar my course;
or few or many, far or nigh,
in every place, and in all hours,
against their fierce hostility,
I bind to me these holy powers.

Day 5

Psalm 91:4–8   Daniel 1:20   Luke 10:18–20

When Patrick arrived at Tara it was Easter Eve
and he lit a fire so he could keep vigil. God
had arranged it that by this timing he would
be brought to give an account of the hope he
had in Christ, for it was also a Druid festival
for which every fire in the land must be put
out in preparation. Patrick's Easter light shone
boldly, so he was brought before the King.

Against all Satan's spells and wiles,
against false words of heresy,
against the knowledge that defiles,
against the heart's idolatry,
against the wizard's evil craft,
against the death-wound and the burning.

the choking wave and poisoned shaft,
protect me, Christ, till Thy returning.

When King Laeghaire tried to have Patrick killed as he left Tara it was from jealousy, for Patrick had preached to many and turned them to Christ away from the magic and old religion of the Druids. The would-be murderers saw only a company of stags pass by. It would seem that the Breastplate prayer was answered!

Day 6

Psalm 139:5–8   *Deuteronomy 33:27*
Luke 23:33–34

Christ be with me, Christ within me,
Christ behind me, Christ before me,
Christ beside me, Christ to win me,
Christ to comfort and restore me,
Christ beneath me, Christ above me,
Christ in quiet, Christ in danger,
Christ in hearts of all that love me,
Christ in mouth of friend and stranger.

Christ beneath me

Beneath are the everlasting arms – and they bear the print of the nails. No matter how far I have sunk, He descends to lift me up. He has plumbed all the hells of this world that He may lift us upwards. He is our firm support.

David Adam
The Edge of Glory

Day 7

Psalm 96:11–13   Jeremiah 33:3   1 John 1:1–5

The mighty God, the Everlasting Father, the
Prince of Peace, Wonderful, Counsellor, the
One who said 'I Am that I Am', that is My
Name, comes when we call. He comes, but
not because we are lords and He our slave.
The God who comes awaits our signal, our
vigil fire lit to welcome His coming. He longs
to be with us, to love and protect us. The
Breastplate prayer ends as it begins; like the
inter-weaving of Celtic design it really has no
ending, only eternity in which the design
brings us back to the same place, more secure
in the knowledge that our life is eternal and
interlocked with His own.

I bind unto myself the name, the strong name of
   the Trinity; by invocation of the same,
   the Three in One, and One in Three,
of whom all nature hath creation;
   Eternal Father, Spirit, Word:
praise to the Lord of my salvation,
   salvation is of Christ the Lord.

Day 8

Psalm 23:3–4   Joel 2:25   John 4:28–30

I know the plans I have for you, says the
Lord, to give you a future and a hope
(Jeremiah 29:11). God can take events of the
past and weave them so skilfully into a new
plan for us that not only do we find there is a

future for us after all, but it is as if there have been no wasted years.

Christ behind me

There He walks in your past. He walks in all the dark rooms you pretend are closed, that He may bring light. Invite Him into your past. Experience His forgiveness, His acceptance of you. Offer especially all that you are ashamed of . . . all that you wish to forget . . . all that still pains and hurts you . . . all the hurt you have caused others. Walk there in the places you are afraid of, knowing that He walks with you and will lead you on!

Christ before me

He forever goes before us to prepare a place for us. He is on the road we tread. Wherever life is leading us, He has gone before. Perhaps we have no clue about what lies ahead; we know *who* is ahead of us, so the future is not quite unknown.

David Adam
The Edge of Glory

Day 9

Psalm 139:15–17   *Isaiah 66:3–4*
            Hebrews 11:24–25

The future is not a foregone conclusion. But when we give God permission to intervene and bring about His will in us, still again and again He offers us choices, perhaps between one good and another. This is so that we can create through our choices, enabling Him to bring into being things He had long ago planned for us. He constantly plans for me in love, and in His mercy he never allows me to see the might-have-beens that only He could see.

In one of Charles Williams' poems he describes the images of possibilities as carved in stone and rock hidden for ever under the sea unless our choices call them into being, until they become visible and become realities:

Before the making of man or beast
the Emperor knew all carved contingent shapes . . .
These were the shapes only the Emperor knew.
Sideways in the cleft they lay,
and the seamews' wings everywhere flying,
or the mist, or the mere slant of the things
seemed to stir them,
then the edge of the storm's shock over us
obliquely split rock from rock . . .
Did you not see, by the dolorous blow's might,
the contingent knowledge of the Emperor
floating into sight? . . . the sculpture,
the living sculpture, rose and flew!

from Taliessin through Logres

Day 10

Psalm 148:3-8   Joel 3:14-6   Acts 26:16-18

Patrick placed all these things in prayer as a shield between him and those who sought to take his life. It worked; they passed through unseen, Patrick and his companions, including

a young boy called Benignus. The ambush
party waiting for them saw only 'a company
of stags with a little fawn running behind
them'. Coincidence? The escape at Tara
enabled Patrick to continue his mission in
Ireland. Perhaps you can replace 'Tara' with
the name of where God has you, as you pray:

At Tara today in this fateful hour,
I place all heaven with its power,
and the sun with its brightness,
and the snow with its whiteness,
and fire with all the strength it hath,
and lightning with its rapid wrath,
and the winds with their swiftness
along the path,
and the earth with its starkness:
all these I place, by God's almighty help
and grace,
between myself and the powers of darkness.

Day 11

Psalm 94:16–20   Genesis 12:1–3   Luke 9:60–62

Columba was from an Irish royal family, but
chose the life of a monk. Nonetheless he
managed to quarrel with King Diarmait, chief
of the kings of Ireland, over two incidents.
Diarmait had executed Curnun, a relative of
Columba's, for manslaughter after a sports
incident and imprisoned Columba for giving
him sanctuary. He also ruled that a hand-
copied book of Psalms must stay in Clonard
monastery with the original from which
Columba had copied it. Columba told his

kinsmen and soon they and neighbouring clans went to war to avenge the injustice. Thousands of men were killed or wounded, and Columba poured out his grief to a holy man called Laisren. The penance he gave Columba was to leave Ireland and to go as a missionary. 'Rest not until as many souls are won for Christ's Kingdom as you have caused to fall by the sword,' he said. Columba and his friends came first to Oronsay, then sailed to Iona from which no glimpse of Ireland could be seen. There he looked back to make sure.

'Every time I saw those hills across the water I should want to go home, and one day the want might have been too stroong for me,' he thought. They call that place The Bay of the Coracle where Columba's boat is supposed to have come to land.

Day 12

Psalm 84:9–11   *1 Chronicles 15:23–28*
John 14:2–3

Columba established a fine missionary base on Iona, and he and his monks travelled far over the sea in their frail coracles, preaching the Gospel in the Orkney and Shetland Islands, in the Faroes and the Hebrides. One evening in June in the year 597 he went out into the fields where the brethren were working and called them to him. 'The time is near for me to be parted from you,' he told them. 'At dawn tomorrow I shall yield up to the Lord the precious thing with which He has trusted me for so many years.' The monks knew that he

meant his soul, and they were very sad, but
Columba himself was full of joy. The last text
he copied out was Psalm thirty-four, verse ten:
'they who seek the Lord shall want no manner
of thing that is good.'

Almighty Father, Son and Holy Ghost,
eternal, ever-blessed, gracious God, to me, the
least of saints, to me allow that I may keep a
door in Paradise;
that I may keep even the smallest door,
the furthest door, the darkest, coldest door,
the door that is least used, the stiffest door,
if so it be but in Thine house, O God!
if so it be that I can see Thy Glory,
even afar and hear Thy Voice, O God!
and know that I am with Thee – Thee, O God.

W. Muir
Prayer of Columba

Day 13

Psalm 104:23   Isaiah 43:21   Colossians 3:17

The first two years of Columba's residence in
Iona were spent in learning the language, tilling
the soil, training followers, and generally
organizing the community. The days were
filled with prayer, study, and manual labour,
and in this last Columba, with his great
spiritual and intellectual gifts, was always
ready to share. In dairy, granary, or in the
fields, each worshipped God in his appointed
task, and made his toil a sacramental thing . . .
The secret of the early Celts lay in this, that
they linked sacrament with service, altar with
hearth, worship with work.

F. M. McNeill/Troup

For us, too, it is important to discover the rhythm of praying as we work and through our work. Sometimes a simple manual task can even assist the praying heart in its focus. Prayer-baskets were woven simply out of reeds as monastics framed their prayers. The simplest task can become for us a prayer-basket.

Day 14

Psalm 72:1–4   *Jeremiah 31:21*
1 Corinthians 2:2–5

King Oswald, a man beloved of God, when he was about to give battle to the heathen, set up the sign of the holy cross, and kneeling down, asked God that He would grant His heavenly aid to those who trusted in Him in their dire need. It is told that, when the cross had been hurriedly made and a hole dug to receive it, the devout king with ardent faith took the cross and placed it in position, holding it upright with his own hands until the soldiers had thrown in the earth and it stood firm. Then he summoned his army with a loud shout, crying, 'Let us all kneel together, and ask the true and living God Almighty of His mercy to protect us from the arrogant savagery of our enemies, since He knows that we fight in a just cause to save our nation.'

The whole army did as he ordered, and advancing against the enemy at the first light of dawn, won the victory that their faith deserved. To this day they called this place Hefenfelth meaning 'the heavenly field'.

Bede

The cross at Heavenfield was set up as a waymark, and the Kingdom of Christ began to come in Northumberland.

Day 15

Psalm 127:1 Isaiah 28:9–11 1 Corinthians 3:1–2

When King Oswald originally asked the brothers of Iona to send someone to teach the Faith of Christ to his people, they sent him a man of a more austere disposition. Meeting with no success in his preaching, for the people refused to listen to him, he returned home and reported to his superiors that he had been unable to teach anything to the nation to whom they had sent him because they were an uncivilized people of an obstinate and barbarous temperament. The Scots fathers, therefore, held a great conference to decide on the wisest course of action, for although they regretted that the preacher whom they had sent had not been acceptable to the Northumbrian folk, they still wished to meet their desire for salvation. Then Aidan, who was present at the conference, said to the priest whose efforts had been unsuccessful,

'Brother, it seems to me that you were too severe on your ignorant hearers. You should have followed the practice of the Apostles, and begun by giving them the milk of simpler teaching, and gradually instructed them in the word of God until they were capable of greater perfection and able to follow the sublime precepts of Christ.'

All who were at the conference paid close attention to all he said, and realized that here was a fit person to send to instruct the ignorant and unbelieving, since he was particularly endowed with the grace of discretion. They therefore consecrated him, and sent him to preach.

Bede

Day 16

Psalm 126   *Exodus 4:11–17*
         1 Corinthians 14:20–21

On Aidan's arrival, the king appointed the island of Lindisfarne to be his base, as he asked. As the tide ebbs and flows, this place is surrounded by sea twice a day like an island, and twice a day the sand dries and joins it to the mainland. The king always listened humbly and readily to Aidan's advice, and diligently set himself to establish and extend the Church of Christ throughout his kingdom. And while Aidan, now their bishop, who was not yet fluent in their language, preached the Gospel, it was most delightful to see the king himself interpreting the word of God to his thanes and leaders; for he himself had obtained perfect command of the Scottish tongue during his long exile.

Bede tells us that other helpers came from Scotland, proclaiming the word of God with great devotion in all the provinces under Oswald's rule. Many were baptized, and churches were built in several places. People flocked gladly to hear the word of God – not just when it was Aidan preaching and their beloved king standing by his side as interpreter, his own eyes glowing at the privilege of proclaiming the truth he loved.

Day 17

Psalm 121:7–8   *Isaiah 35:8*   *Acts 8:35–40*

How many times must Aidan have looked up at the Cheviots and said to himself, 'I will lift up my eyes unto the hills . . . my help comes from the Lord who made heaven and earth!' Bede tells us that he walked almost everywhere, and all who accompanied him, monks or lay-folk, were required to meditate, that is, either to read the Scriptures or to learn the Psalms. This was their daily occupation wherever they went. They also lived what they taught and this was the highest recommendation of their belief. He never cared for any worldly possessions, unless it was so he could give them to assist the poor. Always travelling on foot, unless it was absolutely necessary to ride, in town or country this gave Aidan the opportunity to stop and speak with whoever he met as he went, be they high or low in status. If they were heathen, he urged them to believe and be baptized; if Christians already he would strengthen their faith and inspire them by word and example to live a good and generous life. The Cheviots stand and remember. Even so the Lord will not forget to be our shield, preserving the comings and goings of His own. A causeway shall be there and a way . . .

Day 18

Psalm 72:12-13   *Proverbs 21:13-14*
James 2:17-18

Oswald at length brought under his sceptre all
the kingdoms and provinces of Britain
speaking the four languages of British, Pictish,
Scottish and English. Although he wielded
supreme power, Oswald was always
wonderfully humble, kindly and generous to
the poor and strangers. The story is told how
on the Feast of Easter one year, Oswald sat
down to dine with Bishop Aidan. A silver dish
of rich food was set before him, and Bishop
Aidan had just raised his hand to bless the
food when the servant who was appointed to
relieve the needs of the poor came in
suddenly and informed the king that a great
crowd of needy folk were sitting in the road
outside begging alms of the king. Oswald at
once ordered his own food to be taken out to
the poor, and the silver dish to be broken up
and distributed among them. The bishop, who
was sitting beside him, was deeply moved to
see such generosity, and taking the king's right
hand, exclaimed, 'May this hand never perish.'
Later events proved that his prayer was heard,
for when Oswald was killed in battle, his hand
and arm were severed from his body, and, says
Bede over 200 years later, 'remains
uncorrupted to this day'.

Day 19

Psalm 63:1–4   Jeremiah 6:16   1 Timothy 2:8

It is said that Oswald often remained in prayer
from the early hour at which prayers were
said, known as Lauds, until dawn, and that
through his practice of constant prayer and
thanksgiving to God, he always sat with his
hands palm upwards on his knees. It is also
said, until the saying became a proverb, that
'his life closed in prayer', for when he saw the
enemy forces surrounding him and knew that
his end was near, he prayed for the souls of
his soldiers, saying as he fell, 'God have mercy
on their souls.'

Bede's History

Express again the reality that God is there.
There for your life. There in your prayer.

Between each thought and each action
place the Presence.
Between each encounter and event
place the Presence.

David Adam

Day 20

Psalm 49:1–3   Isaiah 58:6–8   2 Timothy 2:2

Aidan, bishop of Lindisfarne, 'culvitated peace
and love, purity and humility; he was above
anger and greed, and despised pride and
conceit; he set himself to keep and to teach
the laws of God, and was diligent in study and
prayer. He used his priestly authority to check

the proud and powerful; he tenderly
comforted the sick; he relieved and protected
the poor. To sum up what could be learned
from those who knew him, he took pains
never to neglect anything that he had learned
from the writings of the apostles and prophets,
and he set himself to carry them out with all
his powers.'

Bede

It was Aidan who would free slaves whenever
he was able, and a number of these became his
closest disciples. It was he who broke ground
winning people for Christ across
Northumberland, and always learning himself,
imparted to others the life he had embraced
and carried as a torch.

O Lord, I pray that in You,
I'll break ground both fresh and new.
As a student make me stand,
break the hardness of the land
with Your forgiving Father-hand.

Paul Stamper

Day 21

Psalm 78:70–72   *2 Kings 2:8–14*
Hebrews 12:22–23

On the night when St Aidan died, a shepherd
lad was tending his flocks upon the Northumbrian
hills. As he watched his sheep he looked up
from time to time at the great belt of stars
which is called the Milky Way, and thought to
himself that that was the pathway by which the
souls of the dead go to heaven. And while he

was gazing upwards, he saw a sudden vision. He has described it for us in graphic words:

Methought I saw a dazzling radiance shine suddenly out of the darkness, and in the midst of the streaming light a choir of angels descended to earth and lo! they were bearing away as in a globe of fire a happy soul.

The shepherd boy was named Cuthbert, who afterwards was to become one of the most famous of the bishops of Lindisfarne. The vision that he saw is known as the Passing of St Aidan.

Cuthbert was an orphan and lived with a poor widow who loved him as though he had been her own son. 'He longed to be a soldier, but also wanted to serve God. At age fifteen he mounted his horse and carrying the weapons he had trained himself to use, set off for adventure, intending to dedicate his strength to God. His horse led him to the door of the Abbey of Melrose, where Eata one of Aidan's disciples in turn discipled him.'

Day 22

Psalm 107:23–30   Jonah 1:4–15   Mark 4:36–41

In Aidan's school were four brothers, the youngest of whom was called Chad. Chad eventually came to have charge of the Abbey at Lastingham, and ruled over the same in love and peace. From him his monks learned gentleness and humility. One brother whose name was Trumhere noticed that if a gale arose while Chad was reading or doing

anything else he would at once call upon God
for mercy, and pray Him to have mercy upon
mankind. And if the wind increased in
violence, he would close his book and
prostrate himself on the ground praying even
more earnestly. But if there was a violent
storm of wind and rain, or the earth shook
with thunder and lightning, he would go to
the church, and say prayers and psalms
continuously until the tempest had passed.
When questioned why he did this, he told his
monks, 'Do you not know that it is the Lord
who moves the air, raises winds, darts lightnings,
and thunders from heaven to incite the people
to fear Him, and to put them in mind of the
future judgement? Wherefore it is indeed a
time for us to show due fear and love.'

Day 23

Psalm 103:19–22   *Exodus 3:2–5*
                  2 Timothy 4:7–8

Chad was eventually sent as bishop of Mercia,
and built a cathedral and monastery at
Lichfield and with humility, simplicity and
gentleness reached out to the people in that
whole area. His influence spread and
continued over the next two and a half years.
Then one day he was alone in his oratory, and
Brother Owini working outside heard the
sound of sweet and joyful singing coming
down from heaven to earth. It approached the
building, then entered the oratory filling the
place and the surrounding air. Half an hour
later the song rose through the roof and

returned to heaven with inexpressible
sweetness. Owini had stood astonished, now
Chad opened the oratory window and bade
him run to fetch seven other brothers, then he
urged them to be faithful and constant,
announcing that soon he was to leave them.
Owini remained behind after they were blessed
and asked Chad about the singing. 'Since you
were aware of it already I will tell you if you
promise not to speak of it yet. They were
angelic spirits summoning me to the heavenly
reward and in seven days they have promised
to return for me.'

Bede

Earth is crammed with heaven,
and every common bush afire with God,
but only he who sees
takes off his shoes.

Elizabeth Barrett Browning

Day 24

Psalm 89:15–16   Ezekiel 34:11–12   James 5:16

When Cuthbert was made prior at Melrose he
did not restrict his teaching and influence to
the monastery, but worked to rouse the
ordinary folk far and near to exchange their
foolish customs for a love of heavenly joys. He
often used to leave the monastery, sometimes
on horseback but more frequently on foot, and
visit the neighbouring towns, where he
preached the way of truth to those who had
gone astray. Cuthbert was so skilful a speaker

and had such a light in his face, and such a love for proclaiming his message that none presumed to hide their inmost secrets, but openly confessed all their wrong-doing for they felt it impossible to conceal their guilt from him. He gladly undertook the task of visiting and preaching mainly in the villages that lay far distant among high and inaccessible mountains which others feared to visit, and whose barbarity and squalor daunted other teachers. He taught with patience and skill, and when he left the monastery it would sometimes be a week, sometimes two or three, and occasionally an entire month before he returned home, remaining in the mountains to guide the peasants heavenward by his teachings and example.

Bede

Day 25

Psalm 55:22 Proverbs 16:1–3 Colossians 3:12–15

When Cuthbert came as prior to Lindisfarne he handed on the monastic rule by teaching and example, but some of the monks preferred their old way of life to the rule. He overcame these by patience and forbearance, bringing them round little by little through daily example to a better frame of mind. At chapter meetings he was often worn down by bitter insults, but would put an end to the arguments simply by rising and walking out, calm and unruffled. Next day he would give the same people exactly the same admonitions, as though there had been no unpleasantness the previous day. In this way he gradually won their obedience. He was wonderfully patient, and though overwhelmed by sorrow at these monks' recalcitrance, he managed to keep a cheerful face.

He urged his people to lift up their hearts and give thanks to the Lord God more by the yearnings of his own heart than by the sound of his voice. Often as they were pouring out their sins he would be the first to burst into tears, tears of sympathy with their weakness.

Bede

Day 26

Psalm 91:14   Isaiah 35:7   Ephesians 6:10–13

Cuthbert was determined to do battle for Heaven, but did not underestimate the strength of the challenge.

'If I could live in a tiny dwelling on a rock in the ocean,' he lamented, 'surrounded by the swelling waves, cut off from the knowledge and the sight of all, I would still not be free from the cares of this fleeting world nor from the fear that somehow the love of money might snatch me away.'

Not till he had first gained victory over our invisible enemy by solitary prayer and fasting did he take it on himself to seek out a remote battlefield farther away from his fellow men. Eventually he moved onto the Inner Farne a few miles out south-east of Lindisfarne. The island was haunted by devils; Cuthbert was the first man brave enough to live there alone. But when the man of God came, he ordered the evil spirits to withdraw, and the island became quite habitable.

Bede

Day 27

Psalm 5:11–12   Isaiah 43:10–11   Revelation 1:8

God to enfold me, God to surround me,
God in my speaking, God in my thinking,
God in my sleeping, God in my waking,
God in my watching, God in my hoping,
God in my life, God in my lips,
God in my soul, God in my heart,
God in my suffing, God in my slumber,
God in mine ever-living soul,
God in mine eternity.

Celtic Prayers

As He is He was: as He was He is.
He shall be as He is and was,
the Eternal forever so be it Amen.
The Forever Eternal so be it Amen.
The Edge of Glory

Day 28

Psalm 22:14–17   Isaiah 53:5   John 21:19–20

A fourteenth-century hermit we know only as the Monk of Farne was one of the people to inherit Cuthbert's call to a solitary life on the Inner Farne. These extracts are from his writings:

All day long I stretched out my hands on the cross towards thee, O man, to embrace thee, O bow down my head to kiss thee when I have embraced thee, I open my side to draw thee into my heart after this kiss, that we may be two in one flesh. There can be safety for thee nowhere else but in me, when the day of wrath and judgement comes. See, I have shown thee the sign thou didst beg; know then how much I love, and fly quickly to me.

. . . precisely because I am a sinnér, I have fled to thee; since there is nowhere I can flee from thee save to thee. Thou dost stretch out thine arms to receive me and bend down thy head to kiss me; thou dost bleed that I may have to drink, and open thy side in thy desire to draw me within . . . I will gladly run to thee albeit a sinner, albeit unclean, for with thee there is merciful forgiveness; thou wilt wash me in thy blood, and I shall be made whiter than snow. I will enter into thee and not stay without, for outside thee there is no salvation.

Day 29

Psalm 15:2–4   *Micah 6:8*   *3 John 5:6*

Just as a table without bread is a needy one,
so absence of charity is ruin to the soul,
for the soul walks by love, and the man who
does not love abides in death.

Monk of Farne

If we do not love, then all we do is to no avail.

Read 1 John 4:8 or 1 Corinthians 13:3.

It is not what we give of ourselves or our resources that is the measure of how we love, but what we hold back.

Day 30

Psalm 16:6   Genesis 18:1-8   Matthew 25:34-40

Celtic rune of hospitality

I saw a stranger at yestere'en.
I put food in the eating place,
drink in the drinking place,
music in the listening place,
and in the sacred name of the Triune
He blessed myself and my house,
my cattle and my dear ones,
and the lark said in her song
often, often, often,
goes Christ in the stranger's guise.

Kenneth MacLeod

Day 31

Psalm 72:6-7   Isaiah 26:3-4   John 21:21-22

Deep peace of the running wave to you
Deep peace of the flowing air to you
Deep peace of the quiet earth to you
Deep peace of the shining stars to you
Deep peace of the Son of peace to you.

Iona Community

APRIL READINGS

The Inward Journey

Day 1   Psalm 86:11
        Proverbs 5:1
        Hebrews 12:11
Day 2   Psalm 86:16
        Proverbs 3:13–14
        Luke 14:28–30
Day 3   Psalm 135:4–6
        Genesis 32:24–31
        Revelation 19:16
Day 4   Psalm 133:1
        1 Kings 5:17
        1 Peter 2:5
Day 5   Psalm 48:8
        1 Kings 6:7
        Revelation 21:18–21
Day 6   Psalm 87:3, 5
        Isaiah 62:12
        Revelation 21:9–11, 23
Day 7   Psalm 102:25–27
        Genesis 22:7–8
        1 Peter 1:18–20
Day 8   Psalm 17:15
        Job 1:7–12, 20–22; 19:23–26
        James 5:10–11
Day 9   Psalm 46:5
        Daniel 2:44–45
        Romans 8:18
Day 10 Psalm 27:13
        Genesis 37:18–20, 24, 28, 36; 39:20
        Romans 8:28
Day 11 Psalm 90:10, 12

James 5:13
Day 24 Psalm 102:1-2, 4
2 Samuel 12:16-23
Hebrews 11:14-15
Day 25 Psalm 37:37
Jeremiah 29:11
Mark 4:37-38
Day 26 Psalm 60:3
Isaiah 55:1-2
Matthew 9:17
Day 27 Psalm 41:9-13
Exodus 17:10-12
Colossians 1:23-25
Day 28 Psalm 22:1, 6-8
Isaiah 53:6-7
Matthew 5:11-12; John 12:23-24
Day 29 Psalm 3:3
Song of Songs 8:5, 7
2 Corinthians 1:6-7, 2:4
Day 30 Psalm 18:41
1 Kings 18:42-43
Luke 22:41-44

Day 1

Psalm 86:11   Proverbs 5:1   Hebrews 12:11

Several years ago Paul and Mary Cullity placed a copy of ***The Inward Journey*** by Gene Edwards into my hand and said, 'You must read this – you'll *hate* it!'

What the book itself had to say was that sooner or later you will reach the conclusion that the Christian life is *mostly* about suffering so you might as well be prepared for it instead of being taken by surprise.

This month we will be using passages from Gene's book for our daily notes, describing what a believer 'might expect to encounter experientially on his way down the road toward transformation.'

A.R.

Day 2

Psalm 86:16   Proverbs 3:13–14   Luke 14:28–30

Gene Edwards talks of the reason he wrote *The Inward Journey:*

I was a very ignorant new Christian when I wandered into the huge bookstore of the Ridgecrest Baptist Assembly grounds in North Carolina. As I entered the store I was absolutely awed by the endless, infinite array of books and the myriad categories they were divided into. Dazed, I walked over to the clerk behind one of the counters and asked, 'Where do you keep the books for new Christians?'

She looked at me rather puzzled, weighed my question, and replied, 'Well, there's no such section.' Then she asked, 'What is it you're interested in?' This still ranks as one of the most incongruous questions ever asked me. I didn't have the slightest idea what there was to be interested in.

Three decades have now passed. I suppose during the years I have read about as many books as a man can afford to buy, borrow or copy.

Until this day I still pick up literature marked 'for the new Christian' and with great disappointment find it either inane, useless, traditional, cranial, old, shallow, irrelevant or carrying within its covers the curse of scholarship. That question still haunts me, 'Where *are* the books for new Christians?'

Day 3

Psalm 135:4–6   *Genesis 32:24–31*
                    Revelation 19:16

It took a lifetime of God at His best to break that man, and even then . . . only when He touched him at the strongest point in his life.

Jacob says,
'That broken hip?
An angel did me a favour.'

Day 4

Psalm 133:1   1 Kings 5:17   1 Peter 2:5

Come with us to a quarry in King Solomon's
time . . .

After the stone is cut free from the earth it is
pulled here to the flat of the earth. The stone
is then cut to an exact, predetermined size,
chiselled with large, coarse instruments until it
has some semblance of shape, then cut with
finer chisels. Next it is coarse sanded, then it
is fine sanded, and last polished.

When the stonemason is finished, the stone
is flawless. From here the stone is taken to a
distant city and to a building site.

All these stones will be taken to that city.
Each is destined to be taken to an already
determined place. It is interesting that when
this happens each stone fits perfectly into its
place. They fit so perfectly in fact, that they
appear to be *one* stone.

Day 5

Psalm 48:8   1 Kings 6:7   Revelation 21:18–21

There are enough stones here to build a city! A
very large city. Can you hear the masons?
They are beginning to return to their work
over there. Hear the hammers? The chisels?
One day, when all these stones are completed,
they will be taken to the site, near the house.
There they will be taken through a door, and
from there to the builders' site itself, where

the stones are being reassembled.
Reassembled, but this time into a house . . .
almost as one vast stone.

At that site, on *that* side of the door, there
will be no hammer, no chisel, no mason work
at all. It is here, on this side of the building
site where all cutting, chiselling, sanding and
polishing *must* take place. Here! Not there. All
the thud of hammer and falling of axes, the
grating of chisels and the grinding of sand . . .
is done *here!* It is the plan of the Masterbuilder
that all the business of making rough rock into
perfectly fitting, polished stone be
accomplished in the stone quarry. *There*, there,
beyond this place, beyond that door, is only
the assembling together of what has been done
here.

Day 6

Psalm 87:3, 5 *Isaiah 62:12*
Revelation 21:9–11, 23

This particular house is very large. Large enough
to be a city, for it shall be a house for God to
live in . . .

'A quarry, I live in the midst of a quarry.
Called Earth.'

The real quarry – you are down there
somewhere, being chiselled on by God, man
and circumstances. But not you alone. Every
believer who has ever lived, those who lived
before His visitation and all those who are yet
to come, one day you all will be lifted out of
this quarry through that door . . . *Then* shall
no hammer be heard, for all of that is done in

the quarry. Nor shall you be there as an
endless array of stones. But together you will
be assembled in one place, as one. A living
city . . . the bride. The New Jerusalem.

Day 7

Psalm 102:25–27 Genesis 22:7–8 1 Peter 1:18–20

The angel Messenger takes Christian to see the
secret God had prepared in Himself before the
beginning of time –

Just before him, lying in a pool of blood,
lay the cold, dead and mangled form of a
snow-white lamb.
For
He was slain
Before the foundation
Of the world.

Day 8

Psalm 17:15   Job 1:7–12, 20–22; 19:23–26
James 5:10–11

We usually learn about *Him* only during
periods of adversity. Few, if any, of us really
seek after a deep, intimate relationship with
the Lord except (1) just before, (2) during, and
(3) right after those periods of calamity,
disaster, catastrophe, suffering and pain! That's
true of the very sinful, the very religious, and
. . . well . . . the rest of us!
I challenge the idea that suffering is first of

all a punishment for our sins. If that were true, then every believer on earth would be hiding under a rock somewhere.

Job lowered his voice, 'It appears we have a God who has supreme confidence in His own judgement. Nor can He be persuaded to show a great deal of interest in explaining Himself. He keeps His counsel to Himself, it appears; nor is He perturbed in the least that we're perturbed about His not being perturbed. 'But,' said he, raising his index finger in a gesture of discovery, 'I didn't need to learn anything else. I saw Him. Getting questions answered seems rather a paltry thing in comparison to having *seen* Him.'

Christian stood there for a long time. 'It's hard to realize that that was the man Satan went after with such a vengeance!'

'Shhh,' said the angel, Messenger. 'He knows nothing of that!'

Day 9

Psalm 46:5   Daniel 2:44–45   Romans 8:18

Perhaps we should place the sign on the wall somewhere in our homes:

> *Church life may be*
> *hazardous to your health.*

The Lord knows something we don't: The Fall has left *all* of us in dire straits. Most of us are either extremely sinful or extremely religious.

Or both! And further, I suspect that neither one of those states pleases God more than the other. Neither impresses Him. What *He* does in us impresses Him!

In the quarry which is Earth each stone was in a different stage of completion. A rough stone was just being pulled free of the mother mountain.

Day 10

Psalm 27:13 Genesis 37:18–20, 24, 28, 36; 39:20
Romans 8:28

Visit JOSEPH, and what do you hear?

– a groan, followed by laboured breathing from the cell's captive.

'They meant it to me for evil
But *He* meant it to me for good.'

Day 11

Psalm 90:10, 12   *1 Corinthians 29:11–16*
2 Corinthians 3:18

See the Quarry: Earth!

Christian, there is but one place you will ever learn to follow Him, to worship Him, to obey Him, to love Him.

Only one place, one time . . . to love Him.

Only one opportunity to be changed into His image.

The place is there . . . the time . . . your 70 years.

Day 12

Psalm 27:7–8   Isaiah 28:13   Philippians 3:7–10

Everyone should be warned: 'Give your life utterly to Christ and you will eventually suffer much more than you can now comprehend.' But there is no way a man can communicate to daring young Christians the amount of suffering they will encounter in one lifetime. Again and again they have been cautioned, in every way known. Yet, each time that sovereign hand of God has fallen on one of them and he (or she) has truly entered into the fellowship of Christ's sufferings, he is always surprised how hard, how unbearable, is the cross.

For better or worse at the beginning they did not have the good sense to run out the door. These were young Christians who loved the Lord, who would not be stopped, not even by the cross.

Day 13

Psalm 2:11–12   Deuteronomy 4:23–24
Hebrews 12:28–29

Our emotions sometimes author one of the greatest problems of our Christian life: to create a God in its own image, a loving, sweet, and precious God who wouldn't dare declare war on a person's dominant emotions. The emotions do not have a franchise on this project. The intellect often sculpts out a God in its own image, a God who is very intelligent, rational, reasonable, very logical, very scriptural, very boxable and definable, and having erected this mind-made God in the centre of life, will vow and declare that this, and this alone, is the true and living God.

Day 14

Psalm 44:17–26   Isaiah 54:11   John 21:17–22

What kind of Christian can best endure suffering? He doesn't exist.

I could handle your problems easily. You could handle mine with a yawn. But it didn't happen that way. I got the ones I couldn't handle; so did you.

Day 15

Psalm 141:3, 9–10   2 Samuel 15:10–14
Acts 14:1–7, 19–23

Many a Christian worker has raised up a work that perhaps was worthy to be called 'church life' or 'body life'. Once built, problems developed. He fought tooth, tong and nail to preserve his work. Why? I wonder. Why fight to preserve it? It will stand if it is Christ. If part of it stands, and that part is really Christ, then having nothing but that little part surviving is far better than a large work that has to be held together by reason, logic, theology, fear, accusation, doctrine or whatever. In my judgement, the worker might seriously consider stepping back, even out – dying to his work, letting the fire fall on that work and seeing just how much of it can survive.

Day 16

Psalm 133:2   *Ruth 1:16–18*   *Acts 2:1–2, 42–47*

There are many great success stories around,
but those works very rarely reflect the bride of
Jesus Christ. Sometimes she seems to be as
elusive as her Lord. Rarely do you see her
beautiful and whole, gathering somewhere in
the city. Rarely will *you* ever gather in a place
where you will sense the deep work of Christ
in the corporate body of people. Being with a
people who have been made one . . . and
whose oneness – tested by the long trek of
time – is found in nothing, absolutely nothing,
but Christ. Such a people is rare, exotically
rare. Rare because that glorious work which
the Father did in the Son was so rare.

Day 17

Psalm 69:20   *Genesis 50:17–20*   *Luke 23:1–2*

Another way to know that the Lord has gained
some ground in your life: when you can
accept criticism, even if viciously served,
without a sense of resentment and with no
need to retaliate.

Joseph said about his brothers, if you
remember, that

'they meant it to me for evil
But *God* meant it to me for good.'

Day 18

Psalm 121:1–8   *Proverbs 14:29–30*
Matthew 10:24–27

Christian workers especially have a tendency to call anything that opposes their little world and their little work as being from the devil. (My, how much of that attitude I have witnessed in these last 30 years.) Such an accusation on the part of a worker, 'I'll tell you, this whole thing is of the devil,' surely makes it rough on the poor brother who is really causing the problem. He wakes up to find all his friends now thinking he's the devil . . . or a reasonable facsimile.

It's an uncomfortable feeling, it is not, to be sitting out there in a meeting and hear that what you are doing is 'the devil's work'. I hope you survive; but frankly the chances are very slim that you will. Sure, I wish Christian workers wouldn't talk that way. Such talk has clubbered my blood for a generation. But they do. For centuries past they have and for whatever centuries lie ahead they will continue to. If the day comes that someone says of you, '*This* is of the devil', I admonish you, check your heart, check your mouth, check your motives. Get clean, get your motives pure, surrender your will, opinions, desires and hopes to the Lord. Then lift up your head to the hills and know that all things are permitted from the hand of the Lord. Sorrow, joy, hope and fear. Refuse to accept *even* this as from the hand of the Lord and chances are you will get bitter. A bitter Christian is a devastated Christian.

Day 19

Psalm 119:8   *Proverbs 3:5*   *Matthew 16:24*

One brother wisely said, 'The cross is usually exactly the opposite of what we thought it was.'

When suffering comes your way, there is one thing that you certainly will do: You will ask the Lord, '*Why* has this happened?' 'There is something else almost as certain.

You will receive no answer.

If the 'why' could be removed, dear brother, most of the transforming power of the cross would disappear. The 'why' factor of the cross is perhaps its sharpest, most effective, most deadly aspect. Remove the 'why' factor of the cross and there really isn't much suffering involved in it.

Day 20

Psalm 141:8   *Daniel 3:14–18*   *Acts 12:1–7*

Then what of those who are delivered, and delivered instantly from their sufferings? And what about this matter of exercising faith and therefore being delivered?

Sitting over there near you are two Christians. One is doing great, the other is in great pain; yet, the second seems to be just as worthy as the first. Why do his afflictions persist? Is it a lack of faith? What a quandary. What are we to believe? Of the two, who is closer to God? Has the afflicted brother failed in faith? Will the proper exercise of faith always triumph over affliction?

He who has been delivered by his faith has triumphed. He who is not delivered, yet faithfully (though weakly) yields – this one has also triumphed!

And if the truth is known, there is yet a third brother, the one who suffers and yet cannot find the strength to yield gloriously. He is only willing not to become bitter under the strong hand of God. He has no glorious story of healing or yielding, but it may just be that the pain he is going through is great enough and the work of God strong enough to penetrate past all his grumblings and groanings and change the inner man. Maybe, just maybe, even this one has triumphed!

Day 21

Psalm 1:2-3   *Isaiah 32:20*   *Matthew 24:32*

I have observed through the years that most Christians have little understanding of the word 'season'. Our Lord is a seasonal God; He comes, He departs. His faithfulness never changes, but His seasons do! There are seasons when the tree is green, there are seasons when it is dry, and seasons when, for the life of us, the thing looks dead. Now, does this mean you are serving some capricious God who comes and goes by whim? Or, could it be, that it is only through *seasons* that true growth may come?

Paul said, 'Does not nature teach us?' Fruit from a tree comes to us as a result of three or four seasons.

The Christian *and* the Lord's body both
need rain and sunshine, cold and hot, wind
and doldrums.

Day 22

Psalm 90:14   1 Kings 18:41–44   2 Timothy 4:2

Seasons of joy, seasons of sorrow, times when
the Lord is so real it seems any activity you
undertake is a spiritual experience.

Seasons of dryness, when things are so bleak
that even a plateful of Sinai sand would be
considered a feast! And are not these seasons
from the hand of God? If so, what is His goal
in the matter? He is taking you to that place
where you can be a man for all seasons.
Where seasons don't faze you . . . no, not
even the glorious ones. An old apostle said it
so well to a young man. 'Be ready in season,
be ready out of season.'

We are all very subject to seasons; yet these
seasons are there to make us eventually
seasonless. There is only one way you are ever
going to learn to triumph over all seasons, and
that is to go through each and every season
. . . many times. When you can reckon the
sound of abundant rain and the hot blowing of
a dry spell exactly the same, then you will be
nearing the land of maturity.

Day 23

Psalm 57:1–11　　*1 Samuel 27:1*　　*James 5:13*

DAVID, author of Psalms, squatting a fugitive on a narrow ledge.

(I thought you might be interested in seeing the music room in which they were penned.)

Day 24

Psalm 102:1–2, 4　　　　*2 Samuel 12:16–23*
Hebrews 11:14–15

What can you do, in your hour of hurting, that might please your Lord? My guarded answer is: very little.

You can rejoice. That's one possibility. You can yield to Him. With joy you can offer up to Him the situation and say, 'Lord, I know this is from Your hand.' But the chances are you are not going to get anywhere near that. So what can you do in the midst of adversity? You can kneel; you can weep, and weep, and weep. *This* you can do.

There is one thing you must not do. Complain if you must, groan if you must, and get angry if you must. But oh, dear brother, stay far distant from bitterness, and from blaming others. Do that and you are dangerously close to forfeiting all future spiritual growth.

Day 25

Psalm 37:37   Jeremiah 29:11   Mark 4:37-38

Is it possible to know if there is true
brokenness in a man? I think so.
  Such a man is not in rebellion toward
anything:
1) nothing in his circumstances,
2) nothing that has to do with what other
   men inflict upon him,
3) and certainly not anything that God
   chooses to lay within his life.
He is at peace in all three circumstances.

Day 26

Psalm 60:3   Isaiah 55:1-2   Matthew 9:17

Some of the wine they sipped was restored
wine, and some of it was new wine, but for
that little band of believers, *it was all new.*
  Not one drop of that wine did they ever sip
except by experience.

Day 27

Psalm 41:9-13   Exodus 17:10-12
Colossians 1:23-25

If you become a worker, remember the words
of that man there in that forsaken cell and
make them your own: 'To suffer for the
church, to suffer *in her place*, for this I was
made a minister!'

On some future occasion when things are really getting rough you might remember those words. Keep reminding yourself of this, 'For *this* I was made a minister.'

Day 28

Psalm 22:1, 6–8   *Isaiah 53:6–7*
Matthew 5:11–12; John 12:23–24

The Lord did not complete His suffering. It has been given to the church to complete the sufferings of Christ. Suffering not yet filled up waits out there for you. You see, the body is also Christ. The body, which is the church, is part of that Christ. There is suffering out there yet to be endured, yet to be known, yet to be embraced by that part of Christ which is called the body. We all thank God that no one member of that body will ever have to know and endure all the sufferings that Jesus Christ experienced while living on earth. But each one of us – because we are in some mysterious way one with Him – will taste some part of His experience of suffering.

One within your fellowship may know *ridicule.* Another will partake of *physical* pain, another will know *rejection,* perhaps someone else may taste what it means to be *vilified* and verbally, socially crucified. And perhaps, just perhaps, there will be one within your fellowship who will touch that awful thing which Christ touched in that last moment on the cross: the dark night of the spirit.

There is one aspect of the cross that none of us will ever know – praise God! We will

never know what it means to be the sin-bearer.
That is one thing which I will never
experience, nor will you. He and He alone has
experienced that. He experienced the one
thing that none of us should have escaped,
and the one thing which He need never have
known. He became the sin-bearer and thereby
took suffering that was truly mine.

Now you must step into your place in the
body of Christ, and you must receive and you
must bear some segment of the suffering
which is Christ's – that is, that part of Christ
which is the church.

Day 29

Psalm 3:3   *Song of Songs 8:5, 7*
2 Corinthians 1:6–7; 2:4

If you ever see a great work of God,
Something joyous,
Alive and real,
Something of Christ,
Something that *is* Christ,
Something enduring,
Then you may be certain of one thing;
Some lonely saint
Silent, alone
Went to the cross,
Suffered, died
And fell into the earth.

And for what did He die?
For that lovely harvest,
That work of God
Which now you see
And declare to be so beautiful.

There must be another day,
And another body of believers.
A day when someone else
Must fall into the earth
And die.
That someone may need be you.

Day 30

Psalm 18:41   1 Kings 18:42–43   Luke 22:41–44

If you cannot *cherish* what it is the Lord is
doing in your life, at least do not *waste* what
He is doing in your life. Lay down the self-
pity, and with all the strength and grace that
He allows you, yield to His work. If you
cannot make it up within you to yield totally
to your Gethsemane (most of us can't) then at
least yield up to the light the dark feelings of
resentment and bitterness that are trying to
hatch inside you.

One day you are going to come to the
conclusion that serving the Lord is mostly
crying . . . and suffering . . . and agonizing.
What can you do in that sad hour? Nothing
really, except bend over double and absorb
into your being those sufferings, sufferings
which really belong to the church. In that
hour, bear her sufferings for her. And if you
happen to look up, you will see her going on
her way, gloriously rejoicing. She will be
oblivious to the fact that she is, at that
moment, so very glorious because you have
suffered.

MAY READINGS

Contagious Community

Day 1 Psalm 78:4
        1 Kings 18:24
        Acts 1:4–5

Day 2 Psalm 119:151
        Habakkuk 2:2
        Acts 1:1–3

Day 3 Psalm 127:1
        Jonah 1:7–10
        Acts 1:7–11, 14–16, 20–26

Day 4 Psalm 130:6
        Joel 2:26–29
        Acts 2:2–4, 12–16, 31–33, 37, 41

Day 5 Psalm 131:2–3
        2 Kings 4:42–44
        Acts 2:5–12, 41, 46

Day 6 Psalm 125:2
        Genesis 2:18a
        Acts 2:42, 44–46

Day 7 Psalm 126:3
        1 Samuel 22:1–2
        2 Corinthians 4:5–7

Day 8 Psalm 131:1–2
        Ecclesiastes 8:16–17
        Acts 2.42, 46–47

Day 9 Psalm 131:2
        Isaiah 52:9
        Acts 3:1–12; 3:25–4:1

Day 10 Psalm 118:22
        Jeremiah 33:1–3
        Acts 4:2–12, 18–20

Day 11 Psalm 125:1

                    Isaiah 54:1–3
                    Acts 4:13–14, 18–20, 32–35
Day 12 Psalm 125:4–5
                    Amos 7:7–8
                    Acts 4:34, 5:1–15
Day 13 Psalm 131:1
                    Isaiah 40:13–14
                    Acts 5:16–21, 29–35, 38–42
Day 14 Psalm 125:2
                    Numbers 11:16–17
                    Acts 6:1–10
Day 15 Psalm 125:1
                    Ezekiel 3:9–10
                    Acts 6:10; 5:13–15, 7:1–3, 48–54
Day 16 Psalm 131:2
                    Judges 16:29–30
                    Acts 7:55–60
Day 17 Psalm 125:1–2
                    Ecclesiastes 3:1, 4, 7
                    Acts 8:1–4
Day 18 Psalm 127:1
                    Isaiah 61:1, 11
                    Acts 8:4–8, 14–17, 25
Day 19 Psalm 130:4
                    2 Kings 6:18–20
                    Acts 9:8–18, 36–41
Day 20 Psalm 131:1
                    Habakkuk 2:1, 3
                    Acts 10:9–19, 11:18–22
Day 21 Psalm 126:3
                    Daniel 4:2–3
                    Acts 11:19–25
Day 22 Psalm 112:6
                    2 Chronicles 35:2
                    Acts 4:36–7; 9:26–28; 11:25–30
Day 23 Psalm 131:1
                    Isaiah 59:10

Acts 12:1–5, 9–16; 13:1–3, 6, 8–11, 49–52
Day 24 Psalm 127:1
Nehemiah 5:16
Ephesians 4:10–15
Day 25 Psalm 125:1
Proverbs 22:6
Acts 13:50–14:5, 19–27
Day 26 Psalm 125:2
Amos 3:3
Acts 15:1–6, 22, 30–41
Day 27 Psalm 32:7
Genesis 39:20–21
Acts 16:6–10, 20–33
Day 28 Psalm 131:1
Proverbs 9:8–10
Acts 17:1–6, 10–16
Day 29 Psalm 125:1
Proberbs 15:1–4
Acts 17:16–31; 18:1–5
Day 30 Psalm 111:6
Isaiah 42:4
Acts 19:8–19; 20:17–18, 22–24, 34–37
Day 31 Psalm 89:52
Lamentations 3:25
Acts 27:33–35

Acts, the fifth book in the New Testament, is not called the good resolutions of the apostles! Faith without works is dead.

Arthur Burt

This month's study is entitled **Contagious Community** and is examining the early chapters of Acts with help from Gene Edwards and . . . the venerable Bede!

Bede at age 59 says: 'I have spent all my life in this monastery, applying myself entirely to the study of Scriptures . . . for my own benefit and that of my brothers.'

Bede had an amazing knowledge of the biblical text, and quotations and verbal echoes from practically all the books of the Bible occur in his Commentary of Acts. Like a Jewish Rabbi he becomes 'a sort of living concordance'. The practice of reading aloud has resulted in 'more than a visual memory of the written words, and instead a muscular memory of the words pronounced and an aural memory of the words heard. The Scripture takes root in the whole person and later bears fruit. It is this deep impregnation with the words of Scripture that explains the extremely important phenomenon of reminiscence whereby the verbal echoes so excite the memory that a mere allusion will spontaneously evoke whole quotations and, in turn, a scriptural phrase will suggest quite naturally allusions elsewhere in the sacred books. Each word is like a book; it catches hold of one or several others that linked together make up the fabric of what is set before us.'

Jean Leclercq

Day 2

Psalm 119:151   Habakkuk 2:2   Acts 1:1–3

Boniface writing to Bede's abbot after his death refers to him as 'that profound student of the Scriptures who, as we have heard, lately shone in your midst as a light of the Church'. Bede made brief extracts from the fathers, and notes of his own, and the immense popularity of his exegetical writings is proved by the huge number of copies of them that have survived across Europe. He made a wide range of authors readily accessible and he set an example of eager curiosity in their use, and although his Acts commentary was an early work he returned to it near the end of his life and wrote two-thirds as much again to update his conclusions after years of study.

Hopefully our own study-notes will make spiritual writers more readily accessible, too!

One of these writers is Gene Edwards who *The Early Church* endeavours to reconstruct what life was like in the days of the Acts. Gene and Bede in their own way each are clear and easy to read. They strive to attract and teach by the power of their story or argument itself, and not by the colours in which they could clothe it.

Right at the beginning of Acts, Bede demands that we pay attention:

Theophilus (verse 1) means lover of God or beloved of God. Therefore, anyone who is a lover of God may believe that this was written for him.

So, listen carefully . . .

Day 3

Psalm 127:1   *Jonah 1:7–10*
                    Acts 1:7–11, 14–16, 20–26

'And a cloud took Him out of their sight. Everywhere creation offers obedient service to its Creator. The stars indicated His birth, clouds overshadowed Him in His suffering, received Him in His ascension, and they will accompany Him when He returns for the judgement.'

Perhaps here Bede is thinking of the 'Dream of the Rood', an ancient Northumbrian poem which says:

'I saw the God of hosts cruelly stretched out. Darkness with its clouds had covered the Lord's corpse, the bright radiance. A shadow went forth, dark beneath the clouds. All creation wept, lamented the king's death, Christ was on the cross.'

For those of us who regularly use 'prayer-pots' from which we draw the names of people to pray for that day, it is interesting that Bede points out that God can direct us through this apparently random choice, or direct by consensus:

'Matthias was appointed before Pentecost and was chosen by lot. The case of the seven deacons came later and there was no shaking of lots but only the disciples' choice; and indeed they were appointed by the prayer of the apostles and the laying on of hands. So if any, under the compulsion of some difficult situation, think that because of the example of the apostles they should consult God with lots, they should see that these same apostles needed only the assembly of the brothers gathered together and prayers poured forth to God.'

Bede

Day 4

Psalm 130:6   *Joel 2:26–29*
Acts 2:2–4, 12–16, 31–33, 37, 41

Bede quotes Pope Gregory explaining, 'The Lord appeared indeed through fire, but by His own interior presence He caused speech to be produced. And God was neither the fire nor the sound, but by what He exhibited exteriorly He expressed what He brought about interiorly.'

It was about 8.45am. Peter began slowly. 'Men and brethren, the people you see here are not drunk, as some of you are saying. It is not even 9am yet.' This concluded Peter's entire planned message. But, even as he made this simple explanation, he noticed that the whole crowd was standing, expectant and silent, wanting some further word. At that moment a thought flashed through his mind. He had told them what all this was not. Why not tell them what it was!

Gene Edwards

Christ not abandoned to hell? (v.31) His soul did in fact descend to those in hell to aid those who needed it, but He was not abandoned there, because returning immediately He sought His body which was to rise again.

By saying (in v.33) that He received from the Father the promise of the Spirit and He poured forth the Spirit both natures of Christ are manifested – for He received the Spirit as a man and poured Him forth as God.

Bede

Each of the eleven took up a spot in the crowd and began answering questions and proclaiming Christ.

Gene Edwards

On the fiftieth day (Pentecost) Moses ordered the festival of the first fruits to be introduced. Now, however, with the coming of the Holy Spirit, it is not sheaves of grain, but the first fruits of souls, which are consecrated to the Lord.

Bede

Day 5

Psalm 131:2–3　　　　　　　*2 Kings 4:42–44*
Acts 2:5–12, 41, 46

Like most tourists they had brought just enough money to get them through the festival. Simply put, the 3,000 are foreigners, they are a long way from home, they are broke, jobless, and homeless! In a city this crowded, where would the Apostles be able to find a place big enough to hold 3,120 people?

Amazingly, there *was* an answer. There was a place in the temple courtyard which was *behind* the temple building. True it was 'open-air' on three sides, and everyone would have to sit on the ground, but it *was* a place to meet. This huge roofed-in area had a name; it was referred to as 'Solomon's Porch'.

It was undoubtedly in this first meeting the Apostles dropped their bomb. They had decided to stay in Jerusalem. Furthermore it was their feeling that all 3,000 of the new converts should stay here, too! Working out the details would be staggering . . . if not downright impossible; but for the moment it was a simple, fantastic, insane, glorious decision. In all church history there has really been nothing quite like that moment!

Gene Edwards
The Early Church

Day 6

Psalm 125:2   Genesis 2:18a   Acts 2:42, 44–46

Without homes, beds, shelter, jobs, money or meals, over 3,000 people had decided to drop everything to gain the depths of the riches of knowing Christ. How they would do it without starving, no one knew . . . nor did they care. Their hearts were set. They would *know* the Lord. Where would they get food, how – in general – would they survive? There were a few people among the 3,000 who actually did live in the city of Jerusalem. These few people volunteered to open their homes to the rest of the 3,000. This was just like the situation of the 120 when they came into Jerusalem, rented a big room, and all piled in together . . . only this time it was 3,000! You can imagine 3,000 people flooding into – and around – about fifty homes. It appears someone who owned his own house came up with this next idea. 'My home is paid for. I can sell it, take the money, rent three homes and buy food!' Soon all the Jerusalem believers were selling not only furniture but also their homes and property. If you find it hard to believe men would do such things, then you have never been in the flood-like joy of church life. In the midst of tidal joy, men laid down all because of their simple, overwhelming love for Christ. And the love grew out of their experience with Him! By now all 3,000 were getting involved in this 'sell everything' experience. The 3,000 who once lived in other cities and other countries began writing back home to have their houses, goods and land sold. They took any kind of job available. The Church cut its teeth on doing the radical. It had its beginning in being practical, not conventional. Church life was born when a bunch of believers, half out of their minds with joy, gave up all they owned and piled into a few houses and started living together. It is hard to explain, this thing called 'church life'. You have to experience it! God never intended you to be His followers without it. The life of a believer was never intended to be experienced alone.

Gene Edwards

Day 7

Psalm 126:3   *1 Samuel 22:1-2*
                2 Corinthians 4:5-7

All day long, the scene at Solomon's Porch was
that of saints coming and going. Those who
had jobs would join the meeting briefly and
return to work; others stayed for the whole day.

No-one knew what would happen tomorrow.
That's one reason you went to a meeting: It
was the only way to know what would
happen next.

. . . Look around, and all over the grounds
you can see young men who are giving their
lives completely to this shaky new enterprise,
the church. Everyone of them has looked at his
own inabilities, his weaknesses, and his mixed-
up life. Each has wondered how he, such poor
material, could ever be a part of the Kingdom
of Christ. They believed, against themselves,
that Christ's life was powerful enough to live
in place of their own lives.

Gene Edwards

Christ's life lived in them realized a quality of
lifestyle that was evangelistic, charismatic and
involved social action and a concern for
justice.

Roy Searle

But contrary to twentieth century propaganda,
Pentecost was not the beginning of a drive to
evangelize the world! Right now their
responsibility is this: to simply, daily,
experience the life of Christ with their
brothers and sisters. No-one will go anywhere
for the next eight years.

Gene Edwards

Day 8

Psalm 131:1–2   *Ecclesiastes 8:16–17*
Acts 2:42, 46–47

The Apostles did not teach the Scripture. The twelve Apostles talked about Jesus Christ! Night and day. That's all you get out of them: Jesus Christ.

Leaving Solomon's Porch and walking along the streets, the disciples praise and sing and chatter, hardly able to contain the glorious things about the Lord which they discovered today. When at last they arrive home they joyfully greet those they live with. It had been this morning that they said goodbye to one another, yet they all greet each other wildly. It has been eight *whole* hours! So much has happened today! Everybody begins talking at once.

Supper is prepared to the accompaniment of uproarious singing, chattering and laughter. After the meal is prepared, everyone sits down somewhere on the floor to eat and they continue to share. As the night grows on, the bedding comes out again, and everyone falls asleep to the sound of laughter and joyful praise. From the time they get home until they went to bed, *the church was meeting!!!* . . . Like twelve men sitting around talking to the Lord! Those 'meetings' (which weren't really meetings at all) which twelve men had while living with Christ, had now become the way the whole church met!

Gene Edwards
The Early Church

Day 9

'Every day they put him at the temple gate called the beautiful.' Bede explains an allegorical reading of this text: The beautiful gate of the temple is the Lord. Whoever enters through Him will be saved. Enfeebled Israel, being unable to walk to this gate, was brought there by the words of the law and prophets, so that she might request help from those who were entering into the interior places of wisdom of the faith which she was to hear. Those who place the prophecies of things to come as it were at the gate are the bearers, but Peter is the guide into the temple. To him, in virtue of his strong profession of faith, the epitaph of 'rock' and the keys of heaven were given. 'Silver and gold I do not have' – Peter, mindful of the Lord's command which was spoken 'Do not possess gold and silver' (Matthew 19:9) did not hoard for himself the money which was put at the feet of the Apostles, but he was wont to reserve it for the use of the poor who had lost their birthright.

Peter and John, surprisingly enough to our century, did not try to capitalize on this spectacular event. The beggar, however, was doing a great deal of advertising. After all, he had been lame from birth! The two men walked on into the temple; so did the beggar – only with a lot more noise, hundreds immediately believed! By this time the story of the healing had filtered back to the *temple rulers*, and a small panic had broken out. The first thing they did was to call out the temple guard; they then rounded up the priests and some Sadducees and rushed over to the Porch to arrest the Apostles. But they arrived a little too late to stop a multitude of people from being converted to Christ. How many were converted that afternoon no one knows. But someone estimated that the total number of men in the church had shot up to about 5,000. This was the second great spurt of growth in the church.

Gene Edwards

'In your offspring all families of earth will be blessed' (3:25). Christ indeed is the offspring of Abraham, and through faith in His name a blessing is promised to all, Jews and gentiles. Notice, however, that the apostle soothed the minds of the Jews to make them more well-disposed to believing by saying that, out of the whole world, the Saviour chose to visit and bless them first.

Bede

Day 10

Psalm 118:22   *Jeremiah 33:1-3*
Acts 4:2-12, 18-20

In a prison cell in the precincts of the Temple Peter stood looking out of the small grille window. It was early morning and a cock crowed. The sound filled Peter with a fearful memory. John heard him whisper: 'Oh, Master, stay near me.' John came to him. 'He told us it would be like this, Peter. Do you remember? That we would be persecuted for His sake.'

'Yes.' The cock crowed again and this time Peter's voice drowned the noise. 'I'll not deny Him this time.'

Joy Harrington
Paul of Tarsus

'The stone rejected by you, the builders, has come to have the chief position in the corner' (4:11). The builders were the Jews, while all gentiles remained in the wasteland of idols. The Jews alone were daily reading the law and the prophets for the building up of the people. As they were building, they came to the cornerstone, which embraces the two walls – that is they found in the prophetic scriptures that Christ, who would bring together in Himself two peoples, was to come in the flesh. And, because they preferred to remain in one wall, that is, to be saved alone, they rejected the stone which was not one-sided, but two-sided. Nevertheless, although they were unwilling, God Himself placed this stone at the chief position in the corner, so that from two testaments and two peoples there might rise up a building of one and the same faith.

'Salvation is not in any other' (4:12). If the salvation of the world is in no other, but in Christ alone, then the fathers of the Old Testament were saved by the incarnation and passion of the same Redeemer, there was agreement in one and the same faith, because through the prophets they learned as something to come the same dispensation of Christ which we learned through the apostles as something which had been done. For there is no redemption of human captivity to sinfulness except in the blood of Him who gave Himself as a redemption for all.

Bede

Day 11

Psalm 125:1   *Isaiah 54:1–3*
Acts 4:13–14, 18–20, 32–35

They were ordinary people, but companions of
Jesus – this was the qualification of their
discipleship, spending time with Him.

R. Searle

The methods of the Early Church, if applied
today, produce the same results. Can anyone
today afford to condemn the miraculous and
insist that his modern methods are more
properly adapted to a modern world when
millions are going to hell and multitudes are
incurably ill? This generation needs the
miraculous power and ministry of Jesus Christ
through Holy Ghost filled Christians as much
as any generation ever needed it.

T. L. Osborn

'The group of believers was of one mind and
heart' (4:32) – Those who had completely left
the world behind by no means pushed
themselves forward, one over the other,
glorying in the nobility of their birth. Rather,
as though born from the womb of one and the
same mother, the church, they all rejoiced in
one and the same love of brotherhood.

Bede

The bond between the people was remarkable,
a living expression of incarnational
Christianity.

R. Searle

Living in common was practised on a far wider scale than most people today realize. In about AD 190 a Christian named Tertullian disclosed, 'We have all things in common . . . except our wives!' That means that 160 years after Pentecost the believers were still practising what was begun in Jerusalem – throughout the *whole* Roman Empire!

Gene Edwards

Day 12

Psalm 125:4–5   Amos 7:7–8   Acts 4:34, 5:1–15

Everyone who had a job gave his entire salary into the common pool. *Then* everyone in the church had their basic needs met by living in common on the money placed in the pool. Everyone got food and a place to sleep. All other needs were met according to i) greatest need and ii) funds available. Ananias' plan was simple. He decided to give only *part* of his salary but to *tell* the Apostles he was giving *all*. By doing this he would be able to save back the rest of his monthly income while the church met *all* his needs! In a period of time, he could easily save a small fortune. Ananias put his plan into operation. He never dreamed what would happen as he came to Peter with the gift and made his statement. Peter's spirit stirred. He saw right into the man's heart. He revealed Ananias' sin and Ananias fell dead on the spot. Later in the day Ananias' wife died in the same manner. The news of their deaths shot through the city. This latest sign, two people dropping dead because they lied to the

Holy Spirit, set off a *fourth* great wave of conversions. The Church had begun as 120, then went to 3,000, then to over 5,000 men, and, by this time, who knew how big! Another wave of healing set in. Great numbers of people were again recovering from disease.

Gene Edwards

Sick people were carried out into the streets so that when Peter came by his shadow at least might fall on some of them – and they were cured! Bede says that 'because Peter is a type of the church, it is beautifully appropriate that he himself walked upright, but by his accompanying shadow he raised up those who were lying down.'

Day 13

Psalm 131:1   Isaiah 40:13–14
        Acts 5:16–21, 29–35, 38–42

News of people being healed in Jerusalem reached the ear of people living in all the nearby towns. Soon people from those cities began flocking into Jerusalem, bringing their sick to be healed by the twelve. Perhaps the people in the other towns were getting jealous. Perhaps they were saying, 'If those Apostles are just going to stay in one city, I'm not going to miss the joy of knowing Christ. If the Church will not come to me, I'll go to it.'

Gene Edwards

The Greek word 'martyr' properly means 'witness'. But so many 'witnesses' laid down their lives for their testimony that the word 'martyr' gradually became understood as 'one who bears witness to his death' and that was the understanding of the word when it was adopted into the English language as 'martyr'. But its original meaning was 'witness' – it denotes one who can or does vouch for, (guarantee, verify, prove) what he has seen or heard or knows.

T.L. Osborn

The Rabbi Gamaliel spoke quietly, but with firm authority. 'God has not made us to be judges of each other. He expects us to be vigilant, not bigoted. We do not know in what age or in what manner He will send His Messiah to His people, but we have been warned by the prophets that there will be signs and wonders that men will not believe though they see them. I think men have come to look for the sort of Messiah they have created out of their imagination. God's ways are not our ways, and time will show whether the teaching of the Nazarenes be true or false.'

And to the Council Gamaliel spoke with urgency, though his voice was calm: 'Men of Israel, take care what you do. I advise you to leave these men alone. For if what they teach comes from men it will die of its own accord, but if it should spring from God, whatever you do, you will be unable to put it down. Take care lest you find yourselves fighting against God.'

Joy Harrington
Paul of Tarsus

Day 14

Psalm 125:2   Numbers 11:16–17   Acts 6:1–10

If you had asked Peter for a good, clear
definition of what an *Apostle* was, and what
the duties of an Apostle were, he would have
had to answer, 'I don't have the faintest idea
. . . all I know is that I am one! Watch me and
find out!' The label – the name – was there
only as a means to describe what those men
already were. The title sought to proclaim
what they had already been doing . . .
organically. The name by which they were
called only described what the Holy Spirit had
already done in them! So what were the
twelve? They were men who lived in the
conscious presence of Christ. Furthermore, the
Apostles had developed a 'habit' during over
three years with Jesus – the habit of *always*
being in the Lord's presence – and they *kept*
the habit even after He ascended! Is that
impossible? No, it is not. Eight years after
Pentecost the Apostles were still experiencing
that same intimate relationship with Christ.
They were *still* living constantly in His
presence.

Gene Edwards

In the courtyard below the upper room seven
men stood waiting. They came from many
different countries and all were dressed in the
Greek style. Yet all save one were of the
Jewish race. Barnabas came down the stairs
with Simon Peter. 'These are the seven we
have selected,' he said as he led Peter over to
the group. 'Philip . . . Prochorus . . . Nicanor

. . . Timor . . . Parmenas . . . Stephen . . .'
Peter embraced each man as he would have
embraced his brother. '. . . Nicholas of Antioch
. . . not born a Jew, but has long been of our
faith . . .' Peter hesitated, just for a moment,
before embracing the Gentile. Then he told the
men to kneel and, placing his hands on each
head in turn, he said a blessing. 'Lord, bless
this Your son, that he may faithfully serve You
and feed Your people, not only with bread
that perishes, but with the true bread of
Heaven that gives life to the world.'

J. Harrington

'The Spirit gave Stephen such wisdom that
when he spoke, they could not refute him'
(Acts 6:10). This is what the Lord himself tells
his martyrs: For I will give you eloquence and
wisdom which all your adversaries will not be
able to withstand or contradict (Luke 21:15). It
was fitting that in the first martyr he should
confirm what he deigned to promise to all
those handed over to martyrdom for the sake
of His Name.

Bede

Day 15

Psalm 125:1   *Ezekiel 3:9–10*
            Acts 6:10, 6:13–15, 7:1–3, 48–54

When Stephen proclaimed the Gospel,
everyone knew his words were honest, his
power real, his humility a fact. He would not
have dared to pretend in front of a group of
people who knew him like a book. Stephen's

devotion to his Lord was a solidly established fact.

. . . What Stephen says today will be heard by *the very men* who crucified the Lord eight years ago. His words are less his own defence than a defence of his Lord. In fact, Stephen will act as a lawyer defending his Lord eight years after *His* trial, when no man was present to defend Him!

Gene Edwards

Stephen speaks of Abraham leaving his land and kin-folk to go where God would lead, and Bede harmonizing this and the Genesis account says that in Mesopotamia the Lord spoke to Abraham who was away from home but held by the hope and desire of returning, and told him to erase the love for that place from his mind, signifying not a physical but a mental departure by which he separated himself for ever from association with the Chaldeans and their nation, (for in one year he left Chaldea, entered Mesopotamia, tarried in Haran, and was brought into the land of promise).

Heaven as God's throne and earth His footstool is not to be understood in a material way, as though God has parts of His body placed in Heaven and on earth as we do when we sit down. Rather, it is to show that He is within and above all things, However, spiritually, heaven stands for the saints, while earth stands for sinners since God watches over the former by dwelling within them, the latter he brings to the ground by condemning them.

Bede

It is obvious to everyone that Stephen does not care at all for his own life. He makes no effort to defend himself or to gain sympathy for himself in answering the charges. Gradually it becomes apparent that Stephen has somehow turned the tables: he has put the Sanhedrin on trial . . . before Heavenly councils.

Gene Edwards

Day 16

Psalm 131:2   Judges 16:29–30   Acts 7:55–60

Suddenly Stephen was standing in the middle of the room gazing at the ceiling, his whole being transfixed, his face glowing with the glory of God. First century believers had a disconcerting way of stepping outside the confines of time and space. This was one of those holy moments. Spellbound, Stephen stands innocently marvelling, oblivious to everyone else in the room. Suddenly he shouts out at what he is seeing.

'Look! . . . I see heaven; it is opened!! I see the Son of Man standing at the right hand of God.' That did it, the whole courtroom went wild. Madness broke out. Men vaulted over benches and chairs. Everyone in the room rushed toward Stephen, putting their hands over their ears as they went, a sign that they could not bear to hear another word of blasphemy from his mouth. It was a scene of utter insanity.? All judicial dignity, form, and position dissolved. There was nothing in the room but a crowd gone wild, intent upon one thing: the death of Stephen.

Gene Edwards

'And casting him outside the city, they stoned him.' The Lord, too, who chose us out of the world for His heavenly kingdom and glory, suffered outside the gate, like Stephen, who, as though he were a stranger to the world, was stoned outside the city. For he had no permanent city here, but with his whole heart he sought the city to come. 'And falling on his knees he cried out with a loud voice saying, "Lord, do not hold this sin against them." ' For himself he prayed standing up; for his enemies he knelt down. Because their iniquity was so great it called out for the greater remedy of falling upon his knees. His zeal was such that he openly reproached his captors for their fault in lacking faith, and he burned so with love that even at his death he prayed for his murderers.

Bede

As the witnesses raised the heavy stones above their heads and hurled them down into the pit, the first martyr of church history very simply slipped to his knees and fell quietly asleep.

Gene Edwards

Day 17

Psalm 125:1–2   Ecclesiastes 3:1, 4, 7   Acts 8:1–4

What was the 'thirty-nine lashes'? They were a punishment just this side of stoning. In that day a Jew would apparently have done anything to escape the physical ·agony and the social humiliation of these stripes. That was about to change . . . and very suddenly! The followers of Jesus Christ showed no sign of shame. The whip has four strips of leather on it, each about three or four feet long, and the disciple's back is bared. The whip, raised high in the air, straightens and comes down with all its might, not on the disciple's back, but, rather, on the top of his shoulders, its strips reaching out beyond to fall hard upon his chest and stomach, instantly causing welts and bruises. Next time the leather lands upon tender, swollen skin and with each blow the disciple's skin becomes more bruised. The welts begin opening, and finally turn into open gashes. After thirteen such lashes across his front the disciple is probably already in shock, dehydrated and nearly delirious with pain, but now the second thirteen lashes are aimed at the back and right side, and still thirteen more lashes make their permanent mark on his left side. Close to death he is cut down and dragged out. If he survives, then across his chest, stomach and back he will forever carry deep furrowed scars as trophies of his love for his Lord.

It was a shocking scene. Saul's plan called for the arrest and trial of 20,000 people – all to face this same ordeal. There was to have been no distinction of gender. Women faced the possibility of this same agony . . . The guardians of the religious system had moved to destroy the church, to obliterate it from the face of the earth; but unwittingly, they had not stopped the church, they had launched it! By all rights those hours should have been a replay of the days just after the crucifixion: a people scattered and defeated. But the opposite was true: the accidental reunions along the road were moments of joy. Bursts of shouting and exultation went up instantly wherever the believers met . . . The Gospel was established in Judaea by ordinary, untrained, untutored men who came into town, stood in the market, and proclaimed the Gospel of Christ. They were simple, ordinary people, common labourers and tradesmen. They were 'the faces in the crowd' who met in Solomon's Porch and gathered in the homes of Jerusalem.

Gene Edwards

Day 18

Psalm 127:1   Isaiah 61:1, 11
                Acts 8:4–8, 14–17, 25

It was a decade after Pentecost before those who were saved on the day of Pentecost began to exercise the *power* of Pentecost. A church must never have its beginning with a whole lot of prophets and teachers present. That would ruin everything! The healthiest experience a church can have is to be born having at least some meetings that are utterly leaderless. The church, any church, has a *right* to such a joyous, dangerous, hair-raising experience! Such meetings build a strong foundation in the church and provide a counter-balance for the day when prophets and teachers *are* raised up. When that day arrives, the church will not be dependent on such men, nor will the meetings be centred around them. They will only be one more added ingredient, not the cornerstone that holds the meeting together. A body of people who *have previously experienced church life* can survive, flourish and advance for a pretty good length of time with absolutely no help.

Church history was nearly nine years old before church life produced the first 'gifted' man . . . and his gift was *evangelism*. God gave something new to the Church in Philip. But God did *not* give His gift to the Church, or to Philip, until Philip had gone through years of incredible preparation.

Gene Edwards
The Early Church

Day 19

Psalm 130:4   *2 Kings 6:18–20*
                 Acts 9:8–18, 36–41

'And when Saul's eyes were opened, he saw nothing' (Acts 9:8).

By no means would he have been able to see well again unless he had first been fully blinded. Also, when he had rejected his own wisdom, which was confusing him, he could commit himself totally to faith.

Bede

And the scales came down from our eyes that day and Saul saw a new life before him and I where I had seen an enemy before now could see a friend.

Ananias, in the song by Ken Medema

Silently now I wait for Thee,
ready, my God, Thy will to see.
Open my eyes, illumine me, Spirit divine.

Clara H. Scott

One believer is used to allow God's power to
touch the life of another. We have seen this
with Ananias and Saul, and now also with
Peter and Tabitha (or Dorcas). 'Giving her his
hand, he raised her up'. When she was
touched by Peter's hand, Tabitha rose again,
since there is no better way for the soul which
has become weak than the example of the
saints.

Bede

Blest be the Tie that binds
our hearts in Christian love!
The fellowship of kindred minds
Is like to that above.

John Fawcett

Day 20

Psalm 131:1   *Habakkuk 2:1, 3*
            Acts 10:9–19; 11:18–22

'Arise, Peter. Kill and eat.' The voice that Peter
heard told him: Arise to make ready to preach
the gospel. Kill in the gentiles what they had
been, and make them what you are; for
whoever eats food lying outside of himself
turns it into his own body.

Bede

God is always bigger than they think at every
turn, and He can't be boxed in.

Roy Searle

HE is not a tame lion.

C. S. Lewis

'Who was I, then, to try to stop God?!!' When they heard this they stopped their criticism and praised God . . . We see that despite their initial caution they made the structures serve the Spirit instead of trying to insist that the Spirit conform to their structures.

Roy Searle

Someone was needed to travel to Antioch, check out the situation, come back to Jerusalem and report what he saw to the Apostles . . . It was a simple decision: an Apostle would not be needed. Barnabas could see what was happening in this 'renegade' work of the Lord. The Apostles did not realize that they had greatly underestimated what was going on in Antioch. But it was a divine error. God had decided, in the simple selection of Barnabas, to give him one of the key roles in determining the destiny of mankind for all time to come.

Gene Edwards

Day 21

Psalm 126:3   *Daniel 4:2–3*   *Acts 11:19–25*

Barnabas was suddenly in a different world, and he knew it!! Maybe, on second thought, these people should not be encouraged to go on in the Lord. If they continued, what on earth might happen? They had no Hebrew heritage to guide them. They had no strong moral fibre. In a word, they were 'loose'. If

Barnabas encouraged them to go on with the Lord in this free way, something terribly different from the Jewish church was going to blossom. What might it eventually look like? There was no guarantee of what might happen if a *gentile* church was allowed to get started. The thought *was* both frightening *and* exciting. But there it was on every face. As Barnabas looked around the room, there could be no doubt. He could see it in their smiles, hear it in their voices. Christ was their Saviour. They *knew* the Lord Jesus. They were redeemed! It was time for Barnabas to speak. What would he do? The decision he had to make at this moment was unprecedented in all the history of the Jewish faith. Would something *not* Hebrew be allowed to live? Would he encourage these people to go on? Call the whole thing off? Make some corrections here and there? At least take them out and have them circumcised? What, Barnabas, Son of Exhortation, you who have been called, 'a good man, full of the Holy Spirit', what will you do?

Barnabas stood up. You could almost hear his thoughts: 'Well, the Lord started this, I didn't. If He started it, He can finish it.' He opened his mouth . . . 'And he exhorted them all to remain faithful to the Lord and to continue in their faith.' And after those gentiles heard this, even more of them believed! And even more, they all rejoiced. On that *day* in that meeting, the church in Antioch was born.

Gene Edwards

. . . What exactly had Saul been doing these last three years in Tarsus? You recall he had spent the first three years after his conversion out in the desert, alone, getting to know the Lord – doing nothing. Well, it seems he had been doing the same thing during these second three years in Tarsus. Saul had spent six years getting to know his Lord.

Gene Edwards

Day 22

Psalm 112:6   *2 Chronicles 35:2*
Acts 4:36–37; 9:26–28; 11:25–30

Barnabas had been in the Jerusalem church from the beginning. This is significant. Though Barnabas did absolutely nothing during that 'beginning', he nonetheless got a ringside seat on what the Apostles did at the beginning. As you know, the twelve had also learned how to begin a work! They had been with the Lord 'from the beginning', and Saul was standing there watching every move Barnabas made in launching the Antioch church! It has fallen to Barnabas' lot to single-handedly raise up the first *gentile* church. For the next four years he will work diligently to build that church in Antioch. Saul, in the meantime, will *start* getting the type of experience Barnabas acquired years ago! Saul will sit at the feet of Barnabas; and for the next four years he will get his first real dose of the powerful daily experience of church life. Saul will watch; he will help; he will learn; but Barnabas will lead.

Gene Edwards

(In 11:29) we are told) 'They proposed to send relief to the brothers dwelling in Judaea! They knew that the famine would rage more severely in Judaea, and especially in Jerusalem, where among the saints there were poor people who had sold their goods, homes, and fields, and had brought the proceeds to the apostles, so that they had no way left to obtain much more money. And some were punished by the unbelieving Jews for their confession of the faith by having their own property taken away. To them the apostle said, 'You joyfully accepted the plundering of your goods' (Hebrews 10:34).

Eusebius tells us that one of these givers of alms was Helen, queen of Adiabeni, who purchased grain from Egypt and most generously provided for the needs of those dwelling in Jerusalem.

Bede

Day 23

Psalm 131:1   *Isaiah 59:10*
    Acts 12:1–5, 9–16, 13:1–3, 6, 8–11, 49–52

Herod Agrippa had James put to death by the sword. Clement of Alexandria reports that the man who turned James over to the judgement of martyrdom was himself moved to confess himself a Christian. Both were led away together to punishment and while they were being led on the way, he asked James to forgive him. James considered for a moment and said, 'Peace be to you,' and kissed him. And so both were beheaded at the same time.

The other disciples say to Rhoda, when she tells them Peter is outside, 'It is his angel.' We always assume it means 'his spirit', and that in body Peter still was in jail, or that it means 'his ghost', and they believed him already dead, but able to be wandering at large. Bede's comments are very different: 'That each of us had angels is found in the *Shepherd of Hermas* and in many places in Holy Scripture. The Lord said of little children, "Their angels always behold the face of my Father" (Matthew 18:10). Also Jacob referring to himself spoke of "the angel who saved me from all evils" (Genesis 48:16). And here the disciples believed that the apostle Peter's angel was coming.'

. . . Simon is a Negro, coming originally from Cyrene, Africa. He is almost unquestionably the man who carried the Lord's cross on the day of the crucifixion.

He was probably a gentile who had become a Jewish proselyte. He was undoubtedly converted to Christ on the day of Pentecost. Eight years later he fled Jerusalem, and by AD 43 he had ended up in Antioch. He is married. He had two sons: one is named Alexander – probably because he was born in Alexandria, Egypt; the other is named Rufus, or Redman.

Gene Edwards

Paul says to Elymas, 'Behold the Lord's hand is upon you, and you shall be blind.' Remembering his own experiences the apostle knew that light could rise again from the darkness of the mind's eyes. One who was working to take away from others the mind's eyes was not worthy to possess physical eyes.

Bede

It was later estimated that the church in Antioch eventually grew to the point that twenty per cent of the population of the city were following Christ. If that is so, then in the last part of the first century about 100,000 people were in the Antioch church, making it perhaps the largest single church in all history.

Gene Edwards

(Acts 13:52) '*And* the disciples were filled with joy and with the Holy Spirit.' The Greek text has '*But* the disciples . . .' so that we may understand that although the Jews persecuted the faith, the disciples on the contrary were endowed with spiritual joy.

Bede

Day 24

Psalm 127:1   Nehemiah 5:16   Ephesians 4:10–15

Each of the early Apostles had been called, at one time or another. They had heard a call from God previous to their sending. This was true even in the life of the very first Apostle, the Lord Jesus.

Jesus Christ was *called by His Father* before the foundation of the world, called to be the first Apostle, called to build the church. Jesus Christ authored the church; *He* built the church. The group of Apostles, the twelve? Were they also called? Along the blue shores of Galilee the twelve were *called* to be Apostles by the Lord Jesus. God the *Father* called Jesus Christ to be an Apostle. God the *Son* called the twelve to be Apostles. What of Barnabas?

We do not know anything about his call, we only know by the testimony of the Holy Spirit that he had been called. But when, where, we don't know. It may even have been that Barnabas did not recognize his call as a call. Not at first. Sometimes it takes the passing of years and a look back to see these things clearly. And Saul? Saul was converted to Christ on a trip to Damascus. He was also *called* that very same day! So in Apostleship, there is first the call. Many, many men today have been called to minister in His Kingdom. But in our age men have the *call* all mixed up with the *sending*. God never sends men who have been called until they have survived (yes, *survived*) the *preparation!* To be called is not a licence to *serve*.

Gene Edwards

Look carefully at your translation of verse 12 of Ephesians 4. For what purpose did Christ raise up the 'equippers' He gives to the Church? 'to equip the saints, for the work of ministry'? If *your* Bible has a comma there, then to be sure God didn't put it there. His purpose was that the *saints* be equipped for the work of ministry. That is His goal, His reason for gifting His Church with each kind of 'equipper'.

Day 25

Psalm 125:1   *Proverbs 22:6*
                Acts 13:50–52, 14:1–5, 19–27

Many Gentiles believed in the Lord and on that
day a church was born in the city of Pisidea–
Antioch, the first Gentile church. For about
the next four months the two men stayed in
the city and nourished the church. Here is a
group of re-generated Christians but with
absolutely no knowledge of the Jewish
religion: they have never read the ancient
Hebrew scrolls. Abraham, Moses and David are
all new names to them!!! They don't know
anything about *anything*. They have little or
no moral character. Obviously Paul and
Barnabas have a great deal of work to do here
in this town. It is going to take a long time to
establish a strong church here . . . Wrong!!!
Persecution drives Paul and Barnabas out of
the area, and the oldest converts they leave
behind have been Christians only five months,
a group of ex-pagans with no building to meet
in, no scripture old or recent. At best they
may have a few copies of the Psalms or can
quote from them. No leader, no organization,
no rules, no building, no past heritage. Praise
God, they have all they need! They have the
living Holy Spirit within them and they have
one another. They have had a total of only
four months of help. They are left alone; they
are surrounded by a hostile city; but they will
be all right. They are saved. They have learned
enough so that they can sense the inner
direction of the Holy Spirit.
   . . .In Derbe there is no opposition or

persecution. We would assume, therefore, that the Apostles would take advantage of this blessing and stay a long time . . . and do a thorough job for a change. But these brothers seem to have learned something from their past experiences. At the end of four months, despite the fact that they *could* stay longer, the two men leave Derbe. Obviously they feel that a new church needs no more time than this before it can be safely left alone (– left to the Lord alone).

Before returning home they begin a difficult journey to visit the other three new churches. The oldest of them, Pisidea-Antioch, was about eight months old. Each of the four churches had received about five months of help. Following this came a period of being left alone, so each church experienced a period of having no help. One church was left alone for one and a half years, another six months. After this period each church received a short visit from the Apostles. This second visit probably lasted only about two or three weeks. The Apostles are now leaving. They are leaving *permanently*. Think of it: in all that vast land, among all those millions of people are hidden four little bands of Christians.

Gene Edwards
The Early Church II

Day 26

Psalm 125:2   Amos 3:3   Acts 15:1–6, 22, 30–41

The approach these early believers made to a problem was direct and simple. There was really an attitude of openness on the part of everyone toward those who had an opinion differing from their own. There was communication; there was open, frank dialogue. Note also that none of these men made any effort (neither in Antioch nor here in Jerusalem) to expose this problem before the whole church! No one used his position or platform to publicly prejudice others to his private view. None took steps that would cause any type of irreparable breach.

Gene Edwards

'But Paul asked that John Mark should not be taken back.' When John Mark placed himself in the very front line of the fray, he had been too luke-warm about taking a stand. Therefore Paul rightly rejected him, lest the strength of others might be corrupted by the contagious influence, so to speak, of this man.

'And a quarrel occurred.' Do not think this a moral fault, for it is not evil to be agitated. Rather it is evil to be agitated unreasonably, when no just reason demands it.

'And Barnabas took Mark and sailed to Cyprus.' Because he loved him as a brother, and because they were relatives (for we read that they were cousins – Colossians 4:10), Barnabas was separated from Paul and returned to his island homeland; none the less he engaged in the work imposed upon him, preaching the gospel.

Bede

Day 27

Psalm 32:7   *Genesis 39:20–21*
Acts 16:6–10, 20–33

It is encouraging to see men of this spiritual
stature not knowing what to do. At the
moment they do not have clear, singular
direction from the Lord. On the other hand
they do know what to do. *They know to wait!*
Gene Edwards

(Acts 16:25) 'But in the middle of the night
Paul and Silas were worshipping God' – The
devotion of the apostles' hearts and the power
of prayer are expressed here together, since in
the depths of the prison they sang hymns, and
their praise moved the earth of the prison,
shook the foundations, opened the doors, and
finally loosened the very chains of those who
had been bound. In other words, anyone of
the faithful considers it all joy when he falls
into various trials. And he gladly glories in his
infirmities, so that the power of Christ may
dwell in him. Such a one undoubtedly sings
hymns with Paul and Silas within the darkness
of the prison, and with the psalmist he recites
to the Lord: You are my refuge from the
distress which surrounds me, my exaltation.

'The jailor washed their wounds and he was
baptized' – A beautiful exchange – for them he
washed the wounds from their blows, and
through them he was relieved of the wounds
of his own guilty acts.

Bede

Day 28

Psalm 131:1   Proverbs 9:8–10   Acts 17:1–6, 10–16

When those preachers arrived in turn, the people said, 'These men that have turned the world upside down have turned up here now' and those words were not a compliment!

T. L. Osborn

Saturday morning, the city of Berea. Three men, just as if they had never been rejected, ill-treated, beaten or imprisoned, make a straight line for the local synagogue. This Paul is the eternal optimist! And at last his optimism is to be rewarded. Paul has finally come to a city where the local synagogue will give him an unanimously warm reception. They were attentive to all he said – if it was true, then the Messiah had finally come. They decided to meet together at the synagogue every day and read the scrolls to one another and check these writings against what Paul had said. With a seeking attitude like this, many came to know the Lord.

Gene Edwards

We see in the book of Acts two totally different sorts of evangelism. Paul preached in the synagogues first, addressing those with a religious background, explaining the scriptures and introducing an experiential knowledge of Christ whose love for them had led Him to the cross. But reaching those with no religious background or cultural predisposition to the gospel was a totally different task – these gentiles had at least not been inoculated against a true knowledge of God, but the message would have to be given in their own language and reach into their life-experience in a real and provocative way. The Church in our day is very good at Jewish-type evangelism, most of our converts had been to Sunday school or know basic Bible stories! We do very little to meet the world on equal terms with a gospel that makes sense to the 'gentiles'.

Roy Searle

On this next journey Paul is not able to return to visit the new churches because of his opponents. Instead he leaves Luke in Philippi, Silas for a while in Berea and sends Timothy back to Thessalonica where the opposition was so persistent. Timothy was probably only about twenty-two, the church in Thessalonica about ten months old and without any help for about five or six months!

Gene Edwards

We see the breaking of new ground. Prepared to take risks – not inflexible. 'By all means to win some' means there can be no rigidity. The purpose of God must not be thwarted.

Roy Searle

Day 29

Psalm 125:1   *Proverbs 15:1–4*
            Acts 17:16–31, 18:1–5

We need to come out from behind our religious walls, and take down those walls inside our life and language so we can engage with the rest of the world in the Spirit's power and enabling.

'God, who made the world and everything in it: since He is the Lord of heaven and earth, He does not dwell in temples made by human hands.'

Follow the steps of the apostle's argument addressing gentiles. He teaches that the one God is originator of the world and all things. We live and move in him, and are His offspring. He should be loved not just for His gifts of life and light, but also because of a certain affinity of kind. Next He shows the founder of the entire world cannot be enclosed in stone temples, has no need of victims' blood, cannot be created by man's hand, or valued in terms of metals. In all this he disposes of opinions that give explicit reason for idolatry. He posits that salvation is given to us through Christ, and at first calls him man, demonstrating by descriptions of his actions that he was more than a mere man, that slowly they might realize and believe he was God. For what difference does it make in what order anyone believes?

'And indeed some of your own poets have said . . .' He spoke not from the Jewish prophets, but with testimony of their own authors. From the falsehoods of these to whom they could not object, he confirmed his own truths. He takes into account the particular individuals who are his listeners.

Bede

The truth is shocking! Paul served the Lord *in his spare time!* That bears repeating. Paul served the Lord, raised up churches and 'he evangelized the world' . . . and he did *all* this *in his spare time!* He gloried in the fact that his service to the Lord was rendered during the few hours he had left over from a hard day's work.

Day 30

Psalm 111:6   *Isaiah 42:4*
    Acts 19:8–19, 20:17–18, 22–24, 34–37

Certainly, deceivers will come, but that is all the more reason for the *real* power of God in demonstration. He who warns against *false* miracles should at least be able to produce the *real* miracles.

T. L. Osborn

(Acts 20:23) When Paul says 'in all the cities the Holy Spirit warns me' he clearly shows that the things that would happen to him had not been revealed to him directly, but to others concerning him. These others include the prophet Agabus and the disciples who when he was staying at Tyre warned him through the Spirit not to go up to Jerusalem.

(20:35) 'It is more blessed to give than to receive.' He does not value the rich, even if they give alms, more highly than those who have left all things and followed the Lord. Rather, he extols most highly those who have given up at once everything they had, and who nevertheless labour, working with their hands at what is good in order to have something to give to one who is suffering need.

Bede

Day 31

'And when it began to grow light, Paul
entreated them all to take food.'

A most beautiful allegorical sense is evident in
this passage. No one escapes the tempests of
this world except those who are nourished by
the bread of life, and one who in the night of
present tribulations depends for all his strength
on wisdom, fortitude, temperance and justice
will soon, with the shining forth of divine
help, reach the post of salvation which he had
sought, provided that, unencumbered by things
of the world, he seeks only the flame of love
with which he may warm his Heart.

Bede

In a dark and needy world we must
demonstrate the light and life of God to those
disillusioned by the church, and to those the
church has never reached in any way. Our
lifestyle should demonstrate our love for each
other and for Jesus in a way that makes other
people jealous, and it is high time we banded
together to do this.

JUNE READINGS

Desert Fathers

Day 1 Psalm 103
       2 Corinthians 5:16–17
       Luke 4:14–21

Day 2 Psalm 6
       Exodus 21:12–24
       Matthew 5:38–48

Day 3 Psalm 57
       Revelation 13:11–18
       Luke 21:8–15

Day 4 Psalm 131
       2 Corinthians 12:11–18
       Luke 17:7–10

Day 5 Psalm 12
       Ecclesiastes 5:10–15
       Matthew 5:38–42

Day 6 Psalm 111
       Romans 12:9–16
       Luke 12:22–34

Day 7 Psalm 104:10–30
       Ecclesiastes 3:1–14
       Luke 7:31–35

Day 8 Psalm 106:24–27
       Exodus 16:1–3
       Mark 8:14–21

Day 9 Psalm 51:1–12
       Job 9:14–15
       John 8:1–11

Day 10 Psalm 52
       Amos 5:21–24
       Matthew 7:21–23

Day 22 Psalm 51
       Romans 3:22–24
       Matthew 9:9–13
Day 23 Psalm 119:89–96
       Hebrews 5:7–10
       John 17:1–5
Day 24 Psalm 26
       Ruth 3:1–11
       John 20:10–18
Day 25 Psalm 37:30–31
       James 3:1–12
       Matthew 5:33–37
Day 26 Psalm 85:9
       Micah 6:6–8
       Matthew 9:9–13
Day 27 Psalm 118:25–29
       Romans 2:1–11
       Luke 18:9–14
Day 28 Psalm 41:1–3
       James 2:14–26
       Luke 10:25–37
Day 29 Psalm 113
       2 John
       Luke 1:46–55
Day 30 Psalm 150
       Revelation 12:10–12
       Matthew 24:4–14

Introduction

The sayings of the **Desert Fathers** and Mothers are our topic this month.

No introduction is really necessary as their words speak for themselves.

As an old Pentecostal preacher used to say:

Watch the witness, brother –
watch for the witness!

For information on the Desert Fathers:
The Wisdom of the Desert Thomas Merton
Publisher: Darley Anderson

(The order of readings this month is, exceptionally, Psalm, Old/New Testament and Gospel.)

Day 1

Psalm 103   2 Corinthians 5:16–17   Luke 4:14–21

Abba Poemen said about Abba Pior that every single day he made a fresh beginning.

Day 2

Psalm 6   Exodus 21:12–24   Matthew 5:38–48

Abba Isaiah said:

When someone wishes to render evil for evil, he is able to hurt his brother's conscience even by a single nod.

A brother who was insulted by another brother came to Abba Sisois and said to him:

'I was hurt by my brother, and I want to avenge myself.'

The old man tried to console him and said: 'Do not do that, my child. Rather leave vengeance to God.'

But he said: 'I will not quit until I avenge myself.'

Then the old man said: 'Let us pray, brother.' And standing up he said: 'O God, we no longer need you to take care of us since we now avenge ourselves.'

Hearing these words, the brother fell at the feet of the old man and said: 'I am not going to fight with my brother any more. Forgive me, Abba.'

Day 3

Psalm 57   Revelation 13:11–18   Luke 21:8–15

Abba Anthony:

The time is coming when people will be insane, and when they see someone who is not insane – they will attack that person, saying:

'You are insane, because you are not like us.'

Day 4

Psalm 131   2 Corinthians 12:11–18   Luke 17:7–10

They said of Abbot Pambo that in the very hour when he departed this life he said to the holy men who stood by him:

'From the time I came to this place in the Desert, and built me a cell, and dwelt here, I do not remember eating bread that was not earned by the work of my own hands – nor do I remember saying anything for which I was sorry, even until this hour.

And thus I go to the Lord as one who has not even made a beginning in the service of God.'

Day 5

Psalm 12 Ecclesiastes 5:10–15 Matthew 5:38–42

Once some robbers came into the monastery and said to one of the Elders:
   'We have come to take everything that is in your cell.'
   And he said: 'My sons, take all you want.'
   So they took everything they could find in the cell and started off. But they left behind a little bag that was hidden in the cell, the Elder picked it up and followed after them, crying out: 'My sons, take this, you forgot it in the cell.'
   Amazed at the patience of the Elder, they brought everything back into the cell, and did penance, saying: 'This one really is a Man of God.'

Day 6

Psalm 111   Romans 12:9–16   Luke 12:22–34

One of the Elders had finished his baskets and
had already put handles on them, when he
heard his neighbour saying:

'What shall I do? The market is about to
begin and I have nothing with which to make
handles for my baskets.'

At once the Elder went in and took off his
handles, giving them to the brother with the
words: 'Here, I don't need these, take them
and put them on your own baskets.'

Thus in his great charity he saw to it that
his brother's work was finished whilst his own
remained incomplete.

Day 7

Psalm 104:10–30   Ecclesiastes 3:1–14
Luke 7:31–35

Once Abbot Anthony was conversing with
some brethren, and a hunter who was after
game in the wilderness came upon them. He
saw Abbot Anthony and the brothers enjoying
themselves, and disapproved. Abbot Anthony
said:

'Put an arrow in your bow and shoot it.'
  This he did.
  'Now shoot another,' said the Elder.
  'And another, and another.'
  Then the hunter said:
  'If I bend my bow all the time it will break.'
  Abbot Anthony replied:

'So it is also in the work of God. If we push
ourselves beyond measure, the brethren will
soon collapse. It is right therefore, from time
to time, to relax.'

Day 8

Psalm 106:24–27   Exodus 16:1–3   Mark 8:14–21

One of the Elders used to say:

'In the beginning when we got together we
used to talk about something that was good
for our own souls, and we went up and up,
and ascended even to heaven.

'But now we get together and spend our
time in criticizing everything and we drag one
another down into the abyss.'

Day 9

Psalm 51:1–12   Job 9:14–15   John 8:1–11

There was a fornicating monk, who kept a
woman in his cell, so indiscreetly that word
began to get around about it. Some of the
monks living nearby decided to do something
about it, and they asked Abba Ammonas who
was visiting the region to go with them.

The offending monk, seeing them coming,
hid the woman in a large water jar. This was
spotted by the Abba when they all went into
the cell. The Abba sat on the jar, while the
others searched the room. They could find
nothing, and went away ashamed. When they
had gone the Abba got up and took the
culprit's hand and simply said to him:

'Brother, pay attention to yourself.'

Day 10

Psalm 52   **Amos 5:21–24**   **Matthew 7:21–23**

Abba Agatho used to say:

> If you are able to revive the dead,
> but not be willing to be reconciled to your
> neighbour – it is better to leave the dead in
> the grave.

AND
Psalm 18:1–6, 16–19
Romans 12:17–21
Luke 6:20–26

There was a certain Elder who, if anyone
maligned him, would go in person to offer him
presents, if he lived nearby. And if he lived at a
distance he would send presents by the hand of
another.

Day 11

Psalm 127:1–2   **1 Corinthians 3:5–15**
                Matthew 17:17–20

As the Elders said:

> The reason why we do not get anywhere is
> that we do not know our limits, and we are
> not patient in carrying out the work we have
> begun.

Day 12

Psalm 25:8-15   *Deuteronomy 6:10-25*
Luke 23:34

Abba Pastor said:

> A man must breathe humility
> and the fear of God just as ceaselessly
> as he inhales and exhales air.

Abba Alonius said:

> Humility is the land
> where God wants us to go and offer sacrifice.

One of the Elders was asked what was humility and he said:

'If you forgive a brother who has injured you before he himself asks pardon.'

A brother asked another of the Elders:
    'What is humility?'
    The Elder answered him: 'To do good to those who do evil to you.'
    The brother asked: 'Supposing a man can't go that far, what should he do?'
    The Elder replied: 'Let him get away from them and keep his mouth shut.'

Day 13

Psalm 132   *2 Thessalonians 3:6-15*
Luke 10:38-42

A brother came to visit Abba Sylvanus at Mount Sinai. When he saw the brothers working hard, he said to the old man:
    'Do not work for food that perishes, for

Mary has chosen the good part.'

Then the old man called his dicsiple: 'Zachary, give this brother a book, and put him in an empty cell.'

Now when it was three o'clock the brother kept looking out of the door to see if someone would call him for the meal. But nobody called him, so he got up, went to the old man, and asked:

'Abba, didn't the brothers eat today?'

The old man replied: 'Of course we did!'

'Then why didn't you call me?,' he asked.

The old man replied: 'You are a spiritual person, and do not need that type of food, but since we are earthly, we want to eat and that's why we work. Indeed, you have chosen the good part reading all day long, and not wanting to eat earthly food.'

When the brother heard this he repented: 'Forgive me, Abba.'

Then the old man said to him: 'Mary certainly needed Martha, and it is really by Martha's help that Mary is praised.'

Day 14

Psalm 53:1–4   *2 Corinthians 9:6–15*
Mark 4:1–12

Once some brethren went out to visit the Hermits who lived in the desert. They came to one who received them with joy, and seeing they were tired, invited them to eat before the accustomed time, and placed before them all the food he had available.

But that night when they were all supposed to be sleeping the hermit heard the visitors saying:

'These hermits eat more than we do.'

Now at dawn the visitors set out to see another hermit – and as they were starting out their host said:

'Greet him from me, and give him this message: Be careful not to water the vegetables.'

When they reached the other hermitage they delivered this message. The second hermit understood what was meant by the words. So he made the visitors sit down and weave baskets, and sitting with them he worked without interruption. And in the evening when the time came for lighting the lamp, he added a few extra psalms to the usual number, after which he said to them:

'We do not usually eat every day out here. But because you have come along it is fitting to have a little supper today for a change.'

Then he gave them some dry bread and salt, then added: 'Here's a special treat for you.'

Upon which he mixed them a little sauce of vinegar, salt and oil, and gave it to them. After supper they got up again and said more psalms, and kept praying till almost dawn, at which the hermit said:

'Well, we can't finish all our usual prayers – for you are tired from your journey. You had better take a little rest.'

And so when the first hour came they all wanted to leave the hermit – but he would not let them go. He kept saying:

'Stay with me a while. I cannot let you go so soon, charity demands that I keep you for two or three days.'

But they, hearing this, waited until dark, and then under cover of night they made off.

Day 15

Psalm 37:1–11   *Song of Songs 2:8–17*
Luke 22:45–46

A certain brother went to Abbot Moses in
Scete, and asked him for a good word. And
the Elder said to him:
   'Go, sit in your cell
and your cell will teach you everything.'

Day 16

Psalm 19:7–11   *James 1:22–25*   *John 14:23–24*

Abbot Pastor said:

If you have a chest full of clothing,
and leave it for a long time, the clothinig
will rot inside of it.

It is the same with the thoughts in our heart.
If we do not carry them out by physical
action, after a long while they will spoil and
turn bad.

Day 17

Psalm 98   Philippians 4:10–20   Matthew 6:25–34

One of the brothers asked an Elder, saying:
   'Would it be all right if I kept two pence in
my possession, in case I should get sick?'
   The Elder, seeing his thoughts, and that he
wanted to keep them, said:

'Keep them.'

The brother going back to his cell, began to wrestle with his own thoughts saying: 'I wonder if the father gave me his blessing or not?' Rising up he went back to him:

'In God's Name, tell me the truth, because I am all upset over these two pence.'

The Elder said to him:

'Since I saw your thoughts and your desire to keep them, I told you to keep them. But it is not good to keep more than we need for our body. Now these two pence are your hope. If they should be lost, would not God take care of you?'

Cast your care on the Lord then, for he will take care of us.

Day 18

Psalm 139:1–18 Ephesianss 6:10–18 Luke 12:1–7

One of the Fathers said:

'Just as it is impossible for a man to see his face in troubled water, so too the soul unless it be cleansed from alien thoughts cannot pray to God in contemplation.'

Another of the Elders said:

'When the eyes of an ox or mule are covered, then he goes round and round turning the mill wheel. But if his eyes are uncovered he will not go round in the circle of the mill wheel. So, too, the devil if he manages to cover the eyes of a man can humiliate him in every sin. But if that man's eyes are not closed he can easily escape the devil.'

Day 19

Psalm 1   *Hebrews 11:20–40*   *Luke 19:11–27*

A brother asked one of the Elders:
  'What good thing shall I do?'
The old man replied: 'God alone knows
what is good. However I heard it said that
someone inquired of Abbot Nisteros, a friend
of Abbot Anthony, and asked: "What good
work shall I do?" And that he replied: "Not all
works are alike. For scripture says that
Abraham was hospitable and God was with
him. Elias loved solitary prayer and God was
with him. And David was humble and God
was with him. Therefore, whatever you see
your soul desire according to God, do that
thing and you shall keep your heart safe." '

Day 20

Psalm 25:8–12   *Philippians 2:1–11*   *Luke 14:7–11*

Abba John the Little said:

  'We have abandoned a light burden, namely
  self-criticism, and taken up a heavy burden,
  namely self-justification.'

Abba Silvanus said:

  'Woe to the person whose reputation is greater
  than his work.'

A brother came to see Abba Theodore, and
started to talk and inquire about things which he
himself had not tried yet. The old man said to
him:

'You have not found a boat, or put your gear into it, and you haven't even sailed – but you seem to have arrived in the city already! Well, do your work first then you will come to the point you are talking about now.'

Day 21

Psalm 50:7-23   *Hosea 6:4-6*   *Luke 12:1-14*

Once the Rule was made in Scete that they should fast for the entire week before Easter. During this week, however, some brothers came from Egypt to see Abba Moses, and he made a modest meal for them.

Seeing the smoke, the neighbours said to the priests of the church at that place:

'Look, Moses has broken the Rule and is cooking food at his place.'

Then the priests said:

'When he comes out we will talk to him.'

When the Sabbath came, the priests who knew Abba Moses' great way of life, said to him in public: 'Oh, Abba Moses, you did break the commandment made by the people – but you have firmly kept the commandment of God!'

Day 22

Psalm 51   *Romans 3:22-24*   *Matthew 9:9-13*

Abba Milos was asked by a soldier whether God could forgive a sinner. After instructing him at some length, the old man asked him:

'Tell me, my son, if your cloak was torn would you throw it away?'

'Oh no!' he replied, 'I would mend it and wear it again.'

The old man said to him: 'Well, if you care for your cloak, will God not show mercy on his own creature?'

Abba Sarnatas said:

'I prefer a person who has sinned if he knows he has sinned and has repented, over a person who has not sinned and considers himself to be righteous.'

Day 23

Psalm 119:89–96   Hebrews 5:7–10   John 17:1–5

It was said about Abba John the Little that he went away to an old Theban in Scete who lived in the desert. Once the old man took a piece of dry wood, planted it, and said to John:

'Water it every day with a bottle of water until it bears fruit.'

The water was so far away from there, that John had to go out late in the evening and come back the next morning. Three years later, the tree came to life and bore fruit. Then the old man took some of the fruit to the church, and said to the brothers:

'Take and eat the fruit of obedience.'

Day 24

Psalm 26   *Ruth 3:1–11*   *John 20:10–18*

Amma Sara said:

'If I pray to God that all might be inspired
because of me, I would find myself repenting
at the door of every house. I would rather
pray that my heart be pure towards everybody.'

Day 25

Psalm 37:30–31 James 3:1–12 Matthew 5:33–37

It was said about Abba Agatho that for three
years he carried a pebble around in his mouth
until he learned to be silent.

Abba Poemen said:

'Teach your mouth to speak what is in your
heart.'

Abba Isidore of Pelusia said:

'Living without speaking is better than
speaking without living. For a person who
lives rightly helps us by silence, while one
who talks too much merely annoys us.'

Day 26

Psalm 85:9   *Matthew 9:9–13*   *Micah 6:6–8*

One of the brethren sinned and the priest told
him to leave the community. So then Abbot

Bessarion got up and walked out with him
saying:

'I too am a sinner.'

Day 27

Psalm 118:25–29   Romans 2:1–11   Luke 18:9–14

Once two brothers were sitting with Abbot
Poemen, and one praised the other brother
saying:

'He is a good brother, he hates evil.'

The old man asked: 'What do you mean he
hates evil?'

And the brother did not know what to reply.
So he said:

'Tell me, father, what is it to hate evil?'

The father said: 'That man hates evil who
hates his own sins, and looks upon every
brother as a saint, and loves him as a saint.'

Day 28

Psalm 41:1–3   James 2:14–26   Luke 10:25–37

A brother asked one of the Elders:

'There are two brothers of whom one
remains praying in his cell, fasting six days at a
time and doing a great deal of penance. The
other takes care of the sick. Which one's work
is more pleasing to God?'

The Elder replied:

'If that brother who fasts six days at a time
were to hang himself up by the nose – he
could not equal the one who cares for the
sick.'

Day 29

Psalm 113   *2 John*   *Luke 1:46–55*

Amma Theodora said:

'A teacher ought to be a stranger to the love of
domination, and a foreigner to vainglory, far
from arrogance, neither deceived by flattery,
nor blinded by gifts, nor a slave to the
stomach, nor held back by anger, but rather
should be patient, kind, and as far as possible
humble. She ought to be self-disciplined,
tolerant, diligent and a lover of souls.'

Day 30

Psalm 150   *Revelation 12:10–12*
Matthew 24:4–14

The Holy Fathers came together and spoke of
what would happen in the last generation.
One of them called Squirion said:
'We now desire to fulfil the commandments
of God.'
Then the Fathers asked him:
'What about those who will come after us?'
He replied:
'Perhaps half will desire to keep God's
commandments, and will seek the Eternal
God.'
And the Fathers asked:
'Those who come after these, what shall
they do?'
He replied and said:
'The men of that generation will not have

the desire of God's commandments. At that time wickedness will overflow and the charity of many will grow cold. And there shall come upon them a terrible testing. Those who shall be found worthy in this testing will be better than we are and better than our fathers.'

JULY READINGS

Pilgrimage

Canterbury
Day 1   Psalm 120:1
        Micah 4:1-2
        Luke 2:40-47

Inner Farne
Day 2   Psalm 120:2-4
        Job 1:6-8
        Luke 4:1-13

Derry
Day 3   Psalm 120:5-7
        Zechariah 8:3-5
        Luke 15:13-20

The high places
Day 4   Psalm 121:1-3
        Habakkuk 3:16-19
        John 10:14, 27

Little Gidding
Day 5   Psalm 121:4-7
        Song of Songs 1:4; 8:14
        Romans 13:9-10

Bamburgh beach
Day 6   Psalm 121:8
        Acts 26:19

Old Bewick
Day 7   Psalm 122:1
        Ezra 5:1-2
        Mark 1:35-36

Cair Paravel
Day 8   Psalm 122:2
        Ezra 3:11-13
        Luke 19:12, 15

Medjugorje
Day 9   Psalm 122:3-9
        2 Kings 4:4-5
        Luke 1:46-53

Walsingham
Day 10 Psalm 123:1
        Genesis 5:24
        Acts 1:7-11

Haddington
Day 11 Psalm 123:2-4
        Isaiah 7:14
        Matthew 2:1-2, 9-11

Patmos
Day 12 Psalm 124:1-5
        Isaiah 35:3-4
        Revelation 5:11-12

Coventry
Day 13 Psalm 124:6-8
        Isaiah 43:18-21
        Revelation 12:7-12

Assisi
Day 14 Psalm 125:1
        Genesis 37:19
        1 Corinthians 11:1

The house with golden windows
Day 15 Psalm 125:2
        Genesis 28:16-17
        Ephesians 3:16-19

Glastonbury
Day 16 Psalm 125:3-5
        Numbers 17:1-11

John 21:15-17

Heavenfield
Day 17 Psalm 126
        Jeremiah 31:21
        Luke 23:26

Iona
Day 18 Psalm 127
        Amos 9:13015
        Hebrews 12:1

Renewing of vows
Day 19 Psalm 128
        Proverbs 20:24-25
        Matthew 18:18-20

Dachau
Day 20 Psalm 129
        Esther 3:13; 4:7; 8:6
        Matthew 25:35-37

Darmstadt
Day 21 Psalm 130
        Jonah 3:5-10
        2 Corinthians 7:8-10

A slice of heaven
Day 22 Psalm 131:1
        1 Samuel 16:14-23
        Acts 16:13

St Cuthbert-d5-s Island
Day 23 Psalm 131:2
        Isaiah 35:1
        Mark 6:30-31

Josslin
Day 24 Psalm 131:3
        Isaiah 35:1
        Mark 6:30-31

Weston Priory
Day 25 Psalm 132:1
       Ruth 1:16
       John 14:27; 15:11-12

Taizé
Day 26 Psalm 132:2-9
       Zechariah 8:1-3
       John 12:20-25

The Via Dolorosa
Day 27 Psalm 132:10-18
       Numbers 6:25
       2 Corinthians 4:6

Roslin
Day 28 Psalm 133
       Isaiah 30:15
       Mark 9:1-8, 14-19

Clonfert
Day 29 Psalm 134:1
       Isaiah 49:8-9
       John 2:5

Lindisfarne
Day 30 Psalm 134:2
       Joshua 5:13-15
       Matthew 28:17

La Verna
Day 31 Psalm 134:3
       Genesis 32:29-31
       Philippians 3:10

Day 1

Psalm 120:1   Micah 4:1-2   Luke 2:40-47

This month's notes are on the subject of
'Pilgrimage', a journeying to a particular
place, in the expectation that such a journey
will have deep significance. It may be to a
place with personal memories, or a holy place
where for generations people have prayed and
sought God. Everyone's starting point and
journey is different, inside - and outwardly.

(The psalms we are using this month are the
Psalms of Ascent used by pilgrims on their
way to Jerusalem.)

All kinds of people go on pilgrimage of one
sort or another, not all of them believers; it is
a chance for things to move, to change,
perhaps even for God to break into their lives.

. . . and they were pilgrims all
that towards Canterbury meant to ride
. . . I soon was one of them in fellowship
and promised to rise early and take the way
to Canterbury.

Geoffrey Chaucer

Day 2

Psalm 120:2-4   Job 1:6-8   Luke 4:1-13

Then I saw that there was a way to hell even
from the gate of heaven, as well as from the
City of Destruction. So I awoke, and behold it
was a dream.

*John Bunyan in
Pilgrim's Progress*

In general we pray, Lead us not into temptation, but at the same time the Spirit of God may draw us into a deserted place to be tested.

The island of Inner Farne which was Cuthbert's 'lonely battlefield' had the reputation of being just such a place. Geoffry of Coldingham, in the twelfth century writes:

Farne, which was formerly the fortress of devils, is now a cloister and a school of saints . . . It always contains, indeed it actually forms, men of virtue, because when someone is led by the Spirit into the desert, he must expect to be tempted by the devil. Consequently he either cultivates sanctity or else he leaves this holy place. And the strength of temptation is greatly increased by the island's poverty and the cold caused by the sea . . . There is a continual assault from the waves and ceaseless conflict with them: Sometimes the island is completely covered with foam, which flows in from the sea and is blown over it by the wind, and this is a great mortification to those who live there, and it makes them cold and afraid. . .

Day 3

Psalm 120:507   Zechariah 8:3-5   Luke 15:13-20

One sort of pilgrimage is to go back to a place full of memories, of joy, of childhood. Many things will have changed, not least ourselves, and it is a bitter-sweet experience.

A popular and famous song talks of one
man's return to Derry:

> But when I returned
> how my eyes were burned
> to see how that town had been brought
> to its knees
> by the armoured cars
> and the bombed-out bars
> and the gas that hangs on to every tree.
> Now the army's installed
> by the old gas-yard wall
> and the damned barbed wire
> gets higher and higher
> With their tanks and their guns,
> oh my God, what have they done
> to the town that I loved so well?

T.S. Eliot writes:

> You are not here to verify,
> Instruct yourself, or inform curiosity
> Or carry report. You are here to kneel
> Where prayer has been valid. And prayer is
> more
> Than an order of words, the conscious
> occupation
> Of the praying mind, or the sound of the
> voice praying.

Day 4

Psalm 121:1-3   Habakkuk 3:16-19   John 10:14,27

The life of the praying person is a journey
farther up and farther in, to places God
Himself has spoken about to the attentive
heart.

On one such occasion the Shepherd said to Much-Afraid,

'When you continue your journey there may be much mist and cloud. Perhaps it may even seem as though everything you have seen here of the high places was just a dream, or the work of your own imagination . . . But you have seen *reality*, and the mist which seems to swallow it up is the illusion. Believe steadfastly in what you have seen. Even if the way up to the high places appears to be obscured and you are led to doubt whether you are following the right path, remember the promise, ''Thine ears shall hear a word behind thee, saying, This is the way, walk ye in it, when ye turn to the right hand and when ye turn to the left.'' Always go forward along the path of obedience as far as you know it until I intervene, even if it seems to be leading you where you fear I could never mean you to go.'

Hannah Hurnard
Hind's Feet on High Places

Day 5

Psalm 121:4-7   *Song of Songs 1:4; 8:14*
Romans 13:9-10

In 1620 Nicholas Ferrar, his mother, brother and brother-in-law with their families restored a derelict village church at Little Gidding. There they said the daily office of prayer. They were Church of England, and tried to combine the monastic values with normal family life.

For many people the name 'Little Gidding' is at first familiar because of the poem of the same name by T. S. Eliot published as one of his 'Four Quartets'. He seems in these verses to capture something of the nature of pilgrimage – the precise directions to somewhere often awkward to find; and you're not sure quite why you came or what it was you're looking for. If you find it, or it finds you, words cannot easily convey what has happened but it becomes part of the journey that continues.

> Not waiting for You, climbing up the hill,
> I slip and stumble. Still, Your hand
> upon my shoulder is so strong;
> and every boulder sings a song of love
> while, high above,
> Your laughter draws me on and on;
> and ever since that morning
> there has been no right or wrong, but love.
>
> *from Hillclimbing for Beginners*

Wherever He may guide me,
no want shall turn me back;
My Shepherd is beside me,
and nothing can I lack.
His wisdom ever waketh,
His sight is never dim,
He knows the way He taketh,
and I will walk with Him.

Anna L. Waring

Day 6

On the mainland opposite Lindisfarne is
Bamburgh, the ancient capital of Northumbria.
Here we think of the faithful King Oswald,
and of Aidan.

The beach itself seems timeless, and full of
memories . . .

The castle towered above them and before
them were the sands, with rocks and little
pools of salt water, and seaweed and the smell
of the sea and long miles of bluish-green
waves breaking for ever and ever on the
beach. And oh, the cry of the seagulls! Have
you heard it? Can you remember?

C. S. Lewis

It was one summer's evening, years ago, at
Bamburgh on the Northumbrian coast, that we
received the call to ministry. Sitting on the
rocks, gazing out to sea and the Farne Islands I
saw a vision of people being rescued and
brought safe onto the rock.

Roy Searle

When Jesus knew for certain only drowning
men could see Him, he said, 'All men shall be
sailors then, until the sea shall free them.'

L. Cohen

I saw a picture of Northumbria, dark, but with
beacons of light growing and pushing back the
darkness, then bands of people travelling
around the area, fanning into flame what God
already was doing in the area.

Don Bridges

Day 7

Beside the little road from Eglingham to
Chatton is a stone Celtic cross, and carved
beneath it are the joyful words,

> I was glad when they said to me,
> Let us go to the house of the Lord.

A narrow drive leads to a tiny chapel hushed
with prayer, where twice a month communion
services still are held, but day by day people
make their way to be alone, to be quiet.

At Easter in 1988 with adults and children
we sang and processed up that little path to
place a wooden cross from Heavenfield in the
hut by the church gate. It was to be used as a
'poustinia', a silent place for prayer.

> Come, occupy my silent place
> and make Thy dwelling there.
> More grace is wrought in quietness
> than any is aware.

John Oxenham

You do not realize it yet, but the preaching of
the Gospel emanates from the *poustinia*,
creates a unity with God, then causes a
confrontation with the world.

Catherine de Hueck Doherty
Poustinia

Day 8

Psalm 122:2   *Ezra 3:11-13*   *Luke 19:12, 15*

Fill this place, Lord, with Your glory! Let what happens here in our day be as great as what happened in the past. But don't let us build monuments to the past. If the foundations were sound, we have hope to build again. We want to work, we must not die. Let Your tender mercies come unto us that we might live again.

C. S. Lewis in his book *Prince Caspian* has the children exploring the place they have been taken to . . .

> 'Have none of you guessed where we are?' said Peter.
> 'Go on, go on,' said Lucy, 'I've felt for hours that there was some wonderful mystery hanging over this place.'
> '. . . we are in the ruins of Cair Paravel itself,' said Peter.

The place may have a powerful significance, but it is God's purposes that must be made visible and tangible. When we say, 'I'm in charge of these ruins,' it must mean we are guardians of a vision, not curators for the department of ancient monuments.

Day 9

Since June 1981 six young people from the village of Medjugorje in the former Yugoslavia claim to have been having visions of Mary, the Lord's mother. She urges them to prayer especially for peace, to love of Jesus and faithfulness to the Gospel, and to Scripture.

David du Plessis, a well-known Pentecostal, was one of the many who have visited there:

'In my two days in that town I never heard an unkind word or criticism of anyone. The love, unity and fellowship I saw there are only possible in the power of the Holy Spirit. I am quite prepared for God to perform miracles in the twentieth century. And if one of these miracles involves messages delivered by the mother of Jesus, I believe God is capable of that. I saw young people reading the Bible. The priests told me that thousands of Yugoslavians, including atheists and Moslems, have accepted Jesus Christ. They told me that their church is crowded to capacity every single day, and on weekends there are so many people waiting outside that they sometimes have fifty priests hearing confessions. The Mother has encouraged the people to confess their sins and to accept Christ's forgiveness. The whole place is charged with the love of God. You can feel it and you can see it.'

The village is in Croatia, and their priests have at times been imprisoned. Despite harassment by the police, there is great peace in the hearts of the villagers and young people. The only spectacular thing most visitors see is the lives of the people, which are really quite impressive. The pilgrims, like the villagers, are moved to repent, to convert their whole lives. Most return home dedicating themselves to prayer, fasting and spiritual growth.

Jim Wallis writes:

The powers and principalities of this world are aware that prayer and its results are the most revolutionary of acts. That is why they consider those who pray to be a threat. Prayer is an action in itself, a potent political weapon to be used in spiritual warfare against the most powerful forces of the world.

Day 10

Psalm 123:1 *Genesis 5:24* *Acts 1:7-11*

In the tiny Chapel of the Ascension at Walsingham the picture behind the altar comes at first as something of a shock: a pair of feet sticking out from a large white cloud. It brings home to us the absurdity of the situation . . . a cloud received Him from our sight. God took Him – and what a way to go! He is gone ahead to prepare a place for us, and in 'a way that baffles description' it is as simple as that.

Help us to understand that the pilgrimage of this life is but an introduction, a preface, a training school for what is to come. Then shall we see all of life in its true perspective. Then shall we not fall in love with the things of time, but come to love the things that endure.
Peter Marshall

. . . they have left their house and home,
and turned pilgrims, seek a world to come,
and they have met with hardships in the
way and they do meet with troubles night
and day.

John Bunyan

He walks with God
    who turns his face to Heaven,
and keeps the blest commands
    by Jesus given;
his life upright,
    his end untroubled peace.

author unknown

Day 11

Psalm 123:2-4   Isaiah 7:14   Matthew 2:1-2, 9-11

The annual pilgrimage to Haddington in
Scotland is quite an occasion. Time for
ecumencial liturgy, for buses and sandwiches
and quiet excitement. Then suddenly the
moment as you look at the scene of Mary
holding up her child and the royal visitors
kneeling before Him: the wonder of it all, He
came right down to me!

In the white falling snow
the pilgrim travels on.
his face towards the sun.
Beyond the open road he travels on
past the lamp shining windows
and faces by the fire
before the midnight hour,
for Christmas time has come around again . . .

Chris Simpson

Say, shall we yield Him, in costly devotion,
odours of Edom and offerings divine?
Gems of the mountain and pearls of the
    ocean,
myrrh from the forest or gold from the mine?
Vainly we offer each ample oblation,
vainly with gifts would His favour secure;
richer by far is the heart's adoration,
dearer to God are the prayers of the poor.

                                    R. Huber

T. S. Eliot in his 'Journey of the Magi' writes
as if he were one of the pilgrims who came
from so far away. To us their significance lies
in the moment of their arrival, their kneeling,
their gifts and adoration. For them, too, there
is a problem for they return where they came
from, but changed, no longer at ease as they
were before.

Day 12

Psalm 124:1-5   Isaiah 35:3-4   Revelation 5:11-12

'Your task is a simple one, walk with Me,
    show Me to those who have seen Me,
and to those who have been near,
    but are afraid,' says the Lord.

And as he spoke he no longer looked to them
like a lion; but the things that began to
happen after that were so great and beautiful
that I cannot write them.

            from The Last Battle *by C. S. Lewis*

Read the words of John at the end of his Gospel (21:25). Then, again, he was chosen to describe the indescribable, not just what he had felt and touched, but what he had seen in a vision.

Liz Bell shares with us some of her memories of a visit to Patmos where John the Apostle was exiled, where he received his Revelations:

Worship in the cave itself – this small cave some 2,000 years ago gave shelter to the beloved disciple of Jesus. Patmos – God's love just drenched the place like the 'thousand stars'. We walked two or three miles in the pitch dark down a rocky track with our candles singing for joy and hearts burning with love.

On our final day we went looking for the Holy Well where God had provided the spring:

All men from all lands, kneel before you go.
Bend down low, lost son, sad daughter,
    bend down and drink;
I am the water of the well.

Day 13

Psalm 124:6-8   *Isaiah 43:18-21*
            Revelation 12:7-12

Coventry Cathedral was very badly damaged by bombing in World War II and the ruins now stand alongside the beautiful modern cathedral that draws so many visitors to wonder at it. It has many remarkable features:

stained glass windows, a twisted cross of
metal. But on the outside wall is the amazing
sculpture of Michael the archangel subduing
the fallen Lucifer!

Satan, in case you want me
   then you will find me
      in the Presence of God,
and in that presence you cannot follow
   'cos I'll be resting
      in the Spirit of God,
and there is no fellowship
   twixt darkness and light;
and there is no compromise
   twixt wrong and right.
      I'm gonna keep my life bright!

Satan, you're forgotten,
   we're out to get you, so tell me
      how does it feel?
Have you seen Coventry – at the Cathedral?
   there is an angel,
      and you are under his heel.

from Star Wars of Darkness and Light
by Bill Davidson

Day 14

Psalm 125:1   Genesis 37:19   1 Corinthians 11:1

He was born in the small town of Assisi in the
year 1182. Even today, as you walk through
the Umbrian countryside, the peace of St
Francis seeps into your soul and you begin to
believe that perfect joy is possible. When the
light of the Spirit was dying out all over the
world, this man, this little man, this one man

re-enkindled the flame. He was only 45 years old when he died, but he left behind a Dream to dream and a Journey to challenge every man.

Murray Bodo

In Assisi the past is not history,
but the life of Francis is now,
    just as Christ is now.
And because Francis holds Christ's hand
    and so do we: there is no time-gap.

Norma Wise

I dreamt I saw a procession of saints, holy men and bishops in their fine robes and rich clothes. Behind them walked many poor people. and the poor had their eyes on the ground, searching it to be certain they could see the footprints of Jesus there and step in them. At the very back of the line was a little man, not very handsome and dressed in rags, but his head was held back, for his eyes were on heaven all the time. Poor fool. Poor, poor fool.

from the play 'Poor Fool'
by Northumberland Theatre Company

There have been thousands of footsteps
    around Assisi, but through them all,
the footsteps of Francis
    seem freshly there, unaltered,
        calling out for us to walk in them,
            and learn.

B. G.

Day 15

Psalm 125:2 Genesis 28:16-17 Ephesians 3:16–19

This is a story told of a young boy who lived with his parents in a cottage on a hillside, overlooking a wide valley. His greatest joy was to sit on the doorstep on summer evenings, and gaze across the valley to a house miles away on the opposite hillside, for, just as the sun was sinking in the west, the windows of that house would burst into flame, shining dazzlingly with golden light. How perfectly happy the people must be who live there, he thought! One day he packed sandwiches and set off to find the house with the golden windows, but it was farther off than he expected, and it was already towards sunset as he climbed steeply uphill. To his disappointment the house was a plain cottage after all, and the windows ordinary windows. The good people there offered him supper, and made up a bed in the kitchen, for it was too late now for him to return. That night, in his dream, he asked directions of a girl about his age. 'The house with the golden windows? Yes, I've seen it.' And she pointed. He woke to the early song of the birds. Drawing the curtain aside he looked out. There far across the valley, was his own house - and, wonder of wonders, its windows flashed with gold in the brightness of the morning sun.

And the end of all our exploring
will be to arrive where we started
and know the place for the first time.

T. S. Eliot

Day 16

Glastonbury is a place of legend and pilgrimage. Its Christian history is very early, and Joseph of Arimathea is said to have visited there, and given witness to Christ.

Other legends say that Patrick and Brigid came there, either of which is possible. Its connections with Arthur and Merlin have fascinated Christians and occultists alike, and today it is a place of deep spiritual conflict.

Pray for the believers in that town, because as the song says,

> It's hard to dance
> with the Devil on your back.

Pray that their love of Christ will grow ever stronger.

> The most important thing in my life
>   is that I chose to follow Jesus.
> No-one makes me.
>   I chose to.
> I have chosen to follow Him
>   because He loves me
> and love makes all the difference.
>
> *Ann Kiemel*

The ancient Glastonbury carol says,

> The bells of Paradise, I heard them ring.
> And I love my Lord Jesus above everything.

Day 17

Psalm 126   *Jeremiah 31:21*   *Luke 23:26*

Many a commemorative cross stands by
roadside or in field, but few as significantly as
that which stands at Heavenfield. It reminds us
of good King Oswald, returning from Iona to
unite his land, and win its people to Christ.
He did not shirk his responsibilities, but
fulfilled them with honesty and faith, as a
Christian first, and only secondly as a king.
We can only imagine with what mixture of
emotions he knelt before the cross that day.

God has a place for you to fill,
but it will take all of you to fill it.

Hugh Redwood

He walks with God who, as he onward
   moves,
follows the footsteps of the Lord he loves,
and keeping Him for ever in his view,
his Saviour sees and His example, too.

author unknown

I'm going where He goes –
out into the world
of lonely people.

Ann Kiemel

If this is not a place
   where tears are understood,
      then where can I go to cry?
Ken Medema

Day 18

Psalm 127   *Amos 9:13-15*   *Hebrews 12:1*

The mountaineer and the fisherman and the
shepherd of the Isles live their lives in lonely
places, and the winds and waves bear to them
messages from the unknown beyond.

Wilkie

This, then, is the Iona of Columba.

There is the bay where the little, sea-tossed
coracle drove ashore. There is the hill – the
Hill of Angels – where heavenly visitants shone
before him. There is the Sound across which
the men of Mull heard vespers sung by hooded
monks – heard the Lord's song sung in a
strange land. There is the narrow strip of
water across which holy men came to take
counsel, sinners to do penance, kings to be
crowned. The little island speaks with a quiet
insistence of its past – for was it not at once
the fountain and the fortress of the faith, at
once the centre of Celtic learning and of
Christian charity?

Troup

In Iona of my heart, Iona of my love,
instead of monk's voice
    shall be lowing of cows;
but ere the world shall come to an end
Iona shall be as it was.

attributed to Columba

How wonderful it is to walk with God
along the road which holy men have trod.

Theodore H. Kitching

> Follow the example of good men of old,
>   and God will comfort you and help you.
>
> *Columba*

Day 19

Psalm 128 Proverbs 20:24-25 Matthew 18:18-20

Go back to the old wells, to the sweet waters,
Isaac dug the wells again which they had used
in his father's day. Returning to 'the old wells'
may mean the renewing of a promise. Many
couples in particular renew their vows, or
return to places that for them hold important
associations.

> The union of your spirits here
>   has caused Him to remain,
> for wherever two or more of you
>   are gathered in His Name
> there is love.
>
> *Noel Paul Stookey*

> We seek a clear light to shine
>   upon our troubled way.
> We ask You to give us clearer directions
> Where we have missed the way
>   and wandered far, bring us back
>   at whatever cost to our pride.
> Take away our stubborn self-will,
>   for we know that in Your will alone
>   is our peace. We seek that peace.
>
> *Peter Marshall*

Day 20

If I said 'Yes, I forgive, but I cannot forget,' as though God, who twice a day washes all the sands on all the shores of all the world, could not wash such memories from my mind, then I know nothing of Calvary love.

Amy Carmichael: 'If'

Not every pilgrimage is a pleasantly inspirational experience! Art Katz in his testimony-book *Ben Israel* writes of his visit to the concentration camp at Dachau:

I was totally unprepared for what greeted me at this museum of death . . . the gas rooms with the jets still in the ceiling. Here my brother-Jews had been herded like cattle into cars. Women and children. Stripped naked. Old men and young boys. Why was the ear of God silent to the shrieks and prayer of these helpless, innocent ones who were slaughtered like cattle? My stomach turned sick and my eyes blurred with tears . . . Outside were the conveyor belts where the bodies were dispatched to the giant ovens . . . the mutilated bodies were slowly and systematically fed into the flames. The huge smokestacks never ceased their ugly belching – twenty-four hours a day as the ovens were stoked with the House of Israel.

And later, on the train that took him on his way . . . In an instant the truth dawned: Katz, except for the accident of birth, the caprice of

time and place, you might have been born a
German Aryan. It could have been you stoking
bodies into the ovens. He shuddered and
looked long into the blue eyes of the German
man opposite.

'I have been to Dachau,' he said quietly.

Day 21

Psalm 130   Jonah 3:5-10   2 Corinthians 7:8-10

In my dream, behold I saw a man clothed in
rags, standing in a certain place, with his face
from his own house, a book in his hand, and a
great burden upon his back. I looked, and saw
him open the book, and read therein, and as
he read he wept and trembled . . .

John Bunyan

Repentance is seen by many as unfashionable
and outmoded. Like sin, it is not to be talked
about. But John the Baptist and Jesus himself
made it central to their teaching of the
Kingdom of God.

In Darmstadt, on State Highway 3 between
Frankfurt and Heidelburg, stands a small
chapel. Its building was the first of many
victories for the sisters in establishing their
Land of Canaan. Basilea Schlink and her
community of Mary Sisters believed for the
land, the finance, the permission, and with
each obstacle, they sought deeper repentance
lest any inward attitude blocked the release of
God's blessing. Repentance is at the heart of
their community, repentance, the joy-filled life.

As Christian walked on he came to a hill
which grew steeper and steeper. The load on
his back was very heavy as he climbed. Near
the top there was a cross, and just as Christian
came to the cross his burden fell from his
back. It rolled and tumbled down the hill until
it fell into a dark hole, and he saw it no more.

Pilgrim's Progress

Day 22

Psalm 131:1　　*1 Samuel 16:14-23*　　*Acts 16:13*

'Come and see my place where I pray, it's like
a little slice of heaven,' said my friend. A place
of quiet by the river, where the dog can run
about, and a shelter be built. And music is
born out of quiet like this.

He walks with God
    who speaks to God in prayer,
and daily brings to Him his daily care.

author unknown

In every man lies a zone of solitude
    that no human intimacy can fill:
        and there God encounters us.

Brother Roger of Taizé

Speak to me, Lord, give me Your peace
Show me the way to go.
I need Your love, I need Your strength,
All of my needs You know.

Be by my side, be in my heart.
Be in my every prayer.
Filling my life, filling my soul,
all of the time be there . . .

Give me Your love
  – give me Your peace . . .
      Ros Robertson

Day 23

Psalm 131:2   **Isaiah 35:1**   **Mark 6:30-31**

St Cuthbert's Island adjoining the shore of
Lindisfarne is a wonderful parable of quiet, for
it is always in sight of the main island, and yet
for hours and hours at a time it is completely
cut off. It seems designed especially to
experience a day of solitude, long enough to
limit your freedom, but not as inaccessible as
the life of the true hermit.

Here Cuthbert, and almost certainly Aidan
before him, escaped from the pressures of
community and of missions and turned their
face towards God.

Thank you, Lord, that You have set aside
places, special trysting places where we can
meet with You.

A. Eberst

How wonderful it is to talk with God
when cares sweep o'er my spirit like a flood;
how wonderful it is to hear His voice,
for when He speaks the desert lands rejoice.
      Theodore H. Kitching

We've all got little cells in our hearts, little
hermitages that God wants to fill, For some
there's a physical place of silence. It's hard to
be silent. It's hard to stop. To know God in
the quiet is worth a lot – it's there we'll get

our vision and our peace to come through whatever hits us.

A. R.

Turn to Psalm 73 and read verses 25, 26 and 28.

Day 24

Psalm 131:3   Isaiah 6:1-9   Revelation 4:6-11

. . . Brittany was of special interest, for we knew our Celtic Christian fathers had journeyed there with the good news of Jesus. Visiting the small town of Josslin with its castle we noticed a small out-of-the-way church. Walking up the hill towards it, praying in tongues I felt on the verge of a discovery, although the building was not beautiful, and inside showed signs of decay and desolation, as if the Christian community here had lost hope. I went into the lady chapel, prayed for the people in the town, for a visitation of the Holy Spirit. Then my eyes caught sight of a small wooden screen, almost hidden, in a corner, which would usually be set on the altar. Its unusual, almost Jewish, design was identical to our own sanctuary roof at Old Bewick in Northumberland: a blue background with gold stars - all it lacked was the familiar inscription, 'Holy, Holy, Holy, is the Lord.'

Later that day when we visited the town's parish church, almost cathedral-like in size and grandeur, it was for the simplicity of a small side-chapel that I headed, once inside. I lit a candle, and prayed once again for a fresh visitation of the Spirit on the town - and throughout Brittany. There on a small table beside the simple altar was an illuminated model of a tiny church which I recognized immediately as the one we had visited. In its grounds were a band of monks, at prayer and work. It had been an old monastic church. Celtic? Who knows? I prayed again that the Wild Goose would come, that Brittany would know again the Celtic fire, ablaze with the love of Jesus.

J.T.S.

Day 25

Psalm 132:1   Ruth 1:16   John 14:27; 15:11–12

Wherever we go to New England we make a point of visiting Weston Priory in the Vermont hills. The peacefulness of the place itself, the wooden chapel, the beautiful songs of the brothers at prayer . . .

Peace I leave with you, My friends . . .
I have called you now . . .

and their involvement in the Sanctuary movement and God's heart for justice . . .

Because of our belief in God as Spirit
we choose to affirm and encourage
the prophetic voices
that recognize both the sin
    and the need of our time.

Because of our belief in
    the Church as community
we choose to have no superiors or
    inferiors among us.

We choose to be a community
that dances and sings,
in spite of the tendencies of our times
to despair and cynicism.

Renewal of baptismal vows,
Weston Priory

Be glad with dance and song,
let joy ring free:
God's love renews our hope.

Philip Franckiewicz, Weston

This morning during the common prayer I
suddenly became aware of the quality of my
brothers and I am moved to the depths of my
heart. They give their life – all their life. They
pay dearly the price of their commitment. I
know that better than any. Then I can no
longer say if my admiration is for my brothers
or for Christ who has to set his mark on them.

Brother Roger of Taizé

Day 26

Psalm 132:2-9   Zechariah 8:1-3   John 12:20-25

Thou art the Way, none other dare I follow.

Arch. R. Wiggins

My failure to understand made me sad, and by
way of comforting myself I read my Bible. In
this way I followed the main road for five
days.

The Way of a Pilgrim

Each year thousands of pilgrims make their
way to Taizé in France, most of them young
people, and a large proportion not Christians

in any recognized sense. Their time there is carefully prescribed, but non-directive. Their own conversations, the communal prayer, and the ecumenical life of the brothers all have a profound impact.

Brother Roger of Taizé says,

> Some people come to Taizé in a last attempt to find something in the Church. Are my words going to drive them away for good, and without any hope? . . .
>
> And to find some kind of reply, I search deep within myself for some word, some image. And maybe it is I who am most surprised of all by the words I utter . . .
>
> It is the thirst that I sense in the young people on the hill. For them, as for every generation, it is strong to the point of anguish . . .

Day 27

Psalm 132:10-18   *Numbers 6:25*
               2 Corinthians 4:6

In the middle of a busy conference in Jerusalem two of us took a short while to wander through the narrow streets of the Old City. Glancing above me I saw a Roman numeral on the wall, and realized suddenly that we were upon the Via Dolorosa, only yards from the spot where tradition has it that a woman called Veronica held out a cloth to wipe the face of Jesus as He struggled under the weight of His cross.

Look on the face of Jesus Christ, you will

find it *is* still the answer; no hurt you have experienced can have taken you to the place He has not been. He has been wounded. The hurt on His face, in His eyes. The healing for you will be as you also look into His face.

> Faith builds a bridge
>   across the gulf of death.
> Death's terror
>   is the mountain faith removes.
>
> *John Bunyan*

> Christ of the human road,
>   let us reach out to touch You,
>   and, sweet Christ,
>   show us Your lovely face.
> As we see Your face by faith,
>   we learn to become like You,
>   Lord Christ,
>   that the world may see Your glory.
> Show us Your lovely face.

Day 28

Psalm 133   Isaiah 30:15   Mark 9:1-8, 14-19

In the village of Roslin in Midlothian you will eventually find the Community of Transfiguration. A condemned property with minimal facilities and an enclosure with several wooden huts, and one larger hut which serves as a chapel. It is ironically appropriate, for was it not on the mount of transfiguration that Peter wanted to build huts to remain there in the reflected glory of the face of Jesus? It is possible to visit Roslin on retreat, for a day or longer on your own in one of the huts, shut in with God and with yourself.

The things that come out of a man are they
that defile him, and to get out of them a man
must go into himself, be a convict, and scrub
the floor of his cell.

George MacDonald

I undervalue my silence too much. Too often I
move from action into silence instead of the
other way about.

R. Morrison

When you come down from the mountain air,
be on your guard against catching cold.

Hugh Redwood

At Roslin, the other usual visitors are wayfarers
who are fed and given shelter in the house.

. . . thanking him for his kindly hospitality, I
went on my way; where to, I did not know
myself.

The Way of a Pilgrim

Day 29

Psalm 134:1   *Isaiah 49:8-9*   *John 2:5*

Nearby the ancient Clonfert Cathedral, old
farm-buildings have been rebuilt and new
buildings erected to serve the needs of
Emmanuel House of Providence. In the land
where Brendan walked and prayed, the work
of prayer and evangelizing goes on today. The
bell above the main house, and the beautiful
circular oratory, are what draw your attention.
The laughter of the children and their running
feet the gravel. A car arrives with a middle-
aged couple who walk to the silent oratory,

writing the name of a troubled friend in the book of prayer-intentions. A whole camp for young people or for families, a school retreat or prayer-meeting. A cross of reconciliation.

I asked Ken Wise to put into words what his visit to Clonfert had been like:

> When you walked through the gates you knew you had come to a different place, a very godly place. It's not just friendliness, there's a presence there. We went not knowing what to expect. It seemed to be that God's presence was all round the place. I admit I was apprehensive, but when we got there it was totally different.

> How wonderful it is to walk with God along the road that holy men have trod. How wonderful it is to hear Him say, Fear not, have faith 'tis I who lead the way.

Theodore H. Kitching

Day 30

Psalm 134:2   Joshua 5:13-15   Matthew 28:17

> Down the wide open road the pilgrim travels on, his face towards the sun, beyond the open road he travels on.

> And the waves steal the footprints of the summer from the sand;

beneath the silver moon
the North wind blows the
fading leaves again.
Chris Simpson – 'Seasons'

And now perhaps our travels will bring us
again to the Holy Island of Lindisfarne like so
many, pilgrims and tourists alike. Most will
venture over only between the tides when the
island is an island in name only. The tide
comes in and the place becomes quieter. With
tourist and holiday-maker less in evidence,
islander and island speak, and smile, then
leave us to thoughts of our own. It has always
been that way.

Here was a sequence both of access and
inaccessibility. There were hours when the tide
closed it for prayer.

Ronald Blythe

The tide did now its flood-mark gain,
and girdled in the Saint's domain;
for, with the flow and the ebb, its style
varies from continent to isle;
dry-shod, o'er sands, twice every day,
the pilgrims to the shrine find way;
twice every day, the waves efface
of staves and sandalled feet the trace.
Walter Scott

Day 31

Never forget:

> If a man wishes to come after Me,
> he must deny his very self,
> take up his cross,
> and begin to follow in My footsteps.

> Hold Thou my feet,
>   let there be no returning
> along the path which Thou
>   hast bid one tread.
>
> *Arch. R. Wiggins*

Francis wished with all his heart to stand beneath the cross of Christ, assuring Him of his love, that he would be there with Him, ever present on the hill of Calvary throughout the ages till the Risen Christ returned in all His glory and the cross would be no more! It was with such an intention that Francis had made his final journey to the top of La Verna, that holy mountain far to the north of Assisi. There on that mountain he had asked in fear and trembling that Christ would let him experience and share some of His sufferings on the cross. It was as if his whole life had begun and ended there. La Verna was the impossible Dream and eternal journey come true. And yet it remained only as a memory, except for the wounds of Jesus in his feet and hands and side. And they, of course, made all the difference between the poor man who walked up the mountain and the poor man who limped down.

Murray Bodo

AUGUST READINGS

Iona

Day 1   Psalm 137:4–6
            Deuteronomy 3:23–27
            Philippians 2:8–11
Day 2   Psalm 96:10–13
            Genesis 28:11–12
            Ephesians 6:18
Day 3   Psalm 133:1–2
            1 Chronicles 12:1, 18
            John 21:8–10
Day 4   Psalm 48:9–13
            1 Kings 8:55–58
            Philippians 4:4–6
Day 5   Psalm 29:3–11
            Exodus 19:18–19
            Revelation 12:10–12
Day 6   Psalm 24:7–10
            Proverbs 8:3–12
            Acts 12:7–11
Day 7   Psalm 97:1
            Isaiah 52:7
            Galatians 6:14
Day 8   Psalm 36:5–6
            1 Kings 18:43
            1 Corinthians 2:1–5
Day 9   Psalm 107:29–30
            Proverbs 25:25
            Acts 27:15
Day 10 Psalm 90:9–10, 12
            Isaiah 2:5
            Matthew 25:1–7
Day 11 Psalm 55:22

Isaiah 62:1
Acts 5:14
Day 12 Psalm 31:14–16, 19–20, 24
Genesis 12:1–3
2 Corinthians 11:26–29
Day 13 Psalm 103:20–21
Genesis 28:16–17
Luke 2:20
Day 14 Psalm 71:5–8
Amos 3:7
Philippians 1:20–26
Day 15 Psalm 84:1–7, 10
2 Kings 23:4
Luke 17:7–10
Day 16 Psalm 23:4–5
Genesis 49:29–30, 33
Matthew 20:17
Day 17 Psalm 102:7
Exodus 15:11
Luke 1:47–50
Day 18 Psalm 139:6–12
2 Samuel 15:21
Revelation 12:11
Day 19 Psalm 22:4–5
Genesis 44:16–17
1 Corinthians 10:15–16
Day 20 Psalm 123:2
Numbers 24:16–17a
Revelation 22:16–18
Day 21 Psalm 48:1–3, 12–14
Isaiah 61:4
2 Peter 3:8–9
Day 22 Psalm 51:18
Haggai 1:2–5
Matthew 17:24–27
Day 23 Psalm 101:4–5
Proverbs 30:12–13

John 8:3–9
Day 24 Psalm 25:4
Jeremiah 29:12–13
Luke 5:1–3
Day 25 Psalm 127:1
Exodus 35:30–36:1
John 15:26
Day 26 Psalm 91:1–7
Daniel 2:20–22
1 Timothy 4:1–2
Day 27 Psalm 148:1–8
Daniel 3:9–18
Acts 28:2
Day 28 Psalm 148:9–14
Daniel 3:19–25
Luke 19:37–40
Day 29 Psalm 45:1
Ecclesiastes 3:1–3
Mark 4:30–33
Day 30 Psalm 102:13–22
Amos 9:14–15
Revelation 12:17
Day 31 Psalm 5:11–12
Genesis 12:2
Hebrews 12:14–17

Day 1

Psalm 137:4-6   *Deuteronomy 3:23-27*
Philippians 2:8-11

In February 1992 twelve men in association with Northumbria Ministries went together to the island of *Iona* to pray. This month we ask you to journey there with us in prayer. Iona was home to Aidan; and Oswald lived there for years also, but chiefly it is Columba's story we will recall.

> Dun I is the homeland mountain, that brooded over the first church, and the huts of Columba's brothers.
>
> *Margaret Cropper*

We walked up to the top of Dun I to pray and there we sang 'Jesus, we enthone You', and discovered someone else had laid out small stones there on the ground, declaring JESUS IS LORD.

Next day we stood with Ken from Belfast, near the place where Columba landed and looked to be sure he could no longer see his native Ireland, and there again we prayed and sang, 'Jesus, Lord of all, Name above all names'.

> Cul ri Erin, the back turned towards Ireland;
>   farewell to the known and dear,
>   advance to the unknown,
>   with its formidable hazards,
>   its sharp demands.
>
> *M.C.*

Day 2

Psalm 96:10–13 Genesis 28:11–12 Ephesians 6:18

Columba and his brothers lived in simple huts,
praying for each other, and for all those far
and wide whose lives they were to influence.

A central hut upon a rising ground
served as Columba's cell. He watched
in prayer for the small company
assembled round, and for the mighty
int'rests everywhere, which claimed
his anxious heart. The stone was here
which served him as a couch for
needful sleep.

Richard Meux Benson

Columba, disdaining the luxury of straw, used
to lie on a stone, with another rounded stone
for a pillow. A stone with a Celtic cross on it
is preserved in Iona Cathedral and legend says
that this is the very stone used by Columba for
his pillow.

Remember the holy places, the Cathedral,
full of gracious light, and the stillness
of the stone, with its carven capitals,
its timeworn arches, its store of
patterned grave stones, and the hard
pillow where Columba laid his head.

Margaret Cropper

Day 3

Psalm 133:1–2   *1 Chronicles 12:1, 18*
                    John 21:8–10

Some stories tell of Columba being exiled from Ireland because of so many being killed in a battle fought on his behalf. He vowed to win as many lives for the Kingdom's sake.

In this poem by Fiona Martin, warden of Bishop's House, Iona, more monks from Ireland are arriving to join Columba's community.

Columba's Bay

Sea-polished stones
did you welcome them
as they waded ashore,
guiding with calloused hands
coracles among the rocks?
And did the sucking sea
tug at their feet as
Erin tugged at their hearts?

With what dismay did they
remember the oaks of Derry,
warm hearths and friends?
Cold the cry of seagulls,
curious the bobbing seals,
bleak the mists of
moorland and machair.

Then through the gloom,
glowing as the day dawns,
a fire – and, dimly seen,
arms outstretched in greeting,
Columba stands. Beside him,
some fish, some bread, and
breaking upon their spirits the

reminder of another Man,
another place . . .

F.M.

Day 4

Psalm 48:9–13   *1 Kings 8:55–58*
Philippians 4:4–6

Columba divided his monks into three
classifications. There were the 'Seniors' who
were engaged in intellectual activities, the
conduct of worship, and the copying of
manuscripts in the scriptorum. The 'Working
Brothers' performed and taught the outdoor
farm labour, fishing, and sealing on the shore
of Erraid, a nearby island where seals
congregated. The 'Juniors' were young learners
or novices, candidates for monastic vows. All
had to work hard, and participate in all the
hours of worship.

Edward W. Stimson

Columba's monastic rule, eventually used by
many similar communities, required that the
monks own nothing but bare necessities, live
in a place with but one door, centre
conversation on God and God's Testament,
refuse idle words and the spreading of rumour
and evil reports, and submit to every rule that
governs devotion. They were to prepare always
for death and suffering, offer forgiveness from
the heart to everyone, pray constantly for
anyone who has been a trouble, put
almsgiving before all other duties, not eat
unless hungry, or sleep unless tired, pray until

tears came, and labour to the point of tears, as well, or if tears 'are not free', 'until thy perspiration come often'.

James H. Forest

Day 5

Psalm 29:3–11   *Exodus 19:18–19*
Revelation 12:10–12

John tells us there will be one loud voice in heaven – but whose? maybe . . .?

Columba when singing in the church with the Brothers, raised his voice so wonderfully that it was sometimes heard five hundred paces off, and sometimes one thousand paces. But what is stranger still: to those who were with him in the church, his voice did not seem louder than that of others; and yet at the same time persons more than a mile away heard it so distinctly that they could mark each syllable of the verses he was singing, for his voice sounded the same whether far or near. It is however admitted that this wonderful character in the voice of the blessed man was but rarely observable, and even then it could never happen without the aid of the Holy Ghost.

But another story concerning the great and wonderful power of his voice should not be omitted. It is said to have taken place near the fortress of King Brude (near Inverness). When the saint himself was chanting the evening hymns with a few of the Brothers, as usual, outside the king's fortifications, some Druids coming near to them, did all they could to prevent God's praises being sung in the midst of a pagan nation. On seeing this, the saint began to sing: 'My heart overflows with a goodly theme; I will address my verses to the King, and my tongue will be the pen of a ready writer . . .' (Psalm 45:1). And in the same moment his voice was, in a marvellous manner, so raised in the air like a terrible peal of thunder, that both the king and the people were filled with intolerable dread.

Adomnan

Day 6

Psalm 24:7–10   Proverbs 8:3–12   Acts 12:7–11

One significant interview on Kingdom business was Columba's meeting with King Brude, and on this journey he was accompanied by his friends, Abbot Comgall of Bangor and Kenneth, later abbot of Agaboe, who were visiting him at the time . . .

In the first weariness of the saint's journey to King Brude, it happened that the king, uplifted with royal pride, acted haughtily, and would not open the gate of his fortress on the first arrival of the blessed man.

Adomnan

Brude the pictish King awaits him proudly –
'We cannot heed his message. Let him bring what words he likes! Him and his words we fling in scorn away! Bar well the gates' –
Vain pride!

See angels hosts this monk encompassing!
Columba's hand invoked the Crucified!
That great voice shook the walls,
    and quick the gates flew wide!

R. M. Benson

And ever after from that day, so long as he
lived, the king held this holy and reverend
man in very great honour, as was due.

Adomnan

In an account parallel to Adomnan's in the
Latin *Life of Comgall*, it was Comgall who
made the sign of the cross to break open the
locked gates, Columba forced the door of the
king's house in the same manner, and when
the king threatened them with a sword,
Kenneth caused the king's hand to wither until
he believed in God. Unfortunately, none of the
accounts tell us much we would like to know
about Columba's successful mission, the real
conversion of King Brude, the securing of the
deed to Iona, and the favour of Brude upon
the evangelizing of his kingdom. Yet all of
these things surely took place.

Stimson

Day 7

Psalm 97:1   **Isaiah 52:7**   **Galatians 6:14**

The conflict must be long. Through many a
    year
Columba's feet those distant hills must tread,
strengthen'd by penance still to persevere;
oft 'neath their sores the rocky path grew
    red:

in winter oft the snow became his bed:
but love still bound him to the Crucified.

R. M. Benson

The names of ninety churches and monasteries
are associated with Columba's name, thirty-
seven of these in Ireland, but fifty-three in
Scotland and the Western Isles. Even if
allowance for error is made, the number of his
foundations, especially in the Western Isles and
on the western coast, is tremendous, from
Wigtown in the south to Butt of Lewis in the
north and as far west as Saint Kilda. From
these Christian colonies the light of the
Gospel spread far and wide throughout the
area.

Reeves/Stimson

Day 8

Psalm 36:5–6 1 Kings 18:43 1 Corinthians 2:1–5

For most monastic centres the visible
characteristics of landscape have altered in the
course of only a few generations.

> With Iona the case is very different. We may
> be sure that what we now see is very much
> what Columba saw. Its distinctive features
> depend upon the enduring sea . . . Nothing,
> therefore, can be more certain than that,
> when we look upon Iona, or when we
> range even the wide horizon which is visible
> from its shores, we are tracing the very
> outlines which Columba's eye has often
> traced, we follow the same winding coasts
> and the same stormy headlands, and the

same sheltered creeks, and the same
archipelago of curious islands, and the same
treacherous reefs – by which Columba has
often sailed.

from Iona *by the Duke of Argyll, 1878*

Day 9

Psalm 107:229–30   Proverbs 25:35   Acts 27:15

Columba's journeys in the coracle amidst the lakes

. . . His hide-bound boat
bore him and his where lofty forests frown
reflected in the lake. With joy they float,
their hearts aye buoyant with the truth they
    own.
No sunlit breeze has ere such glory known.
Yea, when the stormy waters have denied
their progress, still in prayer they
    labour'd on.
They sang that heav'n might hear!

Their song was mightier than the howling
    wind:
from the deep cavern of the soul it sprang,
as taught by God, and form'd by Him to find
mysterious echoes. While the strugglers
    sang,
demons took flight, and angel-trumpets
    rang,
op'ning men's weary hearts in regions wild
to hail the strangers' tidings. Awed they
    hung
on words so new, so welcome.

R. M. Benson

Day 10

Psalm 90:9–10, 12   Isaiah 2:5   Matthew 25:1–7

The memories cling – shadows of time long
    past,
when king and Viking, from the storm of
    battle,
in thee with hero-saints found peace at last.

Amid the strife, the gloom, of warring ages,
held by thy sons, the torch of Truth flamed
    high,
lighted for anxious men the shadowed
    valley,
blessed with new hope the nations far and
    nigh.

Fled have the years – the kings and
    kingdoms vanished.
Unchanged art thou: and of a changeless
    clime,
Dear storied isle, art thou not ever speaking,
beyond the reach, beyond the realm of time?

S. Dixon, Iona

Jesus bids us shine with a pure, clear light
   . . . burning in the night
Jesus bids us shine first of all for Him;
well He sees and knows it
   if our light grows dim.

Jesus bids us shine then for all around.
Many kinds of darkness in this world
    abound.
   . . . so we must shine.

Susan Warner

Day 11

Psalm 55:22   Isaiah 62:1   Acts 5:14

A few places in the world are held to be holy,
because of the love which consecrates them,
and the faith which enshrines them. One such
is Iona . . . It is but a small isle, fashioned of a
little sand, a few grasses salt with the spray of
an ever-restless wave, a few rocks that wade in
heather, and upon whose brows the sea-wind
weaves the yellow lichen. But since the
remotest days, sacrosanct men have bowed
here in worship. In this little island a lamp was
lit whose flame lighted pagan Europe. From
age to age, lowly hearts have never ceased to
bring their burthen here. And here Hope waits.
To tell the story of Iona, is to go back to God,
and to end in God.

Fiona Macleod Iona

Many churches in the region of the Picts trace
their origin to the Religious Houses settled by
Columba:

Thus through the hills long clothed in
   heathen night
Columba's rule took root with wid'ning
   sway.
New homes of love beneath its mystic light
learnt by Iona's discipline to pray.
New hearts obey. The hallowing skies
send benedictions down, with God's own
   life to rise.

R. M. Benson

Day 12

Psalm 31:14–16, 19–20, 24   Genesis 12:1–3
2 Corinthians 11:26–29

Alone with none but Thee, my God,
I journeyed on my way:
What need I fear, when Thou art near
O King of night and day?
More safe am I within Thy hand
Than if a host did round me stand.

The child of God can fear no ill,
His chosen dread no foe:
We leave our fate to Thee, and wait
Thy bidding when to go.
'Tis not from chance our comfort springs,
Thou art our trust, O King of kings.

Saint Columba

Day 13

Psalm 103:20–21   Genesis 28:16–17   Luke 2:20

Columba seems to have been no stranger to
visits from angels, and was often aware of
their comings and goings, especially to protect
someone in danger or escort a departing soul
heavenward, even when these occurrences
were at a distance, such that Adomnan says
later 'news' from far away would confirm to
have happened at the exact time he had been
aware of the event. He spoke of them seldom,
but was often in the company of angels as he
prayed.

Hard vict'ries inly won,
make strong the soul
to breathe the sov'reign peace
    which angels share:
Unnumbered hosts
strengthen the loving soul that perseveres!

R. M. Benson

One day, on Iona, he commanded his brothers
to allow him to go alone, un-followed, to The
Machair, the western plain. There on a little
hill he was met by many angels who were
clothed in white and flew at great speed. We
know this because one disobedient monk
spied on the meeting, and thereby cut it short!

The site of this story is still recognizable
today on Iona:

One little hill-top is not rocky,
but rounded, green, distinctive:
the hill where Columba spoke with
holy Angels.

Margaret Cropper

Day 14

Psalm 71:5–8   Amos 3:7   Philippians 1:20–26

Columba explains to Lugne and another man
called Pilu on Iona that after thirty years since
his arrival from Ireland his time at last has
come to die, his angel escort awaits, but the
prayers of others have intervened and caused
God to re-arrange the departure date!

See how this corresponds to Luke 24:29!

My sons, I pray'd that God would not delay
to call me hence, for thirty years are run.
I pray'd that He would end my toilsome
   way.
I know His goodness when my work is
   done,
nor dare I grieve if still that toil lives on.
God heard my prayer. The angels came.
   They stand
on yonder rocks to bear me to God's
   Throne.
But still four years they wait!
   So God's command
yields to the Church's prayers,
   that rise throughout the land.

R. M. Benson

Day 15

Psalm 84:1–7, 10   2 Kings 23:4   Luke 17:7–10

. . . to me, the least of saints, to me, allow
that I may keep a door in Paradise.

Columba

One duty of a door-keeper is to stand guard
against all that is harmful; another is to
welcome whoever may come as a guest.

The One who was no less than God
took on the flesh of lowly man
and came to wash the feet of clay
because it was Your holy plan;
and I, no greater than my King
would ever seek a place
of humble service in Your house.

Oh, let me be a servant,
    a keeper of the door!
My heart is only longing
    to see forevermore
the glory of Your presence,
    the dwelling of the Lord
Oh, let me be a servant,
    a keeper of the door.

Twila Paris

. . . if so it be that I can see Thy glory,
even afar, and hear Thy voice, O God.

Columba

Day 16

Psalm 23:4–5   *Genesis 49:29–30, 33*
Matthew 20:17

On Whitsun Eve, Diarmit conducts Columba to
bless the barn. It is now four years later, and
Columba says to him:
    'This Saturday will be a Sabbath indeed to
me; for it is to be the last of my laborious life
on which I shall rest from all its troubles.
During this coming night, before the Sunday I
shall, according to the expression of the
Scriptures, be gathered to my fathers. Even
now my lord Jesus Christ deigns to call me; to
whom, this very night, and at His call, I shall
go. So it has been revealed to me by the Lord.'

Adomnan

They both were hush'd
  in one absorbing thought
God gave: God takes:
  and death can never break
the bond of love which God's own hand
  has wrought.
Silent they homeward turn.
  No words could make
fit utterance for that love which in
  such silence spake.
Columba's soul was gazing on the Lord:
his weary body scarcely could go on,
though leaning on Diarmit.

R. M. Benson

Day 17

Psalm 102:7   *Exodus 15:11*   *Luke 1:47–50*

According to a legend related in the Old Irish
life of Columba, it was revealed to him that a
human sacrifice would be necessary for the
success of his mission, and Oran, one of his
twelve companions, offered to be buried alive.
Three days later when the grave was opened
Oran is said to have opened his eyes, and
begun to comment, 'Death is no wonder, nor
is hell as it is said.' Columba is said to have
wondered what he would say next, and
promptly buried him again! In truth, Oran was
not the name of one of the twelve, but of a
man buried fifteen years before Columba
landed.

Remember Relig Oran, graveyard of kings,
its narrow deep carved doorway,
   the rough grey walls,
Relig Oran where the dead of Iona,
   king and crofter together sleep their sleep.

Remember the Nunnery, once the sheltering
   home
of women who loved God, now to their
   honour
   set with a flower garden, lavish, sweet,
its broken ruins sprouting valerian
   red and white, in every angle and coign.

Do not forget the buildings that are no
   more,
where the first monks kept fast and feast.
And over the Causeway,
   lost among the hilltops,
is one remaining, the solitary's cell.

Margaret Cropper

Here we came in prayer and pilgrimage, made
our muddy way to the hermit's cell, said a
Benedicite, and sang an Adoramus Te,
murmured a Magnificat in the nunnery ruins,
and in Oran's chapel proclaimed, 'Who is like
unto Thee, O Lord among the gods?' The
stone walls echoed: 'let me be a sweet, sweet
sound in Your ears.'

Day 18

Psalm 139:6–12   *2 Samuel 15:21*
Revelation 12:11

The White Sands of Iona skirt its north-
western shore. They are of unusual whiteness,
and are composed of the powdered shells of
innumerable land-snails. The stretch of sand
known as Tràigh Bhàn nam Manach (White
Strand of the Monks) is believed to have been
the scene of the third slaughter of Iona monks
by the Danes, and the hard steep rock at the
northern extremity is said to have been stained
with the blood of the victims.

(A house nearby is now a 'new age' centre for
the Findhorn Foundation. Please pray.)

> Here I stand, looking out to sea
> where a thousand souls have prayed
> and a thousand lives were laid on the
>   sand . . .

Iona

Please read Psalm 116:15, then this beautiful
poem by Fiona Martin.

The White Strand of the Monks

> Sea-sharp winds
> shriek between rocks,
> hurling gulls seaward,
> shredding their thin cries,
> clawing fragile clouds
> till, remnant-torn,
> their sharp tears
> spatter matted heather,

and cleft rocks
bleed by a white strand
where wide-eyed monks
trembling wait.

Day 19

Psalm 22:4–5   *Genesis 44:16–17*
1 Corinthians 10:15–16

Kenneth Macleod speaks in the same breath of
Iona and of the Holy Grail, that cup which
Christ blessed at His last supper, and which
Joseph of Arimathea is often portrayed as
holding at Christ's wounded side to catch the
drops of His blood. There is at once a
simplicity, a deep mystery, and a faith that
goes beyond purely rational considerations that
is at the heart of the experience which is Iona,
and as with the Grail, if the mystery it points
to is Christ Himself and a love for Him, then
perhaps that is what matters most, through the
ebb and flow of many a tide.

To Iona

For their sake who lived and died in thee,
Sang their faith and taught their joy to me
For their sake I bow the knee,
Iona the blest,
Isle of my heart, my grail.

Kenneth Macleod

Thou Grail-lit Iona

My heart's own shrine
where only lives what seemed to die,
my Grail-lit Isle,
Ebb-tide, flow-tide, Christ is nigh.

Kenneth Macleod

Day 20

Psalm 123:2   *Numbers 24:16–17a*
Revelation 22:16–18

(The ruined nunnery on Iona was established
at the beginning of the thirteenth century, and
the nuns were at first Benedictine, then later
of the Augustinian order.)

Dawn in the Nunnery

Day breaks behind the Bens of Mull
Streaming across the restless Sound
Blessing with shy shadows
Pillars and the ruined arches of
The Nunnery.

Holy place of ancient silence
Basking in prayers of countless years
Etching in the early sky
A benediction while a North wind snatches
The Abbey Bell.

With deep compelling resonance it sounds
Evoking in hearts a hidden longing
Echoes of a vocation long-locked
Within the rosy glow of this rough granite –
A Sacred Call.

Eyes uplifted, elated in expectation,
Our sinful human-ness suffused with
Transforming Grace, we glimpse
In fleeting simplicity of soul
Our Morning Star.

Fiona Martin

Day 21

Psalm 48:1–3, 12–14   Isaiah 61:4   2 Peter 3:8–9

The woodwork on the buildings of the small
village gathered near the pier is so weathered
that it makes them look as timeless as seagulls.
At a monkish distance to the north, amid wide
fields grazed by the island's sheep, the
monastery looks as it must have looked when
the Benedictines finished the premises 700
years ago: the plain square tower of St Mary's
Cathedral and the austere rectangular masses of
the adjoining buildings are all of enduring grey
stone with deep-cut windows under steep
slated roofs. So solid does the monastery
appear that it is hard to picture the ruined
state it was in for four centuries after the
Scottish Parliament outlawed the monastic
life in 1561. Had that Act of Suppression come
two years later it would have been a full
thousand years since the first monks landed
on Iona and began spreading the Christian
faith in Scotland.

James H. Forest, 'Sojourners' magazine, May 1980

The Celtic monks, knowing that same
restlessness and provocation which issues from
the Almighty, depicted the Holy Spirit both as

a dove *and* a wild goose. But where in our
contemporary devotions are there glimpses
that God, in the twentieth century, can be
expected to surprise, contradict, upset or rile
us in order that the kingdom may come?

John L. Bell and Graham A. Maule

. . . and I say a prayer,
that the Wild Goose will come to me.

Iona: 'Here I stand'

Day 22

Psalm 51:18   Haggai 1:2-5   Matthew 17:24-27

In 561 Columba arrived on Iona with his
twelve; in 1938 MacLeod arrived with another
band of twelve, half craftsmen without jobs,
half students for the ministry. They built a
wooden shed to live in by the fallen
monastery and began the work of re-building.

MacLeod recounts that the group needed
money with which to get its project started. 'I
wrote to the richest man I knew. He replied
that I should go see a psychiatrist at once.
Then I asked – me a pacifist, mind you – Sir
James Lithgow, a builder of warships at his
Govan shipyard. He was interested, but asked
if I would give up my pacifism if he gave me
the 5,000 pounds. I said "Not on your life."
"Then," he said, "I will give you your
£5,000." ' Materials were hard to obtain: 'The
war was on and the government
commandeered all timber. But a ship coming
from Canada struck a storm and jettisoned its
cargo of lumber in the Atlantic. The timber

floated 80 miles, finally landed on Mull,
opposite Iona – and all the right length! It
roofs the Iona library today.'

James H. Forest

Day 23

Psalm 101:4–5   Proverbs 30:12–13   John 8:3–9

'Pray for me. I ask you, my brothers and
sisters, to pray for me.' If ever you go to a
black church that's a phrase you'll hear almost
every person use when they stand up or come
forward to testify – sometimes it's just like
punctuation, not heart-felt at all, but it's still
an important reminder.

If you attend mass you will say, 'I ask . . . all
the angels and saints and you, my brothers and
sisters, to pray for me to the Lord our God.'

And George MacLeod, founder of the Iona
Community, as he quotes the old spiritual,
echoes the same words:

It's not my brother or my sister
    but it's me, O Lord:
standing in the need of prayer.
We are so warm in our own self-esteem
that we freeze the folks around us.
We get so high in our own estimation
that we stand isolated on a mountain
    top of self-righteousness.
That is why You came: Lord Jesus:
not to save the lecherous but to turn
    the righteous to repentance
And it is me, O Lord.

from Where Freedom is and Laughter

Day 24

Psalm 25:4   Jeremiah 29:12-13   Luke 5:1-3

Let us speak for a while of the blessed
  island,
Iona, thrust out a little from the land,
like Peter's boat,
  where Christ can speak with men.
The Sound that separates it changes colour
and mood, from the pearl-like glimmer
  of quiet dawns,
to deep sapphire, emerald-edged at noon;
and so, by grey, by silver, to dusk again,
to the white summer tides
  of the long light nightfall.
This is an island of contrast,
  of fierce forbidding rock
jutting out into Atlantic breakers,
  and flower spangled turf
where sheep and cattle graze.

Margaret Cropper

Iona has cast its spell on the sons of men. In
early times, it heard the sweet songs of God
sung by Saint Columba and his followers. In
later days, greater men than we have found
there what they sought. This island set apart,
this mother land of many dreams, still yields
its secret, but it is only as men seek that they
truly find. To reach the heart of Iona is to find
something eternal – fresh vision and new
courage for every place where love or duty or
pain may call us. And he who has so found is
ever wishful to return.

G. E. Troup

Many may visit; only a few can stay, remain on
Iona. Pray that those who leave may be
faithfully planted as mustard-seeds of hope in
the world. Pray that those God wants there for
His purposes may be drawn to Iona, and
others kept firmly away.

Day 25

Psalm 127:1   Exodus 35:30–36:1   John 15:26

From the morning service at Iona Abbey:

Almighty and everlasting God, who of old
didst fill the builders of Thy tabernacle with
Thy spirit, in wisdom, in understanding, and
in beauty, vouchsafe, we beseech Thee, Thy
grace and blessing to us Thy servants:
enlighten, purify, direct and sanctify us: accept
and establish our work for the honour of Thy
house and service: grant us the powerful aid
of Thy Holy Spirit in all our undertakings, that
we may promote Thy glory and further Thy
Kingdom: through Jesus Christ our Lord.
Amen.

God asks, 'Who will go for me?
  Who will extend my reach?
And who, when few will listen
  will prophesy and preach?
And who, when few bid welcome,
  will offer all they know?
And who, when few dare follow,
  will walk the road I show?'

The Wild Goose of Iona
John L. Bell and Graham Maule

Please pray today for the work of the Iona Community in Glasgow, and elsewhere in the world.

Day 26

Psalm 91:1-7   Daniel 2:20-22   1 Timothy 4:1-2

Jesus called the twelve disciples together and gave them power and authority to drive out all demons and to cure diseases (Luke 9:1).

From the *'Life of Saint Columba'*

For in the Name of the Lord Jesus Christ, by virtue of his prayers, he cured men suffering from the attacks of various diseases; and he alone, God helping, drove out from this our Island (Iona) which now has the Primacy, malignant and innumerable hosts of demons warring against him, seen by bodily eyes and beginning to bring deadly diseases upon his Monastic Society.

Adomnan

I feel no conflict here.
from 'Iona', a song on the album by Iona

Do pray for the protection of the work God has raised up on the island of Iona. Many people journey there each year, tourists and pilgrims, seekers of all kinds, many of whom have rejected what they have seen of Christianity so far. How crucial is the witness of those they meet there! Others journey there to the pre-Christian power sources of druidism and magic, for Iona is the focus of much attention from those interested in what is loosely termed 'new age'. Pray for much wisdom for the Christians they will meet on Iona and who engage or interact with them. For all who seek to minister or have been given responsibility at the Abbey, Camas or Macleod centres or at Bishop's House we pray protection from weariness and discouragement, from division and argument, from deception and lies of every kind.

What good are our prayers? A painting I love shows a boy shooting paper aeroplanes at the sky. Coincidence or not, in the exact place his paper aeroplanes were aimed the thick cloud has cleared as if a window were opened to the deep of the heavens.

O Isle from whence the Light streamed far
  and wide
God guard thee from all evil.

Bessie J. B. MacArthur

Day 27

Psalm 148:1–8   *Daniel 3:9–18*   *Acts 28:2*

An Iona Benedicite

O ye angels of the Lord, bless ye the Lord,
  praise Him and magnify Him for ever.
O ye Saints of the Isles, bless ye the Lord.
O ye Servants of Christ who here sang
  God's praises and hence went forth
  to preach, bless ye the Lord.
O ye souls of the faithful, who rest in Jesus,
O ye kindly folk of the Island,
O ye pilgrims who seek joy and health

in this beloved Isle, bless ye the Lord.
O ye sheep and hornèd cattle,
O ye lambs that gambol on the sward,
O ye seals that glisten in the waters,
  bless ye the Lord.
O ye ravens and hoodies,
O ye rooks that caw from the sycamores,
O ye buzzards that float on the
  wind-currents, bless ye the Lord.
O ye gulls that fill the beaches with
  your clamour,
O ye terns and gannets that dive
  headlong for your prey
O ye curlews and landrails,
O ye pied shelduck and Bride's ghillies,
O ye dunlins that wheel in unison over
  the waves, bless ye the Lord.

E. D. Sedding

Day 28

Psalm 148:9-14   Daniel 3:19-25   Luke 19:37-40

O ye larks that carol in the heavens,
O ye blackbirds that pipe at the dawning,
O ye pipits and wheatears,
O ye warblers and wrens that make
  the glens joyful with song,
O ye bees that love the heather,
  bless ye the Lord.
O ye primroses and bluebells,
O ye flowerets that gem the marsh with
  colour
O ye golden flags that deck Columba's
  Bay with glory, bless ye the Lord.

O ye piled rocks fashioned by Nature's
    might thro' myriad ages,
O ye majestic Bens of Mull,
O ye white sands and emerald shallows
O ye blue and purple deeps of ocean,
O ye winds and clouds, bless ye the Lord.
O all ye works of the Lord, bless ye the
    Lord, praise Him and magnify Him
    for ever.

E. D. Sedding SSJE
Ascension Day 1947

Day 29

Psalm 45:1   Ecclesiastes 3:1–3   Mark 4:30–33

Iona: If you have a good map of Scotland you
will find it among the Inner Hebrides off the
southwest tip of Mull, a comma of land
separated by a strait the width of an
exclamation point.

But from today's Iona there are still
offshoots, including one founded by John
Oliver Nelson, Kirkridge, which is in Bangor,
Pennsylvania, for Nelson once spent a summer
laying slate tiles on the roof of the Iona abbey
refectory. 'This place was the start of my life,'
he says of Iona. 'This is home.'

It is home for many. Still, Iona Community
remains small. As big in the eye of the world
as is the island itself on a world map. Small as
a mustard seed, you might say. Small, but
potent and marvellous.

St Columba must be glad with the sight of
it, but little surprised. He had a gift for seeing
the future and knew one day there would be

nothing left of his foundation, but he saw
beyond that time to its restoration. Poet as
well as prophet, he left his prophecy as poem:

Iona of my heart,
Iona of my love,
Instead of monks' voices
Shall be lowing of cattle
But ere the world comes to an end,
Iona shall be as it was.

James H. Forest

Day 30

Psalm 102:13–22   *Amos 9:14–15*
Revelation 12:17

Columba's prophecy

'Vast throngs I see in realms far, far away –
with stubborn pride they challenge Christ's
    appeal:
and thou, dear home,
    though plunged in long decay,
shalt rise anew thine ancient fires to feel,
leading the last long war with holy zeal!
But oh! let none thy blessing dare to claim
who shirk the law of strife! Messiah's heel
must feel the serpent's bruise,
    strong through Christ's name
by vigil, fast, and prayer,
    the serpent's pride to tame.'
His utt'rance ceased,
    but still his eye looked on
as if in distant skies his mind could read
the mysteries of the future.

R. M. Benson

Day 31

Psalm 5:11–12   Genesis 12:2   Hebrews 12:14–17

Please continue to pray for Iona, for the
Community, and for our friends at Bishop's
House – our month of thinking of Iona draws
to a close, but their work goes on . . .

> Iona, of all these things guardian and
>   keeper,
> keeper of men's souls from age to age,
> Iona, where men come to discover God,
> you sent by adventurous hearts over swaying
>   waters
> a word of truth to the nations of old times;
> send that word today, by your countless
>   pilgrims,
> who carry away across the gleaming sound
> a blessed imitation, a stir in the breast,
> a measure of beauty, a kindness in the heart,
> a hallowed secret, shaping the long years.
>> *Margaret Cropper, June 1950*

Farewell, then, to Iona. In old days, when they
said goodbye in the Gaelic, they said
something lovely, but so charged with
meaning. When husband parted from wife,
mother from child, lover from her who was
'half his sight', they remembered that days
might be dreary, friends few, and life hard. But
they looked into each other's eyes, and the
words always came – 'The blessing of God go
with you, and the blessing of Columba'.
>> *G. E. Troup*

SEPTEMBER READINGS

Aidan

Day 1   Psalm 145:2-4
        Isaiah 45:1
        1 Timothy 1:15

Day 2   Psalm 121:5-8
        Proverbs 15:13
        Mark 6:30-33

Day 3   Psalm 58:9-11
        Isaiah 42:2-4
        Luke 7:24, 31-32

Day 4   Psalm 75:8
        Zechariah 12:10
        2 Peter 2:4

Day 5   Psalm 22:1, 7, 17-18, 31
        Song of Songs 8:6b-7
        Hebrews 5:13-14

Day 6   Psalm 32:8-9
        1 Samuel 15:22
        Matthew 8:8-9

Day 7   Psalm 5:11-12
        Jeremiah 1:8-9
        Luke 22:35

Day 8   Psalm 53:1-3
        Lamentations 1:12
        2 Corinthians 6:1-2

Day 9   Psalm 55:17
        Amos 3:3
        1 Corinthians 14:8-12

Day 10 Psalm 119:14
        Proverbs 26:21
        Hebrews 6:1-3

Day 11 Psalm 133:1,3

Isaiah 1:14
John 4:35-37
Day 12 Psalm 37:8
Proverbs 3:17-21
Matthew 28:19-20
Day 13 Psalm 107:23-24
Numbers 23:19-20
2 Peter 1:2
Day 14 Psalm 107:25-28
Proverbs 15:1
Romans 8:28
Day 15 Psalm 107:29-30
Genesis 1:2a
Matthew 8:23-27
Day 16 Psalm 91:1-6
Proverbs 29:8
Hebrews 11:34-35
Day 17 Psalm 119:150
Isaiah 37:14-24, 33-34
Matthew 21:22
Day 18 Psalm 141:8-10
1 Samuel 5:1-5
Acts 17:23-25
Day 19 Psalm 113:5-8
Deuteronomy 15:11
Luke 14:11-14
Day 20 Psalm 109:27
2 Samuel 1:25, 27
Mark 14: 3-9
Day 21 Psalm 147:10-11; 20:7-8
Esther 6:7-9
2 Kings 5:11-14
Matthew 5:41-42; 25:34-40
Day 22 Psalm 116:3
Micah 6:8
Hebrews 11:4
Day 23 Psalm 119:30-32

Isaiah 61:1
1 Corinthians 9:23-26
Day 24 Psalm 48:14
Proverbs 8:14-17
Philippians 4:12-13
Day 25 Psalm 113:3
Genesis 49:33
Ephesians 3:16-19
Day 26 Psalm 34:1
Judges 1:15
Luke 2:25-32
Day 27 Psalm 116:15
2 Kings 2:11-14
2 Timothy 4:7-8
Day 28 Psalm 48:1-3
Haggai 1:13-14
Hebrews 11:4-5
Day 29 Psalm 84:4-7
2 Kings 13:14, 20-21
Acts 6:15
Day 30 Psalm 141:1-4
Ecclesiastes 5:12
Matthew 25:21

Day 1

Psalm 145:2-4   Isaiah 45:1   1 Timothy 1:15

An old *Life of St Aidan* written in verse by
Rev. Arthur Wright MA, one-time rector of Low
Toynton and Canon of Lincoln, is serialized
over this month.
Icolmkill means 'the island of Colum of the
Celts' – in Aidan's time the buildings were of
wood, rather than of stone!

Far, in the desolate North beyond the sound
of seething multitudes of striving men,
where, vext but by the wheeling seamew's
cry or thunderous breaking of the Atlantic
tide, weird silence holds her solitary reign –
there lies an islet – Icolmkill by name,
sometimes Iona on whose weathered heights
sits like a queen her rock built monast'ry,
with lofty arch and graceful pillar wrought
by hands of pious devotees; the pride of
generations past and yet to come. Hence
rises heavenward daily chant and psalm, the
constant orison of saintly souls, which ask
for others not themselves alone that Christ
would save them from their sinfulness and
make them His for evermore.

Day 2

Psalm 121:5-8   Proverbs 15:13   Mark 6:30-33

Iona

The worn and weary here may find a peaceful
rest, a home for meditation and for prayer.

The Council Chamber of the Abbey where
monks are assembled under the presidency of
Segenius, fourth Abbot of the Monastery of
Iona:

The Abbot

'Whence comest thou, good brother?
Travelstained, and sad of countenance thou art,
as if some sorrow had befallen thee. Come in
and stay awhile, and tell us how the Lord hath
blest thy goings out and comings in, since last
we met within the cloistered walls of this
sanctuary.'

Brother Corman

'I thank thee, Sire, for thy warm welcome
which renews my strength, and almost makes
me feel again a man.'

Day 3

Psalm 58:9-11   Isaiah 42:2-4   Luke 7:24, 31-32

Corman has returned to Iona from
Northumbria and is recounting his progress to
the other borders. (Bernicia was the northern
part of all Northumbria – corresponding to the
present-day Northumberland and SE Scotland.)

Alas! I am a miserable reed, which waves its
weakness in th' uncertain air, I left this
house with brave intention, and glowing
expectation, that before the Word of God, as
spoken by my mouth, the citadels of sin

would fall, and those adrift upon the sea of heathenism would anchor safely by the Cross of Christ. I wandered far o'er dark Bernicia's wilds, o'er hill and dale, and tried to gain the hearts of the benighted natives of that land from Satan's power and death for evermore. I told them of the wrath of God, that He did hate their devilish lusts, their barbarous ways, their internecine fightings, and that He was justly angry with them every day for so great wickedness.

Day 4

Psalm 75:8   *Zechariah 12:10*   *2 Peter 2:4*

Corman continues to recount his fruitless attempt to convert the Northumbrians:

I told them too of that vast pit eternal, where lost souls in heat and cold are leaping to and fro in silent agony, suffering for their sins, where bound with chains until the day of doom in torment the rebellious angels writhe; I told them of the persecuting bands of cruel-hearted Jews, who crucified and slew the Lord of all, and thus filled up the cup of trembling for themselves and theirs; yet all in vain: they heeded not: they mocked my earnest warnings of their coming fate, despising them; and now I have come back turning away from such hard-hearted churls who are not worthy of God's grace and help.

Day 5

Psalm 22:1, 17-18, 31   *Song of Songs 8:6b-7*
Hebrew 5:13-14

Aidan is provoked to respond to Corman's
hardhearted judgement of the people of
Northumbria, and gently reproaches him:

> The tender infant takes but milk at first, not
> meat and other stronger kinds of food, I
> pray thee, didst thou tell them of the love of
> Christ – His love divine – transcending far
> all other loves – so wide and free that even
> the universe cannot contain it all, which
> caused the Son of God to feel for us in
> grief, to pray for those who did Him wrong
> and give His life a ransom for mankind? The
> love of Christ – *that* wins and conquers all! I
> would not blame thee, brother, but methinks
> it was thy method, not thy theme that failed.

Day 6

Psalm 32:8-9   *1 Samuel 15:22*   *Matthew 8:8-9*

Perhaps now Aidan wishes he had never
opened his mouth? but his heart is already
awakening to the need, and the challenge, of
Northumbria.

Abbot

'Thou speakest well, good Aidan, and perhaps
it would be better that thou shouldest prove

the virtue of thine argument. Go forth in
God's name, and try the gentler mode of
drawing those to Christ who are astray. The
stubborn colt is trained more easily by soft
and coaxing words than by hard blows.'

Aidan

'My conscience answers to thy call. The rule
of this our household is obedience, and so, Sir
Abbot, when thou bidst us "come" we come,
and when thou sayest "go" we go. And yet I
crave your prayers that God on High may bless
my feeble effort to make known the death of
Christ for saving of the lost.'

Day 7

| Psalm 5:11-12 | Jeremiah 1:8-9 | Luke 22:35 |

Unless he too is to fail in his mission it is
improbable that Aidan will ever again see his
beloved home, Iona.

Abbot

'Thou hast our prayers, good Aidan; may the
Lord be thy defence in danger, and thy guide
throughout life's journey to thy crown at last.'

And so he passed along his lonely road, that
heaven-inspired apostle; neither purse nor
scrip encumbered him: God's Word alone his
light and stay through sorrow's darkest hour.
His thoughtful mien and always upward look
proclaimed at once the scholar and the saint.

He passed across the seas that roll between
Iona's isle and dark Northumbria's strand, and
further – till he reached fair Lindisfarne.

Day 8

Psalm 53:1-3   *Lamentations 1:12*
2 Corinthians 6:1-2

Aidan preaches the Gospel wherever he goes:

And ever, as he went, he lifted the Cross of
Christ, 'Repent for Christ has come' he
cried; 'renounce your worthless fetishes, the
only Son of God has come from heaven to
save you from the pains of death and hell.'

When by his burning words his audience
seemed enwrapt in reverent astonishment,
then with a voice of sweet persuasive tones,
as from his very soul, he pleaded hard for
Jesus' love and His self-sacrifice; 'How shall
you turn a careless ear to Him who did so
much for you, whose precious life He gave
that you might live for evermore: He called
you within His Church's fold and He will
grant that by His Spirit's aid you may work
out with trembling and with fear your own
deliverance: the day is short; the night is
coming on, beneath whose shadow no man
can work: the accepted time is *now*.

Day 9

Psalm 55:17   *Amos 3:3*   *1 Corinthians 14:8-12*

Oswald the king had been educated on Iona,
and was able to act as interpreter when Aidan
spoke to his people.

And if perchance they could not understand
the words of his address, some kindly friend
would tell them what it meant; nor did the
king himself with all his royal majesty
disdain the office of interpreter, Oswald the
king, for having learnt in youth the language
of the North, he could make plain the
preacher's statements to the listening crowd;
and many an act of kindness did he do for
Aidan and his saintly company, and ordained
on the isle of Lindisfarne (which for their
own he gave them) they might build a
daughter home for learning and for prayer
within whose sacred precincts might be
heard morning and evening and at noon as
well the voice of supplication rising up with
praise to God on high, such as arose in days
of old within Iona's fane.

Day 10

Psalm 119:14   *Proverbs 26:21*   *Hebrews 6:1-3*

Aidan's care for the brothers living with him
on Lindisfarne:

Here also would the study of God's word,
His own revealed Will, become the care of
those who lived there, and from time to

time, Aidan, with wise discretion, would explain the regulations of Church government, the doctrines of repentance and good works, of baptisms and laying on of hands, of future resurrection, and at last of final judgement, and sometimes the day when Easter Sunday should be kept became the subject of contentious difference and violent words were passed.

Day 11

Psalm 133:1, 3   Isaiah 1:14   John 4:35-37

Aidan calls his brothers again to 'follow the example of good men of old':

But when debate waxed strong among the disputants would he, Aidan the bishop, allay the rising storm of hot discussion, and reminding them of their forefathers' custom, he would say, 'Wherefore this much ado? Hath not Christ died? yes, rather is risen again! Redemption's work is now complete. Why vex your faithful hearts so sadly on these questions of new moons and solemn feast days? Nay, in such concerns let no man judge you; look upon the fields already white to harvest: fare ye forth and reap them: as the shepherd gathers in his wandering sheep, so do ye gather into the Church of Christ these errant souls for whom Christ died, at present dark through sin and fierce idolatries, that they may live as radiant spirits ever worshipping the one true God before the throne on high.'

Day 12

Psalm 37:8   Proverbs 3:17-21
                    Matthew 28:19-20

Aidan's example reminds the brothers of their
true purpose and mission.

He ceased: and as upon a summer's day
when the wild thunderstorm has spent its
rage the sun shines out, and nature seems at
peace, a deeper peace because of all the
wrong contending elements have wrought;
just so the speech of Aidan shed an
influence mild o'er those assembled, who,
ashamed of such unbrotherly exchange of
angry words and biting sarcasm, then began
to turn to higher aims, and spread
themselves abroad throughout the land,
proclaiming far and wide the tidings of
salvation; multitudes of young and old into
the fold of Christ were brought by holy
baptism; churches rose in town and village;
monasteries too were built up here and
there; so mightily did grow the faith of
Christ through Aidan's zeal.

Day 13

Psalm 107:23-24 Numbers 23:19-20 2 Peter 1:2

Edwin was the fifth King of Northumbria, and
on his assassination his daughter Eanfleda had
been carried away for safety to Kent. Utta
seeks Aidan's blessing before escorting her
north:

And there were times when those in anxious
doubt would come to him for help and
would entreat his blessing on the work they
had to do, believing that with piety so great,
whatever he should bless was blest indeed.

And so it chanced a priest named Utta
came, being ordered far away to Kent to
fetch the royal Eanfleda, Edwin's child, to be
the bride of Oswy, and he asked that for
himself and for his retinue a prosperous
journey might be granted with a safe return
across the sea.

Day 14

Psalm 107:25-28   Proverbs 15:1   Romans 8:28

Utta has come to Aidan for a blessing before
embarking on his journey:

. . . To whom replied the Bishop in
prophetic strain 'To pass along life's ocean
seldom is without some danger – an
unruffled calm – nor will thy voyage
homeward either be exempt from perils:
take this holy oil which I give thee: when
howling storm is wildest, and the waves run
mountains high, then cast this oil upon the
weltering deep: and, just as when a
Christian spirit pours soft words upon the
fiery wrath of man, and stills it, even so the
winds shall cease, the tempest driven waters
fall again, and peace prevail where once was
mad unrest.'

Day 15

Psalm 107:29-30 Genesis 1:2a Matthew 8:23-27

Utta remembers Aidan's warning, and the oil
he had given them:

> The priest attended to the good man's
> words, giving such heed as due respect
> required, and went his way: but, as he came
> again, returning, the woe-laden prophecy of
> Aidan met its fulfilment, and the wind-swept
> ship was hurried to and fro upon the boiling
> waves; with terror filled the seamen rushed
> to Utta crying, 'Lost, lost, lost, we perish,
> who shall save us now from wreck and
> death?' Then in their utmost need, Utta,
> remembering good Aidan's gift, broke in:
> 'Put ye your trust in God, for He who
> calmed the waters of Gennesaret can calm, if
> He sees fit, this revelling storm.' Then
> poured he out upon the troubled sea the
> holy oil, which spreading far and wide made
> smooth the surging deep: the wild winds
> ceased, the rolling billows sank, and once
> again the face of heaven was bright with
> tranquil smiles, and the brave ship sped
> safely on her way.

Day 16

Psalm 91:1-6 Proverbs 29:8 Hebrews 11:34-35

Penda, the King of Mercia, was the great
leader of the heathen resistance to the advance
of Christianity in the North.

It is recorded that one evening hour
compline had just been said at Lindisfarne,
and God's protection reverently sought
against perils of the coming night, when in
there rushed a messenger in anxiety; and
fear reflected on his countenance. 'To arms,'
he cried, 'hither the Merican host with
Penda as its leader hastens on transporting
ruthless murder in its train, and cruel
devastation, and behold! already has it
reached to Bamborough's walls, assaulting
them, but failing in attack direct, has piled
up heaps of wood and reeds, the waste of
prostrate villagers around, and kindling them
is seeking to consume that royal fortress
with devouring flames.'

Day 17

Psalm 119:150   Isaiah 37:14-24, 33-34
           Matthew 21:22

Aidan laments the advance of Penda's army
against Bamburgh, and prays for God's
intervention:

'Alas!' rejoined the Bishop, sorrowing,
'Wherefore now, do rage so furiously these
pagan hordes, on wanton plunder bent and
dire destruction, shouting as they come
"Down with it, down with it, even to the
ground"? O Thou Who heard'st in ancient
days the prayer of good King Hezekiah,
when in vain Sennacherib advanced his
braggart host against Jerusalem, so hear us
now; we pray Thee with Thy mighty arm

drive back this conquering army which with
fire and sword threatens destruction to grey
Bamborough's towers, Thou seest, Lord,
what mischief Penda works, Penda, the
chieftain of the Mercian host, to Thine
anointed, hearken to our prayer.'

Day 18

Psalm 141:8–10   1 Samuel 5:1–15   Acts 17:23-25

Aidan's prayers turn back the flames at
Bamburgh:

He scarce had finished when the Eastern
wind, which hitherto had blown against the
walls, changed its direction, and the blazing
flames fell back at once on those who lit
them up, strewing confusion midst the
hostile ranks of the marauding foe: in wild
dismay they fled, not knowing whither. 'See,'
they said, 'the God who fights for them is
stronger than the gods who fight for us;
Woden and Thor and such old deities have
lost their power to help us in our need, and
so we fail.'

Day 19

Psalm 113:5-8 Deuteronomy 15:11 Luke 14:11-14

King Oswald orders his Easter dinner to be
taken away and given to the poor people who
have come to his door for help:

And in like manner many a tale is told of
Aidan's virtues, and the way in which
Oswald assisted him; for he, the king, was
noble hearted, a God-fearing man, who
loved God's people and religious ways; of
whom 'twas said that on one Eastertide the
banquet was prepared with daintiest food
displayed on glowing silver, and the king
about to satisfy his hungering, when
suddenly his almoner hurrying in told of a
starving multitude without; the sick, the
blind, the lame, who waited for remaining
fragments, and what liberal alms his royal
hand might give them. 'Ah!' quoth he, 'Why
should these fast while I am feasting! God
loves all alike, and not the less the poor, but
rather more; His gifts are for them sent, not
only for the great ones of the earth. Take
these rich viands which before me lie; give
them to those who want them more than
we. This silver charger also, break it up and
make with pieces manifold to each abundant
distribution, and I pray God's benison may
rest upon them all.'

Day 20

Psalm 109:27   2 Samuel 1:25, 27   Mark 14:3-9

Aidan blessed Oswald's generous arm! On 5th
August 642 Oswald was slain in battle at
Maserfield. His arm and hand were cut off
from his body and preserved in a silver casket
at Bamburgh, but his niece Osthrida, Queen of
Mercia, rescued his other remains and had
them buried at 'Beardenau' or Bardney near

Lincoln, (from where they were moved to Gloucestershire nearly three centuries later).

Scarce had these words been spoken when at once the saintly Aidan, of fair Lindisfarne the Bishop, grasping his right hand exclaimed, 'Well said, thou charitable prince! Henceforth the story of this gracious act of thine shall live through future ages, and be sung by coming generations yet unborn: and this right hand which now I hold, God grant, in token of thy care for others' wants, that it may never perish or grow less.' Nor did the holy Bishop speak in vain, for after, as the page of history tells, King Oswald, fighting for East Anglia, was slain upon the plains of Maserfield, his mutilated body, earth to earth, was placed within the shrine of Beardenau, but the white hand which Aidan grasped remained still whole and uncorrupted by decay.

Day 21

Psalm 147:10-11, 20:7-8   *Esther 6:7-9*
2 Kings 5:11-14   *Matthew 5:41-42, 25:34-40*

Oswin has become King of Deira, the southern part of Northumbria, reaching from the Tyne to the Humber.
Good King Oswin gives Aidan a fine horse to help him in his apopstolic travels, only to find he has given it away . . .

Nor yet alone of kings amongst his friends did Aidan number Oswald; Oswin, too, Deira's youthful monarch, held him high in honour, and, noticing by chance one day his look so weary through much travelling, gave him a gallant steed, caparisoned with costly trappings, that with greater ease he might discharge his apostolic work. A short time after, meeting a poor man, Aidan, dismounting, passed the royal gift to him that asked an alms, which when the king Oswin had heard thereof, he took to task the generous bishop for his lavishness.

'Why didst thou give that valuable colt set out for thine own use unto the poor? for such as they a meaner sort would serve.' To whom the Bishop readily replied, 'Is a mere colt more dear than God's own Son, who in the person of the poor is seen?'

The king, regretting the severity of his remonstrance, fell upon his knees, entreating Aidan's pardon for his speech, who, though he bade others rejoice, could not himself rejoice, but shed abundant tears.

King Oswin tries to tell Aidan off, and ends up admitting he is in the wrong instead.

Aidan leaves him in tears himself . . . Why?

Day 22

Psalm 116:3　　　*Micah 6:8*　　　*Hebrew 11:4*

Why is Aidan weeping? By word of knowledge he foresees King Oswin's murder. Oswin ruled alongside Oswy, a successor of Oswald, and was betrayed by Earl Hunwald whom he thought to be his friend; he was killed at Oswy's order at Ingethlingum.

His priest then asked him 'Wherefore so
much grief and why these bitter tears of
thine?' to whom the Bishop answered
mournfully, 'My liege methinks the choicest
flower that blooms within the garden plot is
not the gorgeous rose, nor yet the lily with
its scarlet dress. It is the lowly violet that
shrinks from closer observation; so the best
of all our Christian graces is humility, such
as King Oswin wears who seems alas! too
good for this proud world, for we are taught
that whom God loves in early years He takes
unto Himself in kinder world than ours.'
The good man's forecast was ere long
fulfilled, the king was shortly afterwards
betrayed to Oswy, jealous partner of his
throne, who caused him to be basely put to
death.

Day 23

Psalm 119:30-32   *Isaiah 61:1*
           1 Corinthians 9:23-26

How Aidan was loved by rich and poor alike
whom he taught to love Christ faithfully:

Such stories clung around the name and
fame of Aidan, shewing his nobility and
saint-like character: both rich and poor
revered his wonderful simplicity, and not
the less the dignity with which he held
himself aloof from evil deeds, and evil men,
sternly reproving them. His hallowed zeal
and self denial, too, in travelling far and
wide to tell abroad, one day in royal houses,

and the next in some poor lowly cottage, the
good news and blessed teachings of Christ's
holy Church, raised him to be the foremost
in those days of Christian preachers; and he
was acclaimed a very prince among
Evangelists.

Day 24

Psalm 48:14   *Proverbs 8:14-17*
          Philippians 4:12-13

Aidan had made his life count for the
kingdom's sake, but his physical strength was
wearing out . . .

But not for always could his mortal powers
answer the wider longings of his soul;
footsore and often foodless, he pursued his
solitary round: fightings within, and anxious
fears without afflicted him, which day by
day wore down his wasting strength. And in
due time it came to pass that he, devoted to
his missionary work, was journeying on the
mainland, and within a hermit's tent, near
by a royal house where frequently the king,
as was his wont, would bid him welcome,
and submissively would sit and listen to his
sage advice. 'Twas there he met the
messenger of death, and thus to him, life's
weary warfare o'er, peace came at last: the
Christian soldier's strife was ended.

Day 25

Psalm 113:3   Genesis 49:33   Ephesians 3:16-19

Aidan seemed even closer to heaven as his death approached – the land once a spiritual desert has been irrigated by springs of life coming from Lindisfarne.

As the setting sun flings back its parting splendour, and illuminates the heaven it leaves with an unearthly light, not otherwise when sinking to its rest the sainted soul, its mundane labours past, reflects a splendour from the world unseen by mortal eyes, so glorious that it holds in wondering admiration all around. Such was the death of Aidan. His poor frame shrunk with much fasting and long travelling, no further would it bear him to and fro on works of mercy, and for others' good, and yet the more the outward man decayed the inward man grew stronger and it seemed to watching brethren that though yet he lived on earth, his conversation was in heaven.

Day 26

Psalm 34:1   Judges 1:15   Luke 2:25-32

Aidan's strong prayers are for those who will continue his work and follow him.

The voice of praise was ever on his lips for God's great goodness unto him vouchsafed, mingled with prayers as saints alone can pray, and thus his latest supplications rose in faltering accents, 'Let Thy servant, Lord, depart in peace according to Thy Word, for now mine eyes have seen the mightiness of Thy salvation in this heathen land: Grant, I beseech Thee, that Thy Gospel may shed far its blessings, so that all mankind throughout the length and breadth of this wide world, hearing the tidings of Thy mercy, may own Thee and Thee alone the King of kings and Lord of lords, through Jesus Christ. Amen.'

Day 27

Psalm 116:15   *2 Kings 2:11-14*
              2 Timothy 4:7-8

Aidan died on 31st August 650 and was buried at Lindisfarne.

Uttering these words beneath the Church's shade, the good man sank exhausted, and his soul borne upwards on rejoicing Angels' wings midst strains of softest music passed from its earthly prisonhouse to live in Paradise awaiting its reward. Then homeward was his breathless corpse conveyed by faithful brethren to fair Lindisfarne, to rest within God's acre near the fane where oft he had retired in bygone days for secret prayer: then after many years his bones were stored with loving carefulness beside God's altar, there in peace to lie, till at the Archangel's trump the dead again shall wake upon the resurrection morn.

Day 28

Psalm 48:1-3   Haggai 1:13-14   Hebrews 11:4-5

Aidan holds a very significant place in
Christian history, even though the accounts are
biased against the Celtic Church!

But he being dead yet speaketh, for the seed
of God's own Word sown by his careful
hand, the lessons which he taught of love to
God and man as well: his bright example too
lived onward in the grateful heart of all for
generations, and were handed on to nations
distant both in time and space.

And so 'tis told in records of the past that
floods of precious Gospel truth with which
our northern England was first overspread
flowed from Iona (not from Rome as held by
some), and that large gratitude is due for
knowledge of the tidings of great joy to
preachers from the North, of whom the
chief was Aidan and his saintly following.

Day 29

Psalm 84:4-7   2 Kings 13:14, 20-21   Acts 6:15

The wood that Aidan leant on would not
burn. His memory remains an inspiration, and
his prayers still have powerful impact today.

Yet more – 'tis said of him, as has been said
about Elisha centuries before. Whose mortal
frame while resting in the tomb seemed still
instinct with life, and still gave forth life-
giving influence: thus Aidan too, so great his

saintliness, that common things if touched
by him acquired a sacred power, and, as
tradition tells, the very post 'gainst which he
leaned when at the point of death, so
changed its perishable elements that, though
the consecrated pile of which it formed a
part was burnt, the hungry flames could not
at all destroy, or make it less; and though a
second Church was raised, and that again
consumed, it remained quite whole, and still
unharmed was placed in after years, a sacred
sign of Aidan's holiness, within the hallowed
sanctuary walls of yet another, and was
visited by frequent pilgrims; so the legend
runs, which, whether fabled or of truth,
attests the veneration linked with Aidan's
name.

Day 30

Psalm 141:1-4   Ecclesiastes 5:12   Matthew 25:21

Good Aidan, you were faithful to the call you
first received. Help us to follow Christ as
faithfully, on fire with love for Him.

Sleep softly, sainted soul! life's troubled
dream is past: to thee the choicest gifts of
earth were nothing worth: the incense of
thy thoughts ascended far above such
vanities. Sleep on, until the Judge of all
mankind shall come from heaven to gather
in His own and thou shalt hear His cheering
voice, 'Well done, thou true and faithful
servant! Enter thou within the veil that
sunders world from world, and lie for ever
on thy Saviour's breast.'

OCTOBER READINGS

With Understanding

All your mind
Day 1   Psalm 119:1-4
            Nehemiah 8:2-6
            Matthew 22:37-38

Such were some of you
Day 2   Psalm 119:5-8
            Nehemiah 8:8
            1 Corinthians 6:9-11

Secret Defence
Day 3   Psalm 119:9-11
            Nehemiah 8:9-10
            Romans 12:2

I will not forget
Day 4   Psalm 119:12-16
            Nehemiah 8:11-12
            1 Corinthians 14:14-15

The unseen world
Day 5   Psalm 119:17-24
            2 Kings 6:15-17
            Luke 4:1-13

Exaggeration or enlargement?
Day 6   Psalm 119:25-32
            1 Chronicles 4:9-10
            Philippians 3:13-14

Pain or reproach
Day 7   Psalm 119:33-40
            Isaiah 51:7; 53:3
            John 8:43-46

Before kings!
Day 8   Psalm 119:41-48
          Genesis 41:14-16
          Matthew 10:18-20

My pilgrim song
Day 9   Psalm 119:49-56
          Job 35:9-11
          James 5:13

Bring me into harmony
Day 10 Psalm 119:57-64
          Ezekiel 37:2-4
          Romans 8:19-23

The good of affliction!
Day 11 Psalm 119:65-72
          Genesis 37:23-24; 50:20
          Acts 5:29-35, 38-39

Can I not do with you as the Potter?
Day 12 Psalm 119:73-78
          Jeremiah 18:1-6
          Romans 8:25-26

Make friends of God's people
Day 13 Psalm 119:79-80
          2 Kings 10:15
          Galatians 6:10

Is there anyone else up there?
Day 14 Psalm 119:81-88
          Judges 6:11-14
          Hebrews 12:11-12

Settled in heaven
Day 15 Psalm 119:89–95
          Deuteronomy 17:19
          Revelation 1:3; 5:2-5

Room to grow
Day 16 Psalm 119:96
          1 Samuel 2:18-21

Matthew 5:48

How I love Thy law!
Day 17 Psalm 119:97-104
　　　　Proverbs 2:1-6
　　　　Luke 2:40-47, 52

Proceed (with caution)
Day 18 Psalm 119:105-112
　　　　Isaiah 30:30-21
　　　　Hebrews 4:12-13

Hold me high
Day 19 Psalm 119:113-117
　　　　Isaiah 55:8-9
　　　　Ephesians 1:3; 2:6-7

Fear of the Lord
Day 20 Psalm 119:118-120
　　　　Nehemiah 8:9
　　　　James 3:3-7

Right judgements
Day 21 Psalm 119:121-128
　　　　1 Kings 3:12-13
　　　　Matthew 22:15-22

Wonderful words of life
Day 22 Psalm 119:129-132
　　　　Habakkuk 2:14
　　　　John 7:37-39

No iniquity shall have dominion over me
Day 23 Psalm 119:133-135
　　　　Isaiah 58:6, 8-10
　　　　Romans 6:16-18

Weeping at their neglect
Day 24 Psalm 119:136
　　　　Isaiah 5:1-4
　　　　Luke 13:34; 19:41

Zealous anger
Day 25 Psalm 119:137-140
2 Kings 10:16-17
Matthew 23:4, 13

The greatness of the small
Day 26 Psalm 119:141-143
Jeremiah 9:23-24
Matthew 11:25-26

I shall live
Day 27 Psalm 119:144
Deuteronomy 32:47
Luke 7:1-7

The night watches
Day 28 Psalm 119:145-152
Habakkuk 2:1, 3
Romans 10:13-15

Quicken me
Day 29 Psalm 119:153-160
Jonah 2:5-7
Romans 8:11

Great peace
Day 30 Psalm 119:161-168
1 Samuel 26:2, 7-9, 12-13, 22-23
Titus 3:1-2

Strays
Day 31 Psalm 119:169-176
Nehemiah 8:12
Philemon 4-7

Day 1

This month we will be reading slowly through Psalm 119, the longest psalm, which gives thanks for God's laws which give understanding and bring life. We pray God will teach us to obey Him, to honour Him, and to praise Him *with understanding*.

In John Irving's novel *The Cider House Rules* the rules are carefully posted up where everyone can see them, but it makes no difference because the people who have to keep them cannot read. The rules still apply, and so do the penalties for breaking them. God's laws are in-built in our world, so lack of understanding is dangerous.

In *Winnie the Pooh* by A. A.Milne, Owl is instructing Pooh Bear to follow the customary procedure ...

'What does Crustimoney Proseedcake mean?'
   said Pooh,
'For I am a Bear of Very Little Brain,
   and long words Bother me.'
'It means the Thing to Do.'
'As long as it means that, I don't mind,'
   said Pooh humbly.

The word of God challenges us,
   Do you seek him with all your mind?
And we respond,
   Amen. Lord have mercy!

Day 2

Psalm 119:5-8   *Nehemiah 8:8*
1 Corinthians 6:9-11

The one with the gift of making things clear
brings understanding, and imparts life.

The rules are there for your protection and
you know they make sense. People break
God's rules, and are damaged in consequence.
How we need to explain, to help others
understand! People need the Lord. We can
encourage them to find God and His ways in
their life. What He has done for us He can do
for them, too.

We can be part of the process, fully given to
the purpose of the Lord Christ.

An old Celtic song expresses it this way:

As You reach out to bless mankind,
    I feel Your embrace drawing me close.
I rise with You, dear Jesus, and You
    rise with me.

Day 3

Psalm 119:9-11   Nehemiah 8:9-10   Romans 12:2

The word God speaks can be hidden in our
heart as a secret weapon, to protect us from
sinning against Him. His words alter our
understanding and slowly renew our mind,
changing our way of thinking.

First of all, His word may make us sad for
we realize how far we fall short of His
intentions for us; but He urges us to feed on

His word with joy, and be strengthened. If our thinking is shaped by His word we may be protected from many unnecessary hurts, and destructive ambitions. That is why the psalm pays particular attention to the young man and the cleansing of his ways before habits of sin and wilfulness become deeply ingrained.

Abba Isaiah, one of the Desert Fathers, said to beginners who were off to a good start, obediently following the tradition of the fathers:

'Just as the young branches can easily be corrected and bent, so can beginners who are obedient.'

Day 4

Psalm 119:12-16   Nehemiah 8:11-12
1 Corinthians 14:14-15

'I will not forget Your word,' says the Psalm. There's not a whole lot of point in hearing or reading the words of God if we immediately forget what has been said.

James 1:22-25 says that the person who does that is like someone looking in a mirror, then forgetting what they look like, but that the perfect word of God gives freedom if we continue to act on it.

We should pray and praise with the Spirit, but also with understanding; it's not a case of one or the other. The two ways of praying go together; they are not opposites. Praying with understanding does not mean speaking our mind to God. Instead, we pray first only as the Spirit gives us the ability, and in doing that we find we have understanding we did not have before. Even our ability to pray is His gift to us. As we hear from God we begin to have wisdom and understanding.

A fool may talk, but a wise man speaks.

Ben Johnson

Day 5

Psalm 119:17-24   2 Kings 6:15-17   Luke 4:1-13

All of us use only a fraction of our brain-power, to say nothing of how little we develop our five senses. Often when one sense is impaired, others become more finely-tuned. A paraplegic may manipulate a paintbrush with the mouth, or a blind person develop a keen sense of hearing.

How many of us go through life with our spiritual eyes un-seeing, or fast closed? And how is our spiritual hearing? Can we distinguish the voice of the deceiver from that of the Shepherd?

O God, Your words are my counsellors. Yours is the voice I'll listen to.

In the steep common path of our calling,
Be it easy or uneasy to our flesh,
Be it bright or dark for us to follow,
Be Thou a shield to us from the wiles
    of the deceiver,
From the arch-destroyer with his arrows
    pursuing us,
And in each secret thought our minds
    get to weave
Be Thou Thyself on our helm and at
    our sheet

from Carmina Gadelica

Day 6

Psalm 119:25-31   *1 Chronicles 4:9-10*
                 Philippians 3:13-14

Remove from me the way of lying. Lying is not always even deliberate untruth. It may be to not report accurately, but act as if we were certain of the facts. It may be that to choose the way of truth is to be careful never to exaggerate, to be known as a person of our word.

People should be able to say, They said so, so it must be the case. Being in the right is beside the point. As Hugh Redwood has said, 'Don't bend the truth when you hammer it home!'

The last verse of this section of the psalm is powerful:

> I will *run* the way of Your
> commandments when You enlarge my heart.

If my heart is enlarged I'll have time to hold back, nor will I carry things that hamper my progress.

> Do you love Christ,
> King Jesus, is He yours?
> Then love God more
> and burn with love.
> Hold fast the light He gives,
> Live thou for Him.
> Believer, hold Him high . . .
>   *'Aidan'*

Day 7

Psalm 119:33-40 Isaiah 51:7; 53:3 John 8:43-46

Turn away, O God, the reproach I fear. It can matter a lot what other people say, those who speak wrongfully against me.

> Who steals my purse steals trash,
>   'tis something, nothing,
> 'Twas mine, 'tis his,
>   and has been slave to thousands.
> But he that filches from me my good name
> Steals that which not enriches him,
>   and leaves me poor indeed.
>
> *Iago from 'Othello'*

Even in the poverty of reproach Christ can meet us, and He is all in all.

> Thou, Lord, alone, art all thy children need
>   and there is none beside;
> from thee the streams of blessedness
> proceed;
>   in thee the blest abide.
> Fountain of life and all-abounding grace,
> our source, our centre and our dwelling
> place!
>
> *Mme Guyon*

Day 8

Psalm 119:41-48   *Genesis 41:14-16*
Matthew 10:18-20

By seeking out Your precepts I will walk at liberty! I will speak of You before kings and rulers, standing unashamed.

From *Tomorrow You Die*

As the evening wore on, the men became impatient. The chief complained, 'You refuse to co-operate with us. You refuse to tell the truth. We will imprison you for life.' A chill went down my spine. Life imprisonment in the nation of Albania! More grace was going to be needed to accept this than to accept the death sentence.

For the last time they asked me the question. 'Who sent you to Albania?' Again I replied that I was a Christian who lived and served God, that I had come at his command, and that I was prepared to bear full responsibility for my actions. I had known, when I crossed the border, the possible implications of what I was doing.

One of the interrogators then asked an interesting question: 'Are there other people like you who are doing what you are doing?' Without realizing the impact of my reply, I said that yes, there were hundreds who were responding to the call of Jesus Christ to go to the uttermost parts of the earth - to the areas that have never heard - to reach the entire . . . Undisguised fear was written on his face as he asked a further question, 'You mean others like you will come to Albania?'

Reona Peterson

Day 9

Psalm 119:49-56   Job 35:9-11   James 5:13

In the night Your song will be with me, will
be with me, in the night. A song keeps singing
in my heart for I am Yours and You, Lord, are
mine, and all times are in Your hand.

Lord of my heart,
    give me vision to inspire me,
  that working or resting,
    I may always think of You.
Lord of my heart,
    give me light to guide me, that,
  at home or abroad,
    I may always walk in Your way.
from Celtic Fire

With Your inspiration
the pilgrim is fired,
is filled with courage
to tackle the way.

He treks through Tear Valley
and makes it a spring,
a blessing, like early
rain bringing new life.
He takes the path inward
to stand before God.
The Othona Psalms

Day 10

Psalm 119:57-64   *Ezekiel 37:2-4*
                Romans 8:19-23

The earth is full of Your steadfast love, but
now teach *me* Your commands. It is me that is
out of step, out of tune, discordant and
jarring.

> The brightest colour upon His palette is of
> no use to the Artist if it refuses to blend
> with the others.
>
> *Hugh Redwood*

We need to find our place in God's purpose,
receptive and open to His direction and
inspiration, and all creation waits as it were on
tiptoe in excited anticipation of what can
happen if we assume the destiny for which we
were created, and stand as 'sons of God'. We
become 'Christ -carriers'.

> Believer, hold Him high
> that all may see
> the light of Jesus
> in a son of man.
>
> *'Aidan'*

Day 11

Psalm 119:65-72   *Genesis 37:23-24; 50:20*
                Acts 5:29-35, 38-39

Poor Joseph fell foul of his brothers' jealousy.
In the bottom of his pit it took a lot of
imagination to believe any good could ever
come of it.

He who strives to climb out of a pit will not pray that its sides shall be smooth.

Hugh Redwood

Withdraw not thy hand, O my God, from
  me here,
O Chief of the chiefs, O withdraw not thy
  hand.

from Lochabar

When things seem really bad we might need to hesitate before assuming it's against us and out to get us. As Gamaliel pointed out, we need to be careful *just in case* it's God we'd be fighting in rejecting it.

Great questions stand unanswered before us, and defy our best wisdom. Though our ignorance is great, at least we know we do not know. When we don't know what to say, keep us quiet.

Peter Marshall

Day 12

Psalm 119:73-78   *Jeremiah 18:1-6*
Romans 8:25-26

O God, forgive the poverty and pettiness of our prayers. Listen not to our words, but to the yearning of our hearts. Hear beneath our petitions the crying of our need.

Peter Marshall

God, You hear within us the groanings so deep they cannot even be uttered. Let Your tender mercies come unto us that we may live again.

'Can I not do with you as the Potter?' says the
Lord God. Lord, help me to realize that I am
Your project.

Have Your own way, Lord, have Your own
way
You are the Potter – I am the clay
Mould me and make me after Your will
while I am waiting, yielded and still.

Adelaide A. Pollard

'Can I not do with you as the Potter?'
'Yes.'

Day 13

Psalm 119:79-80   2 Kings 10:15   Galatians 6:10

It is your business and others' to go forth,
confronting them face to face, for that is the
only way of bringing them to Me. For when
you are face to face with them, you love them,
and once you love them, then I can speak
through you.

from Molchanie by Catherine de Hueck Doherty

His love that burns inside me
impels me on the road
to seek for Christ in the stranger's face
or feel the absence of His touch

'Aidan'

If your heart is right with my heart,
   give me your hand,
the right hand of fellowship,
the right hand of brotherhood.
If your heart is right with my heart,
give me your hand.

Make friends of God's children;
help those who are weak;
forgetting in nothing,
His blessing to seek.

William D. Longstaff

Oh the comfort, the inexpressible comfort of
feeling safe with a person; having neither to
weigh thoughts nor measure words, but to
pour them all out, just as they are, chaff and
grain together, knowing that a faithful hand
will take and sift them, keep what is worth
keeping, and then, with the breath of
kindness, blow the rest away.

George Eliot

Day 14

Psalm 119:81-88　　　　　　　　*Judges 6:11-14*
Hebrews 12:11-12

The story is told of a man who tripped and
fell off a cliff. Clutching at the grasses on the
edge of the cliff he found himself for a
moment or two able to hang on and delay his
fall.

'Is there anyone up there?' he cried out
desperately. 'Yes,' came the reply, but no
further response. 'Who are you? Why don't
you help me?' shouted the man. 'I'm God,'
said the Voice, 'and I will help you. But you
must do exactly as I say.' 'O.K.,' whispered the
man, 'what have I to do?' 'First, *let go!*' 'Is
there anybody else up there?' called out the
man.

Poor fearful little Gideon had to do

something just like that to become the mighty man of valour God saw him as. Against an army which far outnumbered them, God's solution was to cut back even further on numbers!!

'With decrease thou shalt have increase. Count not as men count. Do not look into thy hand and say, "I have not enough," for with less, even with decrease, nothing shall be impossible to thee. Like with the army of old – I can do more even with less.'

Day 15

Psalm 119:89-95　　　　　*Deuteronomy 17:19*
Revelation 1:3; 5:2-5

Oh well, I guess it has been settled in heaven, and yet I would have died had my trust not been in Your word.

Prayer is not the privilege of a few. It is a reality easily accessible, for tiny children as for old men. It finds expression in innumerable ways.

Brother Roger of Taizé

Delightful I think it to be
　in the bosom of an isle
　　on the crest of a rock
　　　that I may see often
　　　　the calm of the sea,
that I may pore on one of my books
　good for my soul,
a while kneeling for beloved heaven,
　a while at psalms,
　　a while meditating upon the
　　Prince of Heaven

Columba

Little do men perceive what solitude is . . .

For a crowd is not company,
    and faces are but a gallery of pictures,
    and talk but a tinkling cymbal
      where there is no love.

Francis Bacon

Day 16

Psalm 119:96   1 Samuel 2:18-21   Matthew 5:48

Those of us who are unfamiliar with Greek apparently can miss out on the subtleties of meaning in many New Testament passages.

I am told that one such verse is that which says, Be perfect even as Your Heavenly Father is perfect. The two words used for 'perfect' are slightly different. The one is perfection in a limited, finite way, the other infinite.

What this means is that Jesus' command to be perfect is attainable (at least on a good day!) We are asked to be as perfect as we can be, even like he is as perfect as He can be. We are being asked to eat our dinner like our Daddy, not to eat our Daddy's dinner. As we grow, so does our capacity for such food.

'. . . like an onion: except that as you go in and in, each circle is larger than the last.'

C. S. Lewis

Day 17

Psalm 119:97-104   *Proverbs 2:1-6*
Luke 2:40-47, 52

Oh how I love Thy law! It is my meditation, all the day. 'I have more understanding than all my teachers . . .' Jesus had this, not because He was God, but because He was receptive in His human life to the Voice and direction of His Father. As a boy He had apparently not experienced the anointing of the Holy Spirit yet, but even so by saturating Himself in Scripture He was filled with understanding. Nor did He consider Himself unteachable, unable to learn from others.

Aidan of Lindisfarne had a similar love of Scripture, and especially the psalms which he would memorize, and speak by heart as he travelled on foot with his companions. In Eastern Europe and elsewhere, when copies of the Bible are hard-to-come-by, believers naturally treasure the word, and memorize as much as possible – No authority can remove the word hidden in your heart; it can be meditated upon all day long.

'If we practised silence a little bit more, then when we did speak we'd have something to say.'

J. T. Skinner

I weave a silence on to my lips
I weave a silence into my mind
I weave a silence within my heart
I close my ears to distractions
I close my eyes to attractions
I close my heart to temptations.

Calm me, O Lord, as you stilled the storm
Still me, O Lord, keep me from harm
Let all the tumult within me cease
Enfold me, Lord, in your peace.

David Adam

Day 18

Psalm 119:105-112   *Isaiah 30:20-21*
Hebrews 4:12-13

Your word is a lamp to my feet; where I am
standing now, and the step just before me that
I need not hesitate over. Your word is a light
to my path, shining a little way ahead, giving
me glimpses of direction to reassure me and
give me purpose. You shine faithfully upon my
life, but You cannot and will not take the steps
for me – it is I who must walk in Your way
and become the expression of Your will.

O Lord, give me wisdom. I dare not take a
step without You. When I cannot see all of the
way forward, help me to trust that You will
whisper in my heart or in my ear calling me
back when I might step to right or left of what
You intend for me. When there are snares for
my feet, help me to find the way through, and
continue with a rejoicing heart to the end.

A.R.

When we do not know what to do, let us ask
of Thee, that we may find out. We dare to ask
for light upon only one step at a time. We
would rather walk with thee than jump by
ourselves.

Peter Marshall

'Be Thou my vision, O Lord of my heart.'
(attributed to Patrick)

Day 19

Psalm 119:113-117   *Isaiah 55:8-9*
Ephesians 1:3; 2:6-7

Uphold me that I may live and not be ashamed of my hope. Hold me up and I shall be safe.

Give me a calm and confident trust in Thee. Make me willing to live just one day at a time. May my heart re-echo to Thy promise that only as I rest in Thee can the desires of my heart be given to me. And now help me to do my part in placing a guard around my thoughts, by resolutely refusing to return to my old haunts of distrust. I thank Thee for Thy love for me and for Thy help. Amen.

Peter Marshall

My greatest struggle is
the struggle not to struggle.
Arthur Burt

What the soul has to do in the time of quiet is only to be gentle and make no noise . . . Let the will quietly and prudently understand that one does not deal successfully with God by any efforts of one's own.

Teresa of Avila

I knew a man who always said 'Keep looking down.' 'You mean keep looking up, don't you?' 'No! No! We are seated together with Christ in heavenly places!'

Arthur Burt

Keep looking down, we're seated in the
heavenlies,
    God's mighty power has raised us over all.
Keep looking down, above all principalities
    for we have 'died and risen with the Lord'
And in His Name we have authority,
    and in His Name we shall prevail,
And in His Name we dare to face the enemy
    and in His Name we cannot fail.
      Keep looking down!

Jimmy Owens

Day 20

Psalm 119:118-120   Nehemiah 8:9   James 3:3-7

Man can control all kinds of things, but the
tongue may be the hardest of all. Once a word
is out of our mouth, it is hard to call it back.
Regret will not achieve this.

    God's rulings are not negotiable, either.
When we ignore them we hurt ourselves and
usually others as well. When we see the
damage we cause them we are aware of our
sin, and rightly are frightened of God. His
forgiveness frees us, but if we become
sensitized to His approval, and ask for the
sense of the 'fear of the Lord' this can help us
begin to know wisdom, *and* guard our tongue.

The man who never minces his words is
responsible for a lot of indigestion.

Hugh Redwood

The fear of the Lord can help us also to be
directed in the particular path that will best
help us in our own journey with God. The

paths may be as varied as the people! Specific obedience is what is required.

The way depends on where we live: one may go north, the other south, yet both will get to the city.

Hugh Redwood

Pour down upon us from heaven
the rich blessing of Thy forgiveness;
Thou who art uppermost in the City,
be Thou patient with us.

Grant to us, Thou Saviour of Glory,
the fear of God, the love of God and
    His affection, and the will of God
    to do on earth at all times
as angels and saints do in Heaven;
each day and night give us Thy peace.
Each day and night give us Thy peace.'

from Carmina Gadelica

Day 21

Psalm 119:121-128   *1 Kings 3:12-13*
                    Matthew 22:15-22

O Lord, teach us to number our days that we may apply our heart unto wisdom. Time is short, and no one of us knows how little time he has left. May we be found using wisely our time, our talents, and our strength.

Peter Marshall

Help us to know our judgement and justice, Lord. When Your judgements come, then stand by me, and teach me Your statutes so I can understand what justice really is.

Lord, You know I am Your servant, so give me understanding. Protect me from deception. Give me wisdom. When people try to trick me or confuse me with their questions and clever arguments, help me to see their heart. Help me to know when to say nothing. Help me to know when to answer what they are saying. Help me to know when it is an unspoken question that I should be answering.

Teach me to recognize the moments when You wait to intervene, so I can say, 'It is time – *You* work now, Lord!'

A.R.

Day 22

Psalm 119:129-132 Habakkuk 2:14 John 7:37-39

Jesus stood up and said, Whoever is thirsty, let them come to Me and drink, and drink, and drink.

O Lord, Your word enters and lets in the light. It gives understanding to the simple.

Open-mouthed and longing we come to You. To whom else shall we go? You have the words of eternal life. We have believed, some of us recklessly, some of us hesitantly, but we *have* believed, and have come to know that You are the only one who can satisfy our thirst.

I am an emptiness for Thee to fill;
my soul a cavern for Thy sea.

George MacDonald

Day 23

Psalm 119:133-135   *Isaiah 58:6, 8-10*
Romans 6:16-18

'Be sure your sins will find you out,' the proverb says. But listen to Hugh Redwood's comment on that:

Much better it would be, no doubt,
if Sin could always find us out.
This is the question: Why does Sin
so very often find us in?

Lord, order my steps in Your word. Don't let *any* iniquity have dominion over me; let no sin rule over me. Shine Your face on me, Your servant.

Lord, be Lord of all of me. I want You to be the Master, not my independence, my wrong actions and attachments, my wrong attitudes. None of these should master me.

Do now for me what I cannot do for myself. Break the habit patterns, reverse the direction of my negative thoughts, lift from me once again all anxieties and apprehensions.

Peter Marshall

Day 24

Psalm 119:136   Isaiah 5:1-4   Luke 13:34; 19:41

Centuries ago, Demonax the Cynic said this:

Probably all laws are useless;
for good men do not need laws at all,
and bad men are made no better by them.

We can see that he has a point – up to a point! But the writer of the psalms says, 'Streams of tears flow from my eyes because your law is obeyed.' For this to be *our* response we need to have compassion for those who do not take heed of God's law. For this to be *our* response we need to be touched with the sorrow of God's heart, and long to comfort Him. For this to be *our* response we need to believe that the law of God is good, and just, and given to care for and tend the people He loves.

Does it move us to tears that the law of God is abandoned, ignored, or even scorned? Does it move us to action when we realize that most people have little concept of what the laws of God are? Is our heart under Kingdom rule? or do we have divided loyalties, as if we were citizens of two kingdoms, obeying whichever rule of conduct happens to suit us at the time?

'What more could I have done for you than I have done?' says the Lord, 'for I have loved you!'
And Jesus wept.

Day 25

Psalm 119:137–140   *2 Kings 10:16–17*
            Matthew 23:4, 13

Often in the past, Lord, I have come to Thee with heavy heart and burdened life. And Thou hast answered my prayers and graciously lifted the burden from me. Yet with a strange

perversion, I still refuse to leave my burdens
with Thee. Always I gather them up - those
heavy bundles of fears and anxieties - and
shoulder them again.

Peter Marshall

Some of the strongest words You speak, Lord,
are those condemning
   people who put heavy loads on the backs
      of others,
   people who delight in seeing others
      weighed down by their guilt and failure,
   people whose eyelids judge even their
      friends

Your house should be built of living stones,
not sinking ones. Jesus, the prophecies about
You said that the zeal for Your house
consumed You. May that zeal consume us, too.
Help us to destroy everything that gets in Your
way, but to do so with a pure heart.

My soul is dry dust,
   choking worldly ambition
My soul is wet earth,
   bearing rich fruits of grace
My soul is a flame of fire,
   blazing with passionate love.
from The Black Book of Carmarthen, *Wales*

Day 26

Psalm 119:141-143   *Jeremiah 9:23-24*
          Matthew 11:25-26

'I am small and despised.'
'Yes, but have I not said, "Do not despise the
day of small things!"?'

I'd rather be a little thing climbing up
than a big thing tumbling down.

(old Sunday-school song)

The man to whom little is not enough
will not benefit from more.

Columbanus

Day 27

Psalm 119:144   Deuteronomy 32:47   Luke 7:1-7

Many a man has grown upright because his
tendrils have clung to a cross.

Hugh Redwood

By Your cross and resurrection You have
redeemed the world.
    Say but the word, give me understanding,
and I shall live. I shall not die, but I shall live
and proclaim what You have done, Lord. Just
say the word, Lord. Speak it to me. There is a
power within the word You speak which is
greater than the word itself. Give me
understanding. Only You can impart revelation.
People may explain to me, but only You can
reveal it to me, even then, in a way that makes
me realize it.
    Realize that word within my heart. Realize
Your word in my life. Make it real, Lord, in
me. Let Jesus the Living Word become flesh
again, and live among us, spoken through our
lives to a world that is dying for want of the
knowledge of Him.
    Send forth Your word and heal them. Let
Your glory be over all the earth.

A. R./Arthur Burt

Day 28

Each of the sections of this, the longest of
psalms, has an initial letter as its title,
following the Hebrew alphabet. Like the
month, the alphabet and the psalm are nearing
the end. This section, 'Koph', speaks of a
mature response of dependency and prayer in
difficult circumstances. The soul cries out to
God and waits in silent dependency on Him.

If we are the witness to Christ in today's
market places, where there are constant
demands on our whole person, we need
silence. If we are to be always available, not
only physically, but by empathy, sympathy,
friendship, understanding . . . we need
silence. To be able to give joyous, unflagging
hospitality, not only of house and food, but
of mind, heart, body and soul, we need
silence.

Catherine de Hueck Doherty

Sometimes God will wake us in the night to
watch with Him and see things from a new
perspective. Sometimes it's the only time He
can be sure of getting our complete attention.
Sometimes that is the time, the exact time,
when our prayers are needed.

Day 29

Psalm 119:153-160   Jonah 2:5-7   Romans 8:11

Your word was true from the beginning. Every one of Your righteous judgements endures for ever. Quicken me. Restore me to life. Lord, I believe.

Hal Lindsey is the author of *The Late Great Planet Earth* which (for a short time!) enjoyed immense popularity amongst Christian readers of some years ago. The following incident is from a subsequent book *The Terminal Generation*.

A nurse came up to me after I'd just spoken and said, 'Hal, will you please come and meet a soldier I brought over from the veterans' hospital? He accepted Christ as His Saviour and Lord as a result of my reading your book to him. It really took courage for him to come here tonight – he's in great pain because both arms and legs have been amputated. He lost them in Vietnam.' When I walked up to the wheeled stretcher on which he was lying, the young man looked up with a radiant face and said, 'Tell me, Hal, will my new body have arms and legs?' While choking back tears I turned to Philippians 3:20 and 21 and read:
' "But our citizenship is in heaven. And we eagerly await a Saviour from there, the Lord Jesus Christ, who, by the power that enables him to bring everything under his control, will transform our lowly bodies so that they will be like his glorious body." – Jim,' I said, 'your body will be like Jesus

Christ's glorious body. We know that His resurrection body is perfect, so we know that yours will be, too.'

Day 30

Psalm 119:161-168   *1 Samuel 26:2, 7-9,*
Titus 3:1-2   *12-13, 22-23*

Great peace have they who love Your law; nothing offends them.

Lord, do I love Your law? Is it great peace that I experience? or just medium-sized peace?

Am I easily offended? easily tripped up? easily stumbled?

Give me the peace that never returns evil for evil.

Peace and comfort can be found nowhere except in simple obedience.

François Fénelon

Day 31

Psalm 119:169-176   *Nehemiah 8:12*
Philemon 4-7

This month we have read Psalm 119 and prayed: 'Give me understanding according to Your word.'

'Father, I know now, if I never knew it before, that only in You can my restless human heart find any peace. For I began life without knowledge, but full of needs. And the turmoil of my mind, the dissatisfaction of my life all stem from trying to meet those needs with the wrong things and in the wrong places.'

Peter Marshall

I have strayed like a lost sheep. Seek your servant. Lord, You have found me, loved and fed me. Now I must send something to others for whom nothing has been prepared.

It is everyone's duty to pray to God for their friends. And for all their friends, whether they are numerous or few. To make a habit of it may be to impose considerable demands upon time and memory, but it is not merely worthwhile, it is a matter of supreme importance. If you've only a handful of friends, it won't take long, and, if you're one of the lucky ones, with more friends than you can remember all at once, card-index them. Pray for them in instalments, but pray for them. Nobody knows what they may be doing if they pray for a friend tonight.

Hugh Redwood – God in the Shadows.

NOVEMBER READINGS

Chosen People

Day 1 Psalm 39:13
       Deuteronomy 7:6
       Acts 22:11–6
Day 2 Psalm 98:6–7
       Micah 7:19
       1 Corinthians 15:50–54
Day 3 Psalm 114:7–8; 118:20–28
       Leviticus 23:33, 39–43
       John 7:2–6, 8–11, 14–17, 37–46
Day 4 Psalm 119:96–106
       Jeremiah 31:33–34
       1 Timothy 4:13
       2 Timothy 3:14–4:3
Day 5 Psalm 9:1
       Deuteronomy 6:4–9; 11:13–21
       Matthew 22:35–38
Day 6 Psalm 46:1–3, 6–11
       1 Kings 17:9–16
       John 10:1–10, 14–16, 19, 24–27
Day 7 Psalm 42:7
       Jonah 1:17–2:2
       Matthew 12:38–41
Day 8 Psalm 111:9; 109:13, 17–22
       Exodus 3:13–15
       Isaiah 43:1
       Luke 1:47, 49, 5–14, 21–23, 57–64
Day 9 Psalm 17:10, 14–15
       Deuteronomy 15:7–11
       1 Corinthians 13:3
Day 10 Psalm 89:19–20, 26–29, 34
       1 Samuel 20:30–34, 42

Mark 14:22-24
Day 11 Psalm 68:1, 3
Esther 3:1-6
Luke 1:51-55
Day 12 Psalm 107:43
Deuteronomy 33:3
John 15:15b-16
Day 13 Psalm 39:2
Isaiah 61:1, 3
John 20:1-4, 11-16
Day 14 Psalm 78:3-8
Isaiah 62:1
Romans 11:26-29
Day 15 Psalm 137:4
Genesis 18:16-17, 20-33
2 Peter 3:9, 17
Day 16 Psalm 40:7
Isaiah 58:9
Hebrews 10:7
Day 17 Psalm 105:26-38, 43
Exodus 7:20-24: 8:6-8, 16-19; 9:10-11
Acts 7:36
Day 18 Psalm 136:1-4, 10-12
Exodus 13:1-3, 6-8, 11-15
Mark 14:14-16
Day 19 Psalm 16:9-11
2 Chronicles 30:2-5
1 Corinthians 5:7-8
Day 20 Psalm 147:14
Leviticus 23:9-11
James 1:17-18
Day 21 Psalm 80:7-14, 18
Genesis 4:10
2 Timothy 2:2, 7
Day 22 Psalm 121:3, 5-8
Genesis 24:34, 37-46, 57-58
Hebrews 11:5, 8-10, 13-16

Day 23 Psalm 65:9–13
      Leviticus 23:15–17, 22
      Acts 2:1–2, 44-45
Day 24 Psalm 126:2, 5–6
      Ruth 3:18; 4:13–16
      John 10:16
Day 25 Psalm 19:1–6
      Judges 21:16–25
      1 Corinthians 7:9–12
Day 26 Psalm 116:3–4
      Ecclesiastes 12:14
      Luke 21:21
Day 27 Psalm 30:5b
      Job 1:21–22; 2:9–13
      John 11:32–40
Day 28 Psalm 104:19–23
      Isaiah 45:3, 5–7
      Mark 1:21–22, 29–32
Day 29 Psalm 45:1
      Leviticus 26:2–4
      Romans 8:26
Day 30 Psalm 116:7
      Isaiah 49:15–16
      2 John 12

Day 1

Psalm 39:13   *Deuteronomy 7:6*   *Acts 22:11–16*

An unknown poet once wrote:
  How odd
  of God
  to choose
  the Jews!

This month we will be looking at the life and calling, tradition and history of God's very own *chosen people*, and seeing what we can learn.

When Tevye in 'Fiddler on the Roof' is warned by the constable of the coming 'pogrom' that will be a new wave of trouble for the Jewish community he turns to heaven, and says:

  'Dear God, did You have to send me news like that? It's true we are the Chosen People. But once in a while can't You choose someone else?'

Dave Berg (of 'MAD' magazine) asks:

CHOSEN FOR WHAT? Chosen to lead in the Path of Righteousness? Maybe. Chosen to be a Light unto the World? Maybe. Chosen to bear witness to my Friend, Whose name is GOD? Maybe. OR Chosen to take the BLAME from all the BLAME THROWERS for everything that goes wrong in the world. . . . the old story tells of a wise man talking to his bigoted acquaintance and he says, 'You're right, all the trouble in this world is caused by the Jews – AND THE BICYCLE RIDERS!'
  The bigot asked, 'Why bicycle riders?'
  The wise man says, 'WHY THE JEWS?'

Day 2

Psalm 98:6–7   *Micah 7:19*
1 Corinthians 15:50–54

Rosh Hashana is the name of the Jewish new
year festival, and on the first day of the new
year a ceremony called 'Tashlich' takes place
near a source of water. The ceremony
originated in Germany in the fourteenth
century in a non-Jewish custom – fish were fed
with breadcrumbs as a sign of cleansing from
sins. Now the prayer used is one which is
based on the prophet Micah's words 'and cast
all thy sins into the depths of the sea'.

Corrie ten Boom, whose family loved and
protected the Jews during the Nazi occupation
of Holland, has said:

When God forgives our sins, He separates
them as far from us as the east is from the
west, buries them in the bottom of the
deepest sea, and puts up a sign for the
Devil, saying, NO FISHING!

Day 3

Psalm 114:7–8; 118:20–28 Leviticus 23:33, 39–43
John 7:2–6, 8–11, 14–17, 37–46

The Feast of Tabernacles or booths (Succot) is
the context for John's Gospel chapters 7 to 9.

During the Feast the procession carrying
water from the pool of Siloam would circle
the Temple and pour their libations on the
altar, and this was done seven times in the last

day of the Feast. Palm-branches and fruit were waved before God and psalms 113 to 118 always sung.

> Bonfires were lit, and men of piety danced, holding lighted torches and singing songs and hymns to the accompaniment of harps, lyres, cymbals and trumpets played by Levites.

Talmud

In the evening of the final day of the Feast there was a magnificent sight as the lamps were lit in the Court of the Women. Light streamed forth so that the Temple shone with an incredible brightness of light. It seems that this was the moment that occasioned Jesus' amazing statement:
'I AM the Light of the world.'

Day 4

Psalm 119:96–106   *Jeremiah 31:33–34*
1 Timothy 4:13 2   *Timothy 3:14–4:3*

Simchat Torah, the Rejoicing of the Law, is not a biblically prescribed feast, but occurs immediately after Succot.

The Scrolls of the Law are taken out of the Holy Ark and carried in men's arms. Fathers dance with their children, and women throw sweets on them. According to tradition, the synagogue must be encircled seven times or more. The festival is celebrated on the day on which the reading of the Torah is completed and begun again from Genesis. The Torah is read on an annual cycle, so the Jewish community created a great festival of joy on a day that could have been only a day of tedious re-rolling of the community's scrolls from the end to the beginning. We might also ask, is it not a great cause for rejoicing to complete a reading of the Scriptures by the community and to have the opportunity to begin reading again!

Daniel Juster in his study *Jewish Roots* asks whether the early Messianic Jews would have had an ark.

'I believe they did,' he says. 'We historically know that they read the Torah (ie Genesis to Deuteronomy). In the first century Torahs were kept in an ark! Did they keep the New Testament Scriptures in the Ark? We do not know. However, we do know that ancient eastern churches that stem back to the Syrian church have ark-like structures in which they keep the Scriptures.'

Among some of the Orthodox Hasidic communities today this celebration soars into great heights of joy and energy. For Messianic Jews there is further cause for rejoicing – all true believers in Messiah are accounted righteous and have the joy of God's own Torah written on our hearts by His Spirit.

So GOD went to Moses and said,
   'I have a commandment for you.'
     'How much is it?'
       'Nothing.'
         'Good, then I'll take ten.'
          from 'My Friend, GOD'

Day 5

Psalm 9:1   *Deuteronomy 6:4-9; 11:13-21*
                    Matthew 22:35-38

A mezzuzah (Hebrew for 'doorpost') is a cylinder of metal or wood put aslant on the right-hand doorpost of the house. Inside is a rolled fragment of parchment on which the summary of the Deuteronomy command is written to

Remember God and love Him with your all.

Anyone going in or out is obliged to remember it and may stretch out their hand towards it, and kiss the hand. In such a house the whole course of life ought to be subject to the authority of God's word.

A tale is told of a Gentile buying a house from a Jew, and noticing the mezzuzah, asking its significance. 'This is a mezzuzah,' the Jew explained. 'Inside the case you see is a scroll on which are written the most sacred and holy words of the Jewish law.'

When the transaction was completed, the purchaser of the house was interested to see if the mezzuzah would be taken with the outgoing family. But no, the mezzuzah stayed, and every day he saw it on his way in or out, until finally his curiosity would hold no longer. With a small screwdriver he removed the case, opened the tiny parchments with trembling fingers, and read:

'HELP! I am being held prisoner in a mezzuzah factory.'

To spiritualize the story unmercifully; we too are prisoners, faced day to day with the question, 'Do you seek HIM with all your heart, and with all your soul, and with all your mind, and with all your strength?'

A-men, make us Your captives, Lord, for only then can we be free.

Day 6

Psalm 46:1–3, 6–11   1 Kings 17:9–16
John 10:1–10, 14–16, 19, 24–27

The Feast of Dedication mentioned in John's Gospel is more commonly known as Hanukah, and usually occurs close to Christmas-time. It recalls the days of the Maccabees who led the Jewish people in revolt against their Syrio-Greek oppressors during the inter-testamental period. The accounts of these events will be found in translations of the Apocrypha, or in some Catholic editions of the Scriptures which include deutero-canonical texts.

Jesus' words are about being a good, true shepherd, and are intended as a contrast to the evil shepherd who had compromised their religious practices with those of pagan Greek culture.

The Menorah used during the eight days of Hanukah is a candle-stick with eight stems, lit by an extra candle called the shammas. It recalls how when the Temple was re-dedicated after the victory of the Maccabees and the Menorah was lit they found only enough oil to keep it alight for one day (and this original Menorah was supplied by oil). Only the prescribed oil could be used and it took eight days before it could be prepared. Miraculously the one day's supply was enough for the eight days.

The lighted Menorah in Jewish households of today should be placed in a window so everyone can see it. Each day an extra light is lit in turn.

This song 'Maoz Tzur' is a traditional one sung after the candles are lit:

Rock of Ages, let our song
praise Thy saving power;
Thou, amidst the raging foes
wast our shelt'ring tower.
Furious they assailed us
but Thine arm availed us,
and Thy word broke their sword
when our own strength failed us.

Day 7

Psalm 42:7   Jonah 1:17–2:2   Matthew 12:38–41

'Jonah was in the belly of the fish.'

Many people will say: 'That is impossible, that is a fable.' But God, who can make fishes 100 feet long, says that it is possible. (Can you make a fish one inch long?) And God can do an even greater miracle: Christ says that as Jonah was three days and nights in the stomach of the fish, so He would be three days and three nights in the heart of the earth, in the grave, and then rise from the dead. Jonah says inside the fish: 'Salvation is of the Lord!' Salvation, in Hebrew, is Yeshua, or Jeshua; that is the Hebrew name for Jesus. . .

Professor Samuel Schultz argues that there is

no room for the idea of a harsh vindictive
God of justice in the Old Testament to be
contrasted with a God of love and mercy in
the New. Love and mercy are always offered
before judgement is rendered. Yeshua's
warnings concerning judgement in the New
Testament are as severe as anything in the Old,
even if we argue that the highest personal
revelation of God's love is seen in Yeshua!

Incidentally, the April 4th, 1896 *Literary
Digest* gave a story of a Mediterranean whale
that demolished the harpoon boat.

> Two men were lost . . . One was found alive
> in the whale's belly a day and a half after it
> was killed. James Bartley lived with no after
> effects except his skin was tanned by the
> gastric juices.'

F. J Dake

Day 8

Psalm 111:9; 109:13 17–22   *Exodus 3:13–15*
Isaiah 43:1   Luke 1:47, 49, 5–14, 21–23, 57–64

The Jews would not willingly tread upon the
smallest piece of paper in their way, but took
it up; for possibly, said they, the name of God
may be upon it. Though there was a little
superstition in this, yet truly there is nothing
but good religion in it, if we apply it to man.
Trample not on any; there may be some work
of grace there, that thou knowest not of. The
name of God may be written upon that soul
thou treadest on: it may be a soul that Christ
thought so much of as to give his precious

blood for it; therefore, despise it not.

Samuel Taylor Coleridge

The letters J H W H are a jumble of Hebrew consonants, and a better translation than Jehovah is 'The Lord'. The name of God is so awful, so unpronounceable, that it has never been used by any of his creatures. Indeed, it is said that if, inadvertently, the great and terrible name of God should be spoken, the universe would explode.

Madeleine L'Engle

The Scriptures recognize how important a name is; it denotes someone in particular, and affirms that they have significance. One of the strongest curses ever framed is that someone's name be cut off, remembered no more.

Madeleine L'Engle writes:

> . . . we live in a world which would reduce us to our social security numbers. Area codes, zip codes, credit card codes, all take precedence over our names. Our signatures already mean so little that it wouldn't be a surprise if, by the year 2000, we, like prisoners, are known only by our numbers. But that is not how it was meant to be.

Survivors of the concentration camps still have numbers branded on their bodies; they bear the mark of a system that needed to dehumanize them.

In contrast Judith MacNutt writes:

> I believe my name 'Judith' was given to my mother in prayer; it means 'Jewess'. When I moved to Israel in the mid-'70s that name took on a new meaning. I had felt called to

Israel for several years and responded to that call, not knowing what was in store for me.

When I arrived in Jerusalem, I finally understood what had been obscurely felt in my heart for years, I felt immediately at home with the land and the people, and experienced a deep peace, even though I was in a country torn by war and terrorist attacks. I knew I was in the centre of God's perfect will, and found it easy to love the work He had called me to. I was so happy!

As a Christian, I longed for acceptance in a largely Jewish state. I was mostly greeted with suspicious glances and questions. These people had been greatly persecuted by Christians for centuries and were very guarded. I longed for an open door – and then I gave my name:

'Judith'.

A smile, with a questioning look, would cross their faces, followed by the question

'Are you Jewish?'

Then I could respond with,

'I'm Jewish in my heart.'

Long before I was born, God had told my parents a name, a name that would reflect my destiny and one of the great loves of my life.

Day 9

Psalm 17:10, 14–15   *Deuteronomy 15:7–11*
1 Corinthians 13:3

STOOPING TO HELP SOMEBODY. This position is called 'MITZVAH', a good deed.

This, they say, NUDGES GOD right to the 'BOOK OF GOLDEN DEEDS'. And GOD writes down the MITZVAH in DIAMOND-STUDDED LETTERS TEN FEET HIGH.

In the twelfth century Moses Maimonides devised eight ways to nudge GOD for a MITZVAH while performing CHARITY. EACH ONE HIGHER THAN THE OTHER. The highest degree is to make the man who needs charity SELF-SUPPORTING. The next highest degree is where the one that GIVES and the one that RECEIVES are NOT aware of each other. The third Inferior degree is where the RECIPIENT knows the GIVER, but the giver does NOT know the recipient. A lesser Mitzvah is when the poor man knows to whom he is indebted, but the giver does not know to whom he has given. The fifth degree is where the giver puts alms into the hands of the poor without being asked. The sixth degree is where he puts money into the hands of the poor AFTER being asked. The seventh degree is where he gives LESS than he should, but does so CHEERFULLY. The eighth degree is where he gives RESENTFULLY.

But there's a CATCH to all these MITZVAHS. It's best illustrated by an old story about a Rabbi, who was so addicted to golf that he even snuck off on the HIGH HOLY DAY to play. That day he made a HOLE IN ONE. As he danced about with exultation, there was a rumble of thunder and a clap of lightning, and GOD'S voice boomed down on him. 'SO WHO ARE YOU GOING TO TELL?' THAT'S the CATCH when you earn a MITZVAH. 'SO WHO ARE YOU GOING TO TELL? IF YOU DO, YOU'LL LOSE IT. The question is, what

have you DONE for someone today, that you
DIDN'T HAVE TO DO . . . and whom DIDN'T
YOU TELL?'

from My Friend GOD by Dave Berg

Day 10

Psalm 89:19–20, 26–29, 34
1 Samuel 20:30–34, 42   *Mark 14:22–24*

It is important to the understanding of the
story of David and Saul to understand that
David and Jonathon, Saul's son, had entered
into a covenant relationship with each other.

This agreement was far more than a
friendship or business contract – in some ways
its significance was equal to or greater than
that of marriage. It involved a vow that was
binding for life, sealed by the shedding of
blood, an exchange of possessions, a covenant
meal of bread and wine with the promise,

> This bread is my body, all my strength is
> yours and this wine my blood which I will
> shed willingly on your behalf. Your enemies
> become my enemies, too. All I have is yours
> by right.

Abram and God made such a covenant, and on
the strength of it God could demand the
surrender of his only son. Jesus spoke out his
part of a similar covenant at the Seder meal
with his disciples, and we know that even if
we are faithless He remains faithful.

When Saul suspected David and Jonathan
had become covenant-brothers he was angry
because whether Jonathan lived or died David
became king by right if he should so choose.

Day 11

Psalm 68:1, 3   *Esther 3:1–6*   *Luke 1:51–55*

Purim, which commemorates the deliverance
of the Jews from the hands of Haman through
Esther the queen and her uncle Mordecai, is
the feast of reversals. It reminds us that
eventually the Evil One's machinations will be
tolerated no longer and all shall be well and all
manner of things shall be well.

Purim is the nearest thing Judaism has to a
carnival. The Talmud gives leave to a
worshipper to drink on this day until he
cannot tell the difference between 'Blessed be
Moredecai' and 'Cursed be Haman'. To the
credit of many otherwise non-observant Jews,
they often do their best to comply. In Israel a
public street festival not unlike Mardi Gras has
sprung up, with the name As'lo Yoda, the
Talmud word for 'until he cannot tell the
difference'.

The day before Purim is the Fast of Esther, a
sunrise-to-sundown abstention. At sundown
the synagogues fill up. The marked difference
between this and all other occasions of the
Jewish year is the number of children on
hand. Purim is the children's night in the
house of the Lord. It always has been, and the
children sense their rights and exercise them.

They carry flags and noisemakers, the
traditional whirling rattles called 'groggers',
which can make a staggering racket. After the
evening prayers the reading of the Book of
Esther begins, solemnly enough, with the
customary blessing over a scroll and the
chanting of the opening verses in a special

musical mode heard only on this holiday. The Reader chants through the first and second chapters and comes at last to the long-awaited sentence,

'After these things, the king raised to power Haman the Agagite'

– but nobody hears the last two words. The name 'Haman' triggers off stamping, pounding, and a hurricane of groggers. The Reader waits patiently. The din dies. He chants on, and soon strikes another 'Haman'. Bedlam breaks loose again. This continues, and since Haman is now a chief figure in the story, the noisy outbursts come pretty frequently. The children, far from getting tired or bored, warm up to the work. They do it with sure mob instinct; poised silence during the reading, explosions on each 'Haman'. Passages occur where Haman's name crops up several times in a very short space. The children's assaults come like pistol shots. The Reader's patience wears thin and finally breaks. It is impossible to read with so many interruptions.

He gestures angrily at the children through the grogger storm and shoots a glance of appeal to the rabbi. This, of course, is what the children have been waiting for . . . Thereafter to the end of it is a merciless battle between the Reader and the children. He tries to slur over the thick falling 'Hamans, they trip him every time with raucous salvos. He stumbles on to the final verse, exhausted, beaten, furious, and all is disordered hilarity in the synagogue. It is perhaps not quite fair to make the Reader stand in for Haman on this evening, but that is approximately what happens.

This is my God, Herman Wouk

Day 12

Psalm 107:43 Deuteronomy 33:3 John 15:15b–16

Rabbinic disciples were people who were attached to a particular person and who then themselves decided to follow and accept the teachings of that person. To become a disciple was entirely up to the individual: they chose to follow a rabbi and accept his teachings until they felt able to leave and establish independent status as teachers themselves. Jesus was different. He chose his disciples.

Keith Whitehead, Emmaus Community

In this light it is interesting to look again at the story of Mary and Martha. The contrast between them is not just that between contemplative and active. The expression 'sit at the feet of' is not just a description of what would make a good snapshot of Lazarus, Mary and Martha to put in the family album. Mary sat listening to Jesus, looking up into His face. Instead it is the equivalent of Saul of Tarsus studying for a prolonged period under Rabbi Gamaliel. When Jesus disputed with other teachers he often argued from the rabbinical principle, 'From the minor case to the major', or as Arthur Burt would say, 'The greater includes the lesser'. So if circumcision could be performed on the Sabbath to make a minor member of the body whole before God, then miraculous power could be used on the Sabbath to heal and make a whole body whole. Or if the commandment said to not commit adultery, the greater which included this would say 'not even in your heart'. The

greater includes the lesser, but the small things
mattered, too.

I have a friend you can go to with
your small problems.
My friend's name is
GOD.

Dave Berg

Day 13

Psalm 39:2   Isaiah 61:1, 3   John 20:1–4, 11–16

As a young Dutch-Jewish refugee Johanna-Ruth
Dobschiner found an illustrated children's
Bible in the home she was evacuated to, and
re-read the familiar stories of Noah, Abraham,
Isaac, Jacob, Joseph, Moses and Pharaoh,
Joshua, Saul, David, Solomon, Haman,
Jeremiah, Isaiah, and Malachi . . .

Almost unconsciously I entered a part of
history previously unknown to me, yet
strangely familiar. It still dealt with the
people of Israel but new characters had
entered the scene, names I had never been
taught, names which had never been
mentioned at home or in school lessons.
Scenes which took place in Synagogue and
Temple, according to this Bible, registered a
blank when searching my memory. Yet all
the stories were so obviously Jewish . . .
One person outshone all others in these
stories – a prophet born in Israel. As the
weeks and months passed by, His life
became part of mine. The readings about
Him and incidents concerning Him became

more important to me than anything else in my own environment. I found I could tolerate my isolation without frustration, always longing for the next opportunity to learn more about Him for he had become my hero.

Then the cross:

While still reading of His agonies, in myself I wished for Him to show the power that was His, and free Himself from that cross. I knew He would do it, and as I read on I waited eagerly for the moment when this would be described . . . Instead, 'It is finished.' I had lost the one I loved dearly, although I had never met Him, except within the pages of this book. Now all was lost to me.

According to the custom of my people I mourned for Him seven days. My thoughts were wholly centred on my loss and a deep sense of depression settled upon me. I was weepy, edgy, moody and unhappy. True, I had suffered disappointment, but why not act as an adult and read the remaining pages of the book?

The first day of the week, and Mary finds His grave empty, the body stolen. What next! Having fought back her tears for so long, Mary now gave way to her grief. She felt as I had done during these past ten days, and again I joined in her sorrow.

. . . and then continued reading . . .

Selected to Live, *J. R. Dobschiner*

Day 14

Psalm 78:3–8   Isaiah 62:1   Romans 11:26–29

The atmosphere of the New Testament carried on the Spirit of the Hebrew Scriptures pervasively and profoundly – but Rabbinic Judaism replaces revelation with human reason, and this development was well underway even before the coming of Jesus, and culminated in the rejection of Him and the witness of His Jewish apostles by the first-century Jewish religion leadership. Rabbinic Judaism is the child of the first-century Pharisees who added the prayer of condemnation against Jewish believers and Jesus to synagogue liturgy. This all took place long before the Church had become infiltrated by paganism and begun to reject its Jewish roots.

Sometimes in John's Gospel and other places we are confused by the phrase 'the Jews' being used to condemn the religious establishment, Pharisees, Sadducees and religious leaders: were not John and the other writers also Jews? Americans abroad are called 'Yanks', but in the Southern United States 'Yankee' is used as a sectional term to refer to the North. Galilean Jews referred to Judeans as 'the Jews' since 'Judean' and 'Jew' in Greek are the same word.

Such condemnations were after all in-house criticisms and not intended as ammunition for generations of anti-semites.

Anti-semites never quote any of the following:

John 4:22 'Salvation is of the Jews', that
Jesus was, is and forever will be a Jew
descended from Jacob! or that 'the common
people (Jews) 'heard Him gladly,' that many
wept openly at His death and that the
priestly establishment feared all of Jesuralem
following Him (Luke 20:19, 22:2) that
myriads of Jews did follow Him (Acts 21:20)
that Jewish apostles spread the good news of
Yeshua throughout the world.

The proper Scriptural response is gratitude and
love. Paul says, 'It is not you who support the
root, but the root supports you.'
(Romans 11:18)

Day 15

Psalm 137:4   *Genesis 18:16–17, 20–33*
       2 Peter 3:9, 17

Let me tell you an old Hebrew legend:

It is written that as long as GOD can find 36
JUST MEN, HE'LL keep this world going.

They are called 'Lamed Vornicks' meaning 36.
It is also rumoured that GOD sends out a
prophet in every generation to find these 36
JUST MEN. So far there are only 35 names on
that list. Now I'm not claiming to be a
prophet. But somewhere, reading these
words at this very moment is the 36th JUST
MAN!

*　　*　　*

Now the world is saved!

*   *   *

Dave Berg

Elie Wiesel writes:

> One of the Just Men came to Sodom,
> determined to save its inhabitants from sin
> and punishment. Night and day he walked
> the streets and markets protesting against
> greed and theft, falsehood and indifference.
> In the beginning, people listened and smiled
> ironically. Then they stopped listening: he
> no longer amused them. The killers went on
> killing, the wise kept silent, as if there were
> no Just Man in their midst.
>
> One day a child, moved by compassion for
> the unfortunate teacher, approached him
> with these words:
>
> 'Poor stranger, you shout, you scream,
> don't you see that it is hopeless?'
>
> 'Yes, I see,' answered the Just Man.
>
> 'Then why do you go on?'
>
> 'I'll tell you why. In the beginning, I
> thought I could change man. Today, I know
> I cannot. If I still shout today, if I still
> scream, it is to prevent man from ultimately
> changing me.'

Day 16

Psalm 40:7   Isaiah 58:9   Hebrews 10:7

God desires to look at us with open face and
say, Here I am and I am here for you. The
Hebrew word for this is 'Hineni' – and there

are familiar stories of people responding to God in this way. Hineni means I'm ready, Lord; I'll go if You send me; I'm listening, Lord, tell me what You would have me know.

'Abraham!' 'Hineni,' he replied. 'Take your son, your only son Isaac, whom you love, and go to the region of Moriah. Sacrifice him there.'

Isaac says to Abraham, 'Father?' 'Hineni?' 'The fire and the wood are here, where is the lamb for the sacrifice?'

God called to Moses from the bush that was burning, 'Moses! Moses!'
And Moses said, 'Hineni.'

A voice called in the night. The child Samuel gave answer: 'Hineni – what do you want?'

'Whom shall I send, and who will go for me?' said the voice from the midst of the throne.
And Isaiah responded. 'HINENI.'

Lord God, help us to be willing and available, open to your call, to say 'Hineni Adonai. Here I am.'

Day 17

Psalm 105:26–38, 43
Exodus 7:20–24; 8:6–8, 16–19; 9:10–11 Acts 7:36

The plagues, although grievous physical trials to the Egyptians, represent far more:
The plagues undercut faith in the Egyptian gods and show the powerlessness of the Egyptian gods to protect Egypt from the God of Israel. The Nile, for example, is a 'god'; it

turns rancid. Hupi is the frog 'god' and Egypt is given enough frogs to feast on frogs' legs for decades to come! The sun is a chief 'god'; it is blotted out by darkness. Most alarming is the death of the first born – especially Pharoah's own first born – who would have been considered an incarnation of the sun god!

Egyptian religion was a very sophisticated pagan ritual of magic and superstition. Egypt was the most powerful nation of that age. Therefore, the exodus of this enslaved people was truly a defeat of paganism, of all false gods, of all superstition and magic, a defeat authored by the one Creator – God!

The defeat of Egypt and its gods by the Israelites could only lead to the conclusion that God is the Lord of all the earth. The exodus of Israel struck terror into the hearts of the decadent, utterly corrupt Canaanite people whom Israel was to conquer.

Daniel Juster Jewish Roots

Day 18

Psalm 136:1–4, 10–12   Exodus 13:13, 6–8, 11–15
Mark 14:14–16

The family is gathered for the Seder meal, and a young boy asks the question that demands the recounting of the story of the miracle of the exodus, a story rehearsed from generation to generation.

'Why is this evening
different from all other evenings?'

'Because we were once slaves
of the Pharoah of Egypt;
but the Lord heard our voice:
He felt our sorrow
and understood our oppression;
with His outstretched arm
He led us to Egypt.
Then we were at last set free.
Blessed is the Lord
who promised salvation to Israel:
He has kept His promise
and kept the Covenant
     He established with Abraham.'

Day 19

Psalm 16:9–11   *2 Chronicles 30:2–5*
               1 Corinthians 5:7–8

Jesus and his disciples celebrate the Passover
meal a full day earlier than they should, since
he knows that if they waited it would not be
possible, and he has so desired to share the
feast with them, and will not be disappointed.
(They are only one day out, after all, and in 2
Chronicles we read how God blessed the
reinstitution of Passover even when by force of
circumstance His people were a whole month
out from the correct date.) Jesus would be on
trial all night and nailed to the cross around
nine the next morning. Six hours later he died
at the exact time when the Passover lambs
were also killed. At the sunset the Preparation
would be over and the Passover Feast would
begin which must be observed as Sabbath
(Leviticus 23:4-8) known as the first day of

unleavened bread. Any leaven is carefully
hunted for and swept out of a Jewish home
before these seven days begin. The soldiers are
urged to break the legs of crucified men so
they will die more quickly and be removed
before the Feast Sabbath begins: Jesus is
already dead by now. He is carried hastily to a
borrowed tomb, observed by the women.
Between the Feast and the usual weekly
Sabbath they have time to prepare the spices
for his embalming, then early on the first day
of the week, when it is already 'the third day
since all this took place' they hurry to the
tomb and find him gone. Death could not hold
him.

Day 20

Psalm 147:14   Leviticus 23:9–11   James 1:17–18

On the fourteenth day of that month the
Passover lamb was prepared. After sunset it
was eaten, and this began the Sabbath which
was a high holy day, the first day of
unleavened bread. On the next day, the
sixteenth, the day after this Sabbath day when
no work was done, a priest would search for
the first sprouts of grain in the ground, carry
his find back to the Temple and wave them
before the Lord as the 'first fruits'.

Another seven times seven days, a sabbath of
sabbaths, makes fifty days, 'pentecost', and by
then the grain will have ripened until an
armful can be gathered – but for now it is just
an early sign of life, first fruits from the earth.

Day 21

Psalm 80:7–14, 18 Genesis 4:10 2 Timothy 2:2, 7

During the fifty days between First Fruits and Pentecost (or Weeks) occurs another more modern marked day on the Jewish calendar. This is Holocaust Day – Yom Ha Shoah – the Day of Calamity which recalls the destruction of European Jewry under the unspeakable horrors of the reign of the Nazis. The day is marked in both synagogues and larger communities by services which include memorial prayers, readings from concentration camp poetry and literature and recommitment to the survival of Israel.

> My heart still beats inside my breast
> While friends depart for other worlds.
> Perhaps, it's better – who can say? –
> than watching this, to die today?
> *Eva Pickova, age 12, Auschwitz*

Then they came for the Jews and I didn't speak up because I was not a Jew.
Pastor Martin Niemoller

Day 22

Psalm 121:3, 5–8   Genesis 24:34, 37–46, 57–58
Hebrews 11:5, 8–10, 13–16

> O Lord our God
> and God of our fathers!
> Mercifully direct and guide our steps
> to our destination,
> and let us arrive there

in health, joy and peace!
Keep us from snares and dangers,
and protect us from enemies
that we might meet along the way.
Bless and protect our journey!
Let us win favour in your eyes
and in the sight of those around us.
Blessed are you, O Lord,
who hear and grant our prayers!

Praying with the Jewish Tradition

Day 23

Psalm 65:9–13   *Leviticus 23:15–17, 22*
                    Acts 2:1–2, 44–45

The temple priest returns to the grain field,
now full with ripe crop of grain, ready for
harvest. He cuts and gathers enough to make
two loaves. Back in the temple, he beats and
presses the seed grinding it to flour, adding
water to fashion loaves from the dough and
slips them into the depths of a fired oven. He
waits. It is now about eight in the morning.
Soon the loaf will be ready to lift out from the
oven, take to the altar and lift up to God.
Then the day of Pentecost will have fully
come.

Meanwhile at a house somewhere in the city
people are praying, and the presence of God
bursts upon them. The Day of Pentecost is
fulfilled. Harvest is here. The church is born.

Day 24

Psalm 126:2, 5–6   Ruth 3:18; 4:13–6   John 10:16

Shavuot or Pentecost speaks of harvest
fulfilling the promise of the first fruits. At
Shavuot the Book of Ruth is read for the main
action of the story takes place around
harvest-time.

God called the Jewish people into
relationship with Him in order that they might
in turn reveal His nature, His character and His
greatness to the other nations and be a light to
the world.

The story of God's care and mercy towards
Ruth who was a Moabitess makes beautiful
reading, and reminds us that God's choice of
Israel as his peculiar people was in the nature
of a First-Fruits festival – the full harvest must
embrace all peoples.

Day 25

Psalm 19:1–6   *Judges 21:16–25*
1 Corinthians 7:9–12

The last chapters of the book of Judges can be
summed up in the final verse: they all did
what seemed right in their own eyes. It is a
pantomime of neglect, abuse, reprisals,
massacre, hasty oaths and back-pedalling.

The 600 Benjamite men were given 400
virgins from Jabesh Gilead – the only survivors
respectively from both areas, but that left 200
Benjamites still needing wives, and all the
other Israelites had sworn not to give their
own daughters to a Benjamite.

Instead they turned a blind eye and let the Benjamites hide nearby when the young girls came out to dance through the vineyards at harvest-time. We read of no complaints, their families were satisfied, the couples returned to larger portions of land, and were never able to be divorced. However hastily some of the couples at least had chance to decide for themselves who'd be carried off by whom. Today 'Tu B'Av' is celebrated as the Festival of Love.

At a Jewish wedding ceremony the marrying couple exchange vows under a very special canopy known as a 'hupah'. The rods at the four corners are either able to stand on the ground or are held by the groom's attendants. The top of the canopy is his own prayer tallit (a fringed shawl). The symbolism is that he is taking the bride under his roof and she is becoming part of his house.

> A song shall be heard in the cities of Judah
> and in the streets of Jerusalem
> a song of joy, a cry of gladness
> a song of the Bridegroom, a song of the Bride.
>
> *Jeremiah 33:10–11*

Day 26

Psalm 116:3–4   Ecclesiastes 12:14   Luke 21:21

In AD 70 before the fall of Jerusalem there were several divisions within Judaism – Pharisees, Sadducees and Essenes were the most prominent sects. Nazarene Jews (Jewish believers in Jesus) were another section of the Jewish community. But when the Roman armies approached Jerusalem to quell Israel's rebellion, these Nazarenes fled the city, taking up residence in Petra. They thereby avoided terrible destruction and slaughter by the Roman army. The rest of the Jews distrusted them thereafter and assumed there was treachery afoot. Why did they flee? In Luke 21 and Matthew 24 Jesus predicted that Jerusalem would be surrounded by enemies. His followers were commanded, whenever they saw this beginning to occur, to 'flee to the mountains'. They were not traitors; they were simply following their Yeshua's teaching.

Amazingly, this date, Tisha B'av, was exactly that of the destruction of the first Temple; now 656 years later the second Temple was destroyed (and in 1492 it was on this day the decree of Expulsion of Jews from Spain took effect). This date is still marked by mourning customs.

Now some people argue that, with the birth of modern Israel, mourning for the fall of Zion has become an anachronism.

But the Jewish national memory is long. It is not likely that the given date of the capture of Jerusalem and the ruin of two temples will be forgotten.

In the twelfth century the Crusades set out to free the Holy Land from Arab-Islamic control. The cry then went out that it was inconsistent to seek to rid the Holy Land of infidels when there were infidel Jews within the midst of the lands of Europe. Hence Crusaders held their crosses high as they pillaged and destroyed Jewish lives and property throughout Europe on their way to the Holy Land. Many were burned alive or tortured. Bad theology easily kills – as surely as obedience to the words of Jesus brought life to the Nazarenes at Petra. There is a tendency to read Scripture in such a way that we assume all the negative words to Israel are still addressed to Israel, and that anything nice to say will be transferred to the 'church'.

We may validly receive from Scripture a subjective answer or a word with real prophetic significance to us. What we cannot do is disregard its original intention. ('Upper and Nether Springs' speaks about Northumberland for us, but we are not saying that was the author's original intention, only that God has quickened such an understanding of these passages in addition to their own factual meaning.)

Day 27

Psalm 30:5b Job 1:21–22; 2:9–13 John 11:32–40

Jewish custom was to mourn for the dead three full days and nights known as 'days of weeping' which were followed by four 'days of lamentation' thus making seven days. One rabbinical notion suggested that for three days the person's spirit wandered about the sepulchre hoping to re-enter the body, but when corruption set in the spirit left. For this reason loud lamentations began on the fourth day. When the seven-day mourning period was over, and the visitors had left, the mourner returned to a quiet period of less intense mourning for 30 days, then 11 months to progressively come out of mourning. Close relatives make a practice of saying 'the Kaddish' often in the eleven months – a prayer of praise to God and longing for His Kingdom. Its wording is parallel to that of the Lord's prayer and is often used at other times, as well.

KADDISH: Glorified and sanctified be the Great name of God in the world which He created according to His will. May He establish His Kingdom during your days and during the days of the whole house of Israel at a near time speedily and soon. Say, Amen. May His Great name be praised for ever, glorified and exalted, extolled and honoured, and praised and magnified be the Name of the Holy One, blessed be He, whose glory transcends, yea is beyond all blessing and praise and consolation which is uttered in the world. Say, Amen. May there be great peace from heaven upon us and upon all Israel. Say, Amen. May He who makes peace from the heavens, grant peace upon us and upon all Israel. Say, Amen.

David Kossoff in his book *A Small Town is a World* tells of Rabbi Mark sitting by the death-bed of his friend old Mendel. Mendel sensed the Rabbi's grief and made jokes. But then when his breathing grew shallow he asked the Rabbi for one last wish, his voice by now rather faint. 'Anything, old friend,' said Rabbi Mark, bending forward to hear the words. 'When it's all over,' said Mendel, 'and it's time to lift me into my coffin, promise not to hold me under my arms . . . I'm ticklish.'

A prayer upon waking:

The soul You gave me is pure, my Lord: You gave it life and You preserve it within me, and at the end, when the time comes, You will take it away, only to give it back to me one day. But as long as that soul is in me it will worship You, O Lord my God, the God of my fathers, from whom one day the dead will receive back their souls.

One Jew exclaimed to his friend:

'You should live to be **120 years** and a **couple of months.**'
'**Why a couple of months?**'
'**So you shouldn't die suddenly.**'

Day 28

Psalm 104:19–23   *Isaiah 45:3, 5–7*
Mark 1:21–22, 29–32

Evening comes when You call,
and all nature listens to You
'cause You hold it all.
And now You hold me.
Annie Herring and Matthew Ward

Blessed are You, O Lord our God, King of the universe! At Your word night falls. In Your wisdom You open heaven's gates, You control the elements and rotate the seasons. You set the stars in the vault of heaven. You created night and day. You cause the light to fade when darkness comes and the darkness to melt away in the light of a new day. O ever-living and eternal God, You will always watch

over us, Your creatures. Blessed are You, O
Lord, at whose word night falls.

from The Talmud

In name of the Lord Jesus,
and of the Spirit of healing balm,
In name of the Father of Israel,
I lay me down to rest.

Carmina Gadelica

The rest of the seventh day is a memorial of
creation, but also a sign of the covenant
between God's people and Himself. If a king
were to ratify a treaty or agreement this would
bear a sign, usually an image of the gods he
owed allegiance to, but Israel was commanded
to not make any such image – instead the
sabbath itself would be the sign, and a
representation of His nature. Only Israel had a
seven-day cycle of weeks. We do not sense
today how unique Israel truly was, for the
seven-day week has since become the practice
of the world.

adapted from Jewish Roots.

Day 29

Psalm 45:1   *Leviticus 26:2–4*   Romans 8:26

There is a story told about a Jewish farmer
who, through carelessness, did not get home
before sunset one Sabbath and was forced to
spend the day in the field, waiting for sunset
the next day before being able to return home.

Upon his return home he was met by a
rather perturbed rabbi who chided him for his
carelessness. Finally the rabbi asked him:

'What did you do out there all day in the field? Did you at least pray?'

The farmer answered: 'Rabbi, I am not a clever man. I don't know how to pray properly. What I did was simply to recite the alphabet all day and let God form the words for himself.'

When we come to celebrate we bring the alphabet of our lives. If our hearts and minds are full of warmth, love, enthusiasm, song and dance, then these are the letters we bring. If they are full of tiredness, despair, blandness, pain and boredom, then those are our letters. Bring them. Spend them. Celebrate them. It is God's task to make the words!

Ronald Rolheiser

Day 30

Psalm 116:7   Isaiah 49:15–16   2 John 12

If my lips could sing as many songs
as there are waves in the sea:
if my tongue could sing as many hymns
as there are ocean billows:
if my mouth
filled the firmament with praise:
if my face
shone like the sun and moon together:
if my hands
were to hover in the sky like powerful eagles
and my feet
ran across mountains as swiftly as the deer:
all that would not be enough
to pay you fitting tribute,
O Lord my God.

C3-5 AD

Sleep deserts my eyes and I toss like a ship
in the sea of my yearning for you,
as I imagine these things:
If I were a child in arms and you were my
    mother,
then I should suckle and you would quench
    my thirst.
If I were a stream and you and I sat in my
    garden
I would tend your fruit.
If I were a shelter and you dwelt within me
we would clothe ourselves with joy.
If I were a servant and you were my Lord
I would long to serve You,
O, I would never choose freedom.

Israel Najara C16-17

DECEMBER READINGS

Deeper life

Day 1 Psalm 43:3
Genesis 5:22-24
Hebrews 11:15-16

Day 2 Psalm 86:2-4
Job 23:8-14
Matthew 10:9-10, 16-20

Day 3 Psalm 22:6-7
Exodus 4:2-3a
Matthew 26:6-13

Day 4 Psalm 139:9-10
Job 4:12-13
1 Thessalonians 4:11

Day 5 Psalm 139:5
Song of Songs 8:5a
Mark 1:35

Day 6 Psalm 90:12
Song of Songs 2:10-15
Ephesians 4:26,32

Day 7 Psalm 139:18b
Song of Songs 4:9
Ephesians 5:31-32

Day 8 Psalm 39:13
Isaiah 5:1-2
Luke 22:54-62

Day 9 Psalm 139:17-18a
Genesis 17:3-6, 15-17
Philippians 3:12, 14

Day 10 Psalm 139:14-17
Jeremiah 18:3-6
Philippians 3:12, 14

Day 11 Psalm 40:17

```
          1 Kings 19:9
          Romans 8:27
Day 12    Psalm 38:8
          Jonah 1:17-2:1
          Matthew 6:6
Day 13    Psalm 40:12
          Numbers 13:30-33; 14:1, 36-38
          Luke 4:1-3, 5-7, 9-11, 13
Day 14    Psalm 91:3, 5-6, 13-14
          1 Samuel 5:1-4
          Luke 4:4, 8, 12
Day 15    Psalm 38:4
          Exodus 2:11-14
          Matthew 5:21-22
Day 16    Psalm 137:3
          Nehemiah 2:2
          John 21:24
Day 17    Psalm 66:10-13
          Daniel 3: 26-27
          2 Corinthians 4:6-7
Day 18    Psalm 33:18
          Lamentations 3:55-57
          Luke 18:13
Day 19    Psalm 139: 23-24
          Proverbs 15: 16-17
          1 Corinthians 13: 1-3
Day 20    Psalm 42:8
          Song of Songs 7:10-13
          Philippians 4:12
Day 21    Psalm 40:1, 5
          Hosea 2:14-15
          Matthew 13:31-32, 44
Day 22    Psalm 1:1-3
          Jeremiah 17:7-8
          Matthew 13:3-6
Day 23    Psalm 88:13-14
          Genesis 8:22
```

Romans 8:38-39
Day 24 Psalm 140:1-3
Job 37:5-13
John 17:15
Day 25 Psalm 139:12
Isaiah 45:3, 7
1 Corinthians 4:5
Day 26 Psalm 94:18-19
Song of Songs 1:5
Luke 7:45-47
Day 27 Psalm 51:6
Jeremiah 17:9-10
1 Corinthians 4:4
Day 28 Psalm 130:2-3
2 Samuel 12:5-7a
Romans 12:3
Day 29 Psalm 138:3
Isaiah 6:5-7
Romans 7:24-25; 8:18, 25
Day 30 Psalm 38:8-11, 15, 21
Ruth 1:18-22
Acts 16:23-25
Day 31 Psalm 138-8
1 Kings 9:4-7
2 Corinthians 10:5

Day 1

Psalm 43:3   Genesis 5:22-24   Hebrews 11:15-16

This month's notes are on the subject of the
call to a
Deeper life
   One dynamic of that call is the sense that
where we really belong is somewhere else, that
we have heard something inside us calling us
to 'Come away'. We belong to a different
Kingdom: our home is another country.
   It often is like this:

   'Follow me.'
   'Yes, Lord, I'll follow You . . . But, Lord . . .'
   'Yes?'
   'Where to? Where will I be going?'
   'With me.'

From time to time the sense of alienation from
everything around us may be strong, the sense of
being a stranger, someone on a journey; but the
stranger can see things through different eyes
from those of people who live in that one place
all the time.
   This world is not my home . . .

Day 2

Psalm 86:2-4 Job 23:8-14 Matthew 10:9-10, 16-20

It is a terrible risk to follow even a Friend into
the unknown. It is made worse by the fact that
He so often seems to disappear or go ahead
instead of staying close by.

The instructions He gives us should make it so much easier to continue on the journey: but what instructions?

'Don't provide extra for yourself in case I let you down.'

'Don't worry what to say.'

'I will be there when you need Me, even if it's only at the last moment.'

Instructions like these leave us incredibly vulnerable, but they are only examples of what He really is asking from us: that we choose intentionally, deliberately to make ourselves vulnerable and to walk in that vulnerability!

Day 3

Psalm 22:6-7   Exodus 4:2-3a   Matthew 26:6-13

God tells Moses to throw down even the one thing he still held in his hand.

Jesus, having come to our world as a human being, becomes more humbled still, his life taken from Him in the ugliest of executions – what a waste it looked! His life was poured out in intentional uselessness, like the expensive ointment the woman poured on his head.

Some of us are indignant at the waste, like Judas was.

Some of us are envious of her – at least she had the ointment.

We would like to have something to give, to pour out for love of Him, but we don't have even that. It seems we don't have anything,

Nothing to offer except our uselessness, and our choice to be with Him: and that is a choice that no-one but Him is likely to put any value on.

Day 4

Psalm 139:9-10   *Job 4:12-13*
1 Thessalonians 4:11

In the face of all kinds of pain we find that often there is nothing to say, but it's impossible to be still.

A woman whose child had been killed in an accident talked about her reactions. No one could say anything that would help, she said, and God was silent too, as if He knew better than to try to say anything.

The Scripture says to be still and know that He is God, but she couldn't be still, not at all.

But even when you don't talk to God or have any stillness of your own to bring Him, you can still be met by God in His stillness.

That's what she discovered, and that eventually

'the stillness becomes part of you'.

Day 5

Psalm 139:5   *Song of Songs 8:5a*   *Mark 1:35*

We are asked to follow in the footsteps of our Lord when they are not clear in the road, and even when that road runs through desert.

Going into the desert we are never quite sure what to expect. Being alone can be peaceful, or frightening, or just a dull nothing. But coming out of the desert we find that we are leaning of Him in a new way.

The Russian word 'poustinia' only means 'desert', but is the name given to the wooden hut where someone is shut away for time with God alone.

It is a typical experience for the person undergoing poustinia to feel nothing is happening at all, but as they emerge they find others waiting, pressing them to share what God has given them in the poustinia.

And they will not be disappointed.

Day 6

Psalm 90:12   *Song of Songs 2:10-15*
          Ephesians 4:26, 32

It is important to remember that the deeper life is in fact a deepening of our own relationship with God.

Our experience of other relationships tells us that it is perfectly possible to be with another person for hours day after day without consciously spending time together. In some relationships there may be a deliberate policy of avoiding being together.

Being in relationship with God can be very similar, avoiding time alone, or filling that time with anything at all that can distract from the real question of how much love there is in our heart for Him, and how much being together with Him is a priority, first love for Him freshly re-kindled, the relationship still deepening.

Are you there for Him?

Day 7

Psalm 139:18b   *Song of Songs 4:9*
Ephesians 5:31-32

The pilgrim worried that sometimes he would not have much time to care for his love-relationship with God. Then the Lord spoke to him, and answered his unspoken question.

'Do you have only one minute? Hem it with quietness. Do not spend it in thinking how little time you have. I can give you much in one minute.'

The pilgrim sat by the water, and his dear Lord said to him:

'As the ripples of the river glance up to the light, let your heart glance up to Me in little looks of love very often through the day.'

Amy Carmichael

The old couple sat with each in peaceable silence, and no signal was needed for the kettle to go on, or the tea to be poured, the fire tended to.

'What do you find to do all the time, after all these years?' someone asked the old lady, 'don't you ever tire of each other's company?'

'Oh no,' she replied, 'you see, it's like this: I looks at him, and he looks at me, and we're happy together.'

Day 8

Psalm 39:13   Isaiah 5:1-2   Luke 22:54-62

Jesus turned and looked at Peter.
    Everything was in that look:
disappointment, love, forgiveness. One look,
and he was perfectly known, perfectly
discovered.

> Take me often from the tumult of things
> into Thy presence. There show me what I
> am and what Thou hast purposed me to be.
> Then hide me from Thy tears.
>
> *Hebridean Altars*

Day 9

Psalm 139:17-18a   Genesis 17:3-6, 15-17
Philippians 3:12, 14

The thoughts of the son ran thus:

> 'My hopes painted beautiful pictures, but
> they are fading one by one.'

His Father said:

> 'Destroy all those pictures. To watch them
> slowly fading is weakening to the soul. Dare
> then to destroy them. You can if you will. I
> will give you other pictures instead of those
> your hopes painted.'
>
> *Amy Carmichael*

God doesn't see me the way I do either, I look
all the time into a distorted mirror that
exaggerates some features and makes others
disappear. God sees a true picture of me with

all my faults and limitations, but more than this He sees a picture of all the possibilities and potential I hold.

'Just let Me get my hands on this one,' He thinks, 'and then just wait and see what the finished picture will be.'

Sometimes God gives us glimpses of that picture to encourage us and spur us on. For me it is a long process, but in the end it is all about becoming God's picture of me.

A.R.

Day 10

Psalm 139:14-17   *Jeremiah 18:3-6*
Philippians 3:12, 14

'I am His project' – those were the words on Mary Alice's bookmark, but they were the belief of her heart, too, and however great the problems in her life He would continue to work on that project and bring the work to completion.

Paul, the Apostle, had a similar understanding and so he knew that though he was in Nero's prison he was not Nero's prisoner, but the prisoner of Christ Jesus. Any other arrest or imprisonment was irrelevant. A light shone in the cell.

In the late evening a believer looked over the day and was discouraged, but his Father spoke to comfort him.

'In the early morning did you not bear your beloved ones on your heart? Did you not offer to Me every hour of the day, every touch on

other lives, every letter to be written,
everything to be done? As the hours passed
over you perhaps you did forget; but is it My
custom to forget?'

Amy Carmichael

Lord, You never forget me, even though often I
forget: I am Your project.

Day 11

Psalm 40:17   1 Kings 19:9   Romans 8:27

God is not easily impressed – but then He
never asks us to try to impress Him. It is as if
He turns to us when we are consumed with
our own unworthiness and are tempted to
avoid meeting with Him, then He cuts across
all our excuses and says:

'Relax, I already know you.'

Amy Carmichael captures the feeling of such
an exchange in her book 'His thoughts said
. . . His Father said . . .'

'The son said, But I am not successful.
His Father said, At the end of the day will
   My word be,
Come, thou good and successful servant?
If only thou wilt walk humbly with thy God
   it will be,
Come, thou good and *faithful* servant.'

We are not called to be successful, but faithful
– relax!

Day 12

Psalm 38:8   *Jonah 1:17-2:1*   *Matthew 6:6*

John Skinner's story of the novice monk has
impressed upon many of us the words of
counsel the novice is given:

> Go to your cell,
> and your cell will teach you everything.

The cell is the place of being shut away with
God, and with yourself. This may be a
physical place or just a choice to be opened to
Him in an interior way. We know it is exactly
what we need, but avoid time alone and find
other things to address in order to delay it . . .

The son felt fenced in. His Father took him to
the fence and bid him look; he looked and he
did not notice a hedge of thorn or a barbed
wire entanglement; he saw a fence of feathers.

 'With His feathers shall He make a fence for
you.' The son remembered how once he had
said, 'There are days when little things go
wrong, one after another, and I am distracted
by much serving. Such days are very trying.'
Then the Father had said, 'On such days take
to yourself the words of your Saviour which
you so often have given others. Let them be
your solace and your tranquillity. But tell Me,
when you are under pressure, do you turn first
to your companions or to Me? Your
companions listen and respond, but you never
tell Me about it. Let Me see your face, let Me
hear your voice.'

Amy Carmichael

Day 13

Psalm 40:12   *Numbers 13:30-33; 14:1, 36-38*
               Luke 4:1-3, 5-7, 9-11, 13

Each of us has triggers that activate irrational
fears, psychological monsters that seem
overpowering to us but which probably would
be no problem to someone else.

It may be a temptation to do the right thing
the wrong way, or a lie thrown in our path by
the enemy that anyone else would laugh at for
its foolishness.

The common denominator is the same – it is
a giant bigger than our own courage, and it
comes out when you're alone. All of us have
monsters of some kind, nightmares from our
past or from our subconscious, unwelcome
'visitors'.

But it was the Spirit who drove Jesus into
the desert, God who instructed the Israelites to
subdue and drive out the giants, and He is
bigger than any giant or monster the enemy
may resuscitate or invent.

Sometimes He'd rather the nightmares
appeared and came out into the light to be
recognized for what they are, and robbed of
their power to surprise us.

Day 14

Psalm 91:3, 5-6, 13-14   *1 Samuel 5:1-4*
               Luke 4:4, 8, 12

While we avoid facing up to our personal
'monsters' they actually have more power to
intimidate us.

That is why giving them a name is important – it begins to define them, to make them a known quantity.

Fears need naming, and so do temptations; and lies brought into the light lose their power to destroy.

Day 15

Psalm 38:4   Exodus 2:11-14   Matthew 5:21-22

Years ago I saw an old black and white film about a man with amnesia. Slowly, as the pieces of the murder-mystery come together he begins to realize that although he does not remember it, the truth is that he is the murderer the police are looking for.

The film made quite an impression on me because I was used to films and programmes where the 'good guys' and the villains were clear from the beginning.

From that time on whenever a murder report came on TV, or was in the papers, my instinct was to have immediate sympathy for the murderer, rather than the victim or their family!

All of us have murder in our hearts from time to time, and lots of other unpleasant things. If looks could kill we'd leave plenty of corpses in our wake, some days.

God's concern is not just for the regulating or modifying of our outward behaviour, but for an on-going change in our hearts.

Day 16

Psalm 137:3   *Nehemiah 2:2*   *John 21:24*

When Adrian Plass decided to write the story
of a quiet but remarkable church army officer
turned vicar he called it *A Smile on the Face
of God*. It was a story with lots of loose ends,
unanswered questions and memorable
incidents, a story to make you cry or make
you laugh at other times.

Most of the Christian 'testimony' books you
see are about apparent success stories which,
even if their contents are true, miss out most
of the failures and bad times and ordinary
days. But suppose it was your story that was
being told, what are the memorable incidents?
What impact has God made on your own
story? and have you brought a smile to His
face?

Day 17

Psalm 66:10-13   *Daniel 3:26-27*
                2 Corinthians 4:6-7

A terrible fire ravaged the whole building, and
when, afterwards, she went back to inspect the
remains of her office all she could do was
shake her head and be grateful that she had
not been in the building at the time. Certainly
none of the files of paper had survived.

With one backward glance her eye fell on a
tiny blackened vase still standing on the
charred remains of her desk. She had a new
office now in a different place and was able to

move in there instead. Well, little vase, she
said, you and me have survived and you shall
come with me into my new office.

It stood in the usual place on the corner of
her new desk, but when people came in she
noticed a difference in their reaction. Before,
they would say,
  'Oh, what a beautiful vase,'
now, since it had been through the fire, they
said,
  'Oh, what beautiful flowers.'

Day 18

Psalm 33:18   Lamentations 3:55-57   Luke 18:13

Francis, the great saint of Assisi, considered
himself the most worthless of men, and the
greatest of sinners.

The more the brightness of God's presence
shone upon his heart the more his sin seemed
black in comparison. (We may remember that
Isaiah had a vision of God in His holiness, and
immediately exclaimed 'Woe is me - I am
ruined, for I am a man of unclean lips and my
eyes have seen the King.')

Brother Masseo ran after Francis crying.
  'Why after you? Why after you? Why is the
whole world following after you?' and Francis
was able to only laugh that God had chosen
him because no more worthless creature could
be found on whom to set His mercy.

* * *

A pilgrim looked at the reflection of a
mountain in still water. It was the reflection

that first caught his attention. But presently he raised his eyes to the mountain. Reflect Me, said his Father to him, then others will look at You. Then they will look up, and see Me. And the stiller the water the more perfect the reflection.

Amy Carmichael

Day 19

Psalm 139:23-24   *Proverbs 15:16-17*
1 Corinthians 13:1-3

God doesn't care so much about our outward actions, however sincere, as He does about the heart, its motives, and especially the love for Him that is carried there.

Works of charity may help others, demonstrations of courage and idealism may inspire others to faith and action, but these and even miracles of faith can still flow through a life where the love of Christ has grown cold. If I have not love I am nothing.

I should look to my own heart, and ask how much love for Him it holds.

Day 20

Psalm 42:8   *Song of Songs 7:10-13*
Philippians 4:12

There are times when our times with God seem boring, predictable and routine.

Will we become so discouraged by this that we give up spending time consciously in His company?

Will we persist in the routine of the relationship and hope that the feelings return?

Or will we endeavour to be flexible in our times with Him, keeping the time together varied, finding afresh what pleases Him?

The relationship should grow deeper over the years, not become stale.

Day 21

Psalm 40:1, 5   *Hosea 2:14-15*
Matthew 13:31-32, 44

Be prepared to give God time, just because He matters. Give time for the relationship to develop, and be rooted even more deeply in your life.

Everything in me felt like saying, I am not worthy that You should come under my roof, but instead I said, 'When will You come to me?' I want to wait here with a perfectly-kept heart for I know Your words give me life for ever.

As my thoughts were thus occupied, I found myself on the shore of the sea. And I took a grain of sand from the miles of sand about me and I held it in my hand. Then I knew that my desire for the presence of my Lord was like a little grain for smallness in comparison with my Lord's desire to come under my roof for that was like the measure of the measureless sands. And as my thoughts followed this great thought, Jesus my Lord answered and said to me,

'With desire I have desired to come to you.'
Amy Carmichael

Day 22

Psalm 1:1-3   Jeremiah 17:7-8   Matthew 13:3-6

Our roots need to go deeper than circumstances. It is possible to be rooted deeper than catastrophe.

In the Nazi detention centres many of the Jewish people taught classes, prepared musical concerts, shared reminiscences that would be life-increasing and sustaining. Some gave up instead, and had no will to live. In life or in death, it is important to plant, to invest ourselves, and to glorify God.

His thoughts said:

My longing is to heal the broken and the weak, to defend the maimed, and to lead the blind to the sight of the glory of the Lord. My choice is to be a corn of wheat and fall into the ground and die. Then why these waverings?

His Father said:

Too much of your surface is exposed to the breath of every wind that blows. You must learn to dwell deep.

And the son who had wavered answered humbly,

Renew within me a settled spirit
Establish me with Your directing Spirit.
My heart is fixed, O God, my heart is fixed. I will sing and give praise.

Amy Carmichael

Day 23

Psalm 88:13-14   Genesis 8:22   Romans 8:38-39

The soul goes through many seasons, seasons
of new life and promise, of full fruit, of loss
and then of apparent deadness with hope for
new life again. The secret is to appreciate the
value of these changes and gain the benefits of
each and not become too discouraged.

In Murray Bodo's story of the life of Clare of
Assisi *A Light in the Garden* some of these
seasons of the soul are touched upon:

> The lives of Francis and Clare are themselves
> seasons of every soul, and it has something
> to do with Assisi in the spring becoming
> summer, surrendering to the gentle mists of
> fall, lying seemingly dead in winter, and
> waiting for the poppies of another spring
> . . . You choose your vocation in life over
> and over again. It is not a decision made
> once for all time when one is young. As
> Clare grew in experience and in
> understanding of her commitment, she had
> to say yes again and again to a way of life
> that was not exactly the life she expected at
> the beginning.

Amy Carmichael writes:

> The soul remembered how when she was a
> very little child she had sympathized with the
> grey sea. The blue sea was a happy sea. The
> green sea, when the waves thereof tossed
> themselves and roared, was a triumphant sea.
> But the grey sea looked anxious. So the child
> was sorry for the grey sea. Grey weather she

abhorred. Something of this feeling was with her still. Grey weather was not among the things for which she gave thanks. Then God her Father said to her, All weathers nourish souls.

Day 24

Psalm 140:1-3   *Job 37:5-13*   *John 17:15*

'Each day has enough trouble of its own,' Jesus taught in the Sermon on the Mount. He meant it. He was realistic enough to recognize that this world is too often a place of suffering, for now still in the grasp of the World-hater, the prince of this world.

A day will come when sorrow will be no more and death itself be destroyed, but until then there will always be some poorer than others, some bereaved, mistreated, abused. We must do all we can to protect and to heal, but even the miracles we see are only signs of the Kingdom. That Kingdom is at the same time 'already' and 'not yet'. We are not exempt from trouble, injustice, violence and suffering, just because we are believers. He will allow some of these things to touch us also, even though it is not Him that visits them upon us.

Jesus, who understood that it was necessary for Him to suffer, still questioned, Was there no other way? Job wondered what was going on and in this life was never told what had happened in the courts of heaven over his story of trials. We know that no test is beyond what we can endure, but why this random, faceless violence unleashed at times in our society? The cross begins with an unanswered 'Why?' - and Christ also shouldered the cross.

Day 25

Psalm 139:12   Isaiah 45:3, 7   1 Corinthians 4:5

> Do not be afraid to walk in darkness, for I
> am uncreated light. I will cause you to look
> on darkness and not be afraid.

This was a word spoken to John Skinner some
years ago, but it is a word worth hearing for
many of us.

It will be necessary for many of us to look
on darkness, and when that happens it is
important that it be robbed of its power to
frighten us. There are many kinds of darkness.
The darkness of sin should not surprise us,
and when we confess it, and yield it to God,
we no longer need carry its guilt.

The darkness of despair and of unanswered
questions may require that we reach out and
hold His hand in the darkness, even by faith,
and just keep on walking.

Day 26

Psalm 94:18-19   Song of Songs 1:5   Luke 7:45-47

'I am dark, but comely' says the old
translation of the words of the Shulamite girl
in the Song of Songs.

God, who loves us, is a realist. He knows
our faults and disadvantages, but through all of
that He loves us, He sets His love upon us and
wants to shout to all around about the beauty
that He sees in us.

How can we be down on ourselves, or count

ourselves worthless when He was willing to give everything in order to claim our love?

The knowledge of that love is enough to make that beauty shine from us which till now only He could have seen and no-one else would have guessed at. It comes from within.

Day 27

Psalm 51:6 Jeremiah 17:9-10 1 Corinthians 4:4

When it is just me who has been wronged my lips should most often be silent. And I must see to it that in the hidden person of the heart there is always the gentleness of Christ.

Words of complaint can be so destructive. Let this be my rule:

> Silence, unless the reason for speech will bear the searchlight of Eternity.

Often our heart seems clear and in order, and only the Holy Spirit can begin to make us aware of our self-righteousness, self-conceit, mixed motives and avoidance of unpleasant home-truths.

C. S. Lewis in his poem 'As the Ruin Falls' expresses the idea that it is only foolish talk when he says that he loves someone, since he must recognize that he is 'mercenary and self-seeking' through and through. He wants the one he loves, and God and any or all of his friends to provide exactly what he wants. He 'loves' them precisely because it suits him very well to do so. I think we all know what he means . . .? Having confessed how flawed our love is, we still choose to love and to offer that love as sincerely and truly as we know how.

Day 28

Psalm 130:2-3   2 Samuel 12:5-7a   Romans 12:3

One of the questions in the Ignatian spiritual exercises asks,

> What would I say to someone else in circumstances like my own, what counsel would I give them?

It is very easy for us to be hard on another person, even judgemental in our reactions, but make allowances when we are the offender.

David is very cross with the man Nathan tells him about, and only then can Nathan turn round and say, The man is you!

We should not think too highly of ourselves – we're only as high as we are at our lowest moment, except perhaps by the grace of God which lifts us from the miry clay.

Some people have the opposite problem and can be far more generous and forgiving toward other people, but will never have a good thought or word for themselves.

Let the love of God be reflected in your love for yourself and others. With God in the equation our potential for good is limitless.

Day 29

Psalm 138:3   *Isaiah 6:5-7*
Romans 7:24-25; 8:18, 25

His thoughts said:

> I am not what I meant to be, or what others think I am.

His Father said:

> It is written, 'He restores my soul. The Law of the Lord is perfect, restoring the soul.' Let some word of Mine restore you. Did you think you had a Father who did not know that His child would need to be restored? I will restore health to you: I will heal you of your wounds. I will restore comfort to you. I will restore to you the joy of My salvation. I will renew a right spirit within you. I will not cast you away from My Presence. Child of My love, trust your Father. If the Spirit speaks some word in your heart, obey that word. And, before you're even aware of it, you will know that you are restored.
>
> *Amy Carmichael*

Going deeper in God always involves knowing yourself, including your own sinfulness. That doesn't mean we should be stuck there, we need to look for break-throughs, keys to unlock areas of persistent defeat.

Day 30

Psalm 38:8-11, 15, 21   *Ruth 1:18-22*
Acts 16:23-25

One of the best things about the book of Psalms is that we find that we are not the first person in the world to complain to God, or feel like their prayers come back unheard or that our rivals should be beaten to a pulp, or that the bad guys always win.

Scripture was never intended to be handed to other people as a placebo or as ready-made easy answers. God has many answers for us, but they are rarely easy, and even when freely offered they were often costly . . .

But still the son felt like a long shore on which all the waves of pain of all the world were beating. His Father drew near to him and said, 'There is only one shore long enough for that. Upon My love, that long, long shore, those waves are beating now; but you can be one with Me. And I promise you that there shall be an end, and all tears shall be wiped from off all faces.'

Amy Carmichael

Day 31

Psalm 138:8 1 Kings 9:4-7 2 Corinthians 10:5

Not to make judgements about other people's light, but to obey the light given to you is all that concerns you.

Lord, what shall this man do?
'What is that to you? *You* follow Me!'

So cast down your imaginations – don't try and work it out. It won't be like what you read in books.

Be real with God.
Don't try to re-live someone else's journey.

'What is that to you? *You* follow Me!'

Historical Note

What is the Northumbria Community?

The Community is clearly Christian, but with
members from all kinds of Christian tradition,
and some with no recognizable church
background at all. We are married, and single:
some are unemployed; most are in secular jobs,
some in full-time service which is specifically
Christian; others are at home looking after
families.

The three directors of Northumbria
Community are Anglican, Roman Catholic and
Baptist, and all live in north Northumberland.
Our members are geographically far-flung, but all
feel a special attachment to this area through
prayer.

Some of the most loyal friends of the
Community are not yet committed Christians,
but are encouraged to participate as fully as they
feel they can in our life.

There are now hundreds of individuals and
families who will tell you they 'belong', although
the ways this belonging is expressed are
different. Some will be often found at Hetton
Hall; others are frequent visitors to Holy Island.
For some saying the daily office, and using the
prayer-guide is their main point of identification;
others are part of mission-teams or ministry-
teams representing the Community. Some are
members of local groups identified with the
Community; others are not, but have still
embraced the Community's Rule of availability
and vulnerability as their way for living.

Nether Springs

It was in 1976 that Andy Raine first moved on to the island of Lindisfarne, or 'Holy Island' as it is known locally. Fairly soon the rhythm of daily prayer and attention to Scripture drew his focus on the story of Caleb.

'The passage where Caleb's daughter comes to her father seemed especially significant. The land which was to be her home was darkened and barren, in need of life-giving springs. Her father gave her those springs. The upper springs and the nether (or hidden) springs. The upper springs spoke to us of the intense sense of God's presence, the resonance of centuries of prayer and mission springing from and saturating the Island, that still attract, and compel, and inspire, today.

'The fascinating question it also implied was this, Where, then, were the nether springs to be found?'

John and Linda Skinner had just rented a big house in Berwick-upon-Tweed and for a time Andy came to live with them. They had each been reading Isaiah 58 which speaks of restoring foundations from a time many generations past, of having springs that will not fail, of building out of brokenness.

'Many visitors came to that house – it was a significant taste, even then, of what Community was to mean.'

Chris and Sandra Haggerstone were amongst the group who met at the house. The friends eventually dispersed in various directions as John moved away to complete theological training, and was given an Anglican curacy.

Each year around Easter time a 'Workshop'

would be held in the area and friends would gather from such places as Newton Aycliffe and Edinburgh, Newcastle and the Midlands and Northumberland.

At one of these meetings in Berwick the 'nether springs' had been spoken about, and it was John and Linda, and Chris and Sandra who responded, without really knowing what it would mean.

Years later it meant that the two families would struggle to return to north Northumberland, would eventually rent part of a house, and a farm cottage, do window-cleaning, landscape gardening, picking out eggs – anything that would help them survive, and be in the land they were praying for. They tried to discover what it meant to live as contemplatives with growing children, financial pressure and a constant stream of visitors. 'We were just following what we felt was our own call with no thought of starting something, but people just began to come, and they didn't stop coming. In time we had so many people visiting that we couldn't do our work any more.'

In October '92 the Nether Springs finally had a home – a large house in four acres of ground which is able to be used as a 'mother-house' for the Community. The house, Hetton Hall, has its water supplied from springs and is very close to St Cuthbert's Cave where the saint's body was carried by the monks from Holy Island fleeing from the Viking invaders.

Sandra is now our administrator, and Chris has been over-seeing the task of renovating the semi-derelict stables block into a home for the Skinner family. Nether Springs is 'home' for many of the Community, although only a small number are resident there at any given time. The house is a focus for Community life for its staff, and those who are frequent visitors, those who help with its work in many ways, those who give time, skills and money, those who serve as Trustees. It serves in the areas of spiritual direction, counselling, and has limited refuge facilities. Various courses are taught throughout the year. The house is in constant use for study breaks and directed retreats.

Upper Springs

It was 1976 when Andy was first directed to Holy Island. 'I was asking God the question, where are You sending me? I didn't expect that to be the answer. I'd only been there once before in my life – as a young boy. Years later, we found a black and white photograph of that day trip. A boy in short trousers looking up into the face of the large figure of St Aidan outside the Priory. That picture has been prophetic. Little did I guess that the Island and the people here would become my life.'

In March 1992 Andy moved back to the Island with full support of what has become Northumbrian Community. It has been interesting to see how the Island is the primary point of contact for many in the Community, and over the next couple of years it will be exciting to see how the Upper Springs will be released further.

There are. of course, many other Christian people who have long revered and appreciated these holy places. We are only fellow-pilgrims gathered at the 'springs'. We have no monopoly over them, but we do seek to explore our Celtic

Christian heritage and its potency for the people of God today.

One group who travelled regularly to the Island to meet together were known as 'Northumbrian Ministries'. Roy Searle invited John, then John and Andy to meet with this group. What they explored together was the importance of the Celtic brand of Christianity, its emphasis on monastery and mission, the fire of continual devotion, and obedience to the initiatives of the Spirit. Roy and his friends were waiting for God's instructions, but instead they were given the heart for the vision they already held, that fires would be lit all over the ancient Kingdom of Northumbria and beyond.

New friendships were slowly built, the two trusts in formation combined and eventually Roy gave up his position as a Baptist minister in Sunderland to work full-time with the Community. Roy's own calling to ministry had come, years before, on the rocks of Bamburgh beach so this was in many ways a 'coming home' and the realizing of that vision.

Teams

Some of the folk in the Community are involved, especially at weekends, as teams of musicians, dancers, speakers or whatever else is needed. Sometimes they participate in church events or conferences, but increasingly the focus is towards those who would only have negative concepts of church.

A recent project is the writing of a portfolio of music, story, dance and drama about the Celtic saints which can be presented in all kinds of setting.

A Northumbrian Office

The Office of prayer combines traditional Celtic services with songs and readings which have been part of our journey as a Community. One Easter we tried using the morning, midday and evening prayer together, and found them to be immediately comfortable – simple and strong. We soon had opportunity to print the Office in a small leather loose-leaf binder (Filo-fax/day-timer) if we could order 500 of them! This was more than we needed at the time, but the decision to sell off our surplus copies has led to people far and near praying with us, and coming to have further contact with the Community in some other way.

But to pray regularly with our Office, is for many, their greatest sense of identification with all the others in the Community. Others will play the tapes of the sung versions of the prayers and meditations at home, or in the car on their way to and from work.

The Community prayer-guide encourages those who intercede regularly as they chart the progress of different situations, and familiar names are matched to real people.

We have also prepared additional liturgies drawing on the stories of Aidan, Cuthbert, Oswald, Hild and Brigid.

Vigilance

People again are exploring the idea of pilgrimage – especially around the Celtic sites. We pray increasingly for places such as Iona, Othona, Selcuk (where John-the-Beloved's tomb is), Lindisfarne, Glastonbury, Clonfert and

Heavenfield, and have friends in, or links with, each of these places. Sometimes these sites are contested for by other powers. John explains:

In the early church it was the Celtic monks who were in constant conflict with the Druids. They were powerful men of God and the mistake the Church has made is to put down to legend some of the great things that happened through them. With people getting back to the magic arts, the Church is often impotent in knowing how to deal with them, and needs to grow in its understanding of spiritual warfare. For the early monks, even the sign of the cross was a very powerful spiritual weapon whereby they invoked the power of the protection of the Trinity. The Celtic Church devastated the Druids' hold on Northumbria and overturned the Druidic belief system which pervaded the whole of society at the time. In only 70 years they had converted half the nation although they never built any lasting structures and few churches. Even if we only last ten years, if we leave some new believers we will have done our job. Our call here is to build an altar. The sad thing is that people make pilgrimages to all kinds of new age shrines and Buddhist centres; it's about time we had an altar to the true Lord.

In a number of locations smaller groups meet once a month as an expression of the Community. These endeavour to promote the deeper life of individuals, ensuring that no one need be alone on their spiritual journey, but find appropriate direction or companionship and a sympathetic forum for their struggles. They also try to identify those with a calling to deep intercession in prayer; they recognize it is important to build real friendships with the 'un-churched', or with those alienated from church, and that this must be done in a way that expresses both vulnerability and availability if it is to be authentic.

The Rule

One building-block for the Community is the Community Weekend to which people come exploring the 'Rule' or 'Way for living'. Availability and vulnerability are expressed in a number of ways such as commitment to prayer, hospitality, asking awkward questions, choosing relationship instead of reputation and so on.

If they choose to embrace the Rule, they must say YES to vulnerability and availability and formally commit to this way for living – for a year at first.

On their return home the fruit of this may be a new focus amidst a busy ministry or secular life or it may be a tendency to question the purpose of much of the activity they were previously involved in.

This could be uncomfortable . . . but so are availability and vulnerability.

Resources

Tapes of the Office and meditations, The Rule, Additional Liturgies, selections of many more months of study notes, other books and teaching materials available on request from:

Nether Springs Trust
Hetton Hall
Chatton
ALNWICK
Northumberland
NE66 5SD

or contact for information:

Paul and Mary Cullity
158 Spruce Street
Keene
NH 03431
USA

Acknowledgements

The authors and publisher acknowledge with thanks permission to reproduce copyright material as listed below:

Darley Anderson Books, London, for the extract from *The Wisdom of the Desert* by Thomas Merton.

AMS Press Inc, New York, for the extract from *The Black Book of Carmarthen,* ed. Skene

David Berg for extracts from *My Friend God* published by SPI books, a division of Shapolsky Publishers Inc, New York.

Birdwing Music/Fine Balance Music for the words of the song 'Christ as a Light' by John Michael Talbot.

Chatto & Windus Ltd, London, for the extract from *The Singer* by Calvin Miller.

Christian Literature Crusade, Fort Washington, USA, for the extracts from *If* and *His Thoughts said . . . and His Father Said* by Amy Carmichael.

The Council of Churches for Britain and Ireland, London, for the prayer entitled 'Expressions of Faith', translated for the British Council of Churches for the week of prayer for Christian Unity 1988.

Darton, Longman & Todd, London, and Doubleday, New York, for lines from *Celtic Fire: An Anthology of Celtic Christian Literature,* ed. Robert Van de Weyer.

Faber & Faber Ltd, London, for the lines from 'Little Gidding' from 'Four Quartets' by T. S. Eliot, published in *Collected Poems* 1909-1962

Farrar, Straus & Giroux Inc, New York, for the
extracts from *House Like A Lotus* by
Madeleine L'Engle.

Gill & Macmillan, Dublin, and Sheed & Ward,
Kansas City, USA, for the prayer from *Prayers
of Life* by Michel Quoist.

Chuck Girard Ministry, USA, for the extracts
from the songs 'Don't shoot the Wounded',
'It's easy to love', 'We can love them' and
'That doesn't mean we turn' by Chuck
Girard.

Jugend mit eine Mission (Youth with a Mission),
Schloss Hurlach, Germany, for 'Psalm 90' arr.
Jim Patterson and 'Psalm 31' arr. Marion
Warrington, both published in *The Singing
World*.

Kingsway's Thankyou Music, Eastbourne, for the
extract from the song 'Arise My Love' by John
& Ross Harding, copyright © 1975
Kingsway's Thankyou Music.

Morehouse Publishing Company, Ridgefield, USA,
for the extracts from *Holy Island* by James
Kennedy.

New Dawn Music, P.O. Box 13248, Portland,
Oregon, USA, for the words of the song 'In
the Shadow of Your Wings' by Robert F.
O'Connor, S.J.

Penguin Books Ltd, London, for the extracts
from *A History of the English Church and
People by Bede*, translated by Leo Sherley-
Price and revised by R. E. Latham. Copyright
© Leo Sherley-Price, 1955 and 1968.

Reed Book Services for extracts from *Prayers of
Peter Marshall* Ed. Catherine Marshall,
published by William Heinemann.

Salvationist Publishing and Supplies Ltd, London,
for the words of 'Never Forget', by Arch

R. Wiggins, and 'When Jesus Looked O'er
Galilee' by Catherine Baird.

SPCK, London, for an extract from *Praying with
the Jewish Tradition* by Paula Clifford
(translator), 1988, used by permission.

The Revd Peter Sutcliffe for his prayer entitled
'Peter's Song for Marygate'.

Verlag Evangelische Marienschwesternschaft,
Darmstadt, Germany for the meditation
'Prayer of Victory in the Blood of Jesus
Christ' from *If I only Love Jesus* by M.
Basilea Schlink. We are grateful for the kind
permission of the Sisterhood of Mary to
continue use of the earlier edition, in which
we are fluent, although subsequent
translations from the German have rearranged
the wording.

The Wild Goose Worship Group of the Iona
Community for the words of 'Inspired By
Love and Anger' and 'Stumbling Blocks and
Stepping Stones' both by John L. Bell and
Graham A. Maule.

Every effort has been made to trace copyright
owners, and the authors and publishers
apologize to anyone whose rights have
inadvertently not been acknowledged. This will
be corrected in any reprint.